CITIES

CITIES

THE FIRST 6,000 YEARS

MONICA L. SMITH

VIKING

VIKING

An imprint of Penguin Random House LLC

penguinrandomhouse.com

Library of Congress Cataloging-in-Publication Data

Names: Smith, Monica L. (Monica Louise), author.
Title: Cities : the first 6,000 years / Monica L. Smith.
Description: New York : Viking, [2019] | Includes bibliographical references and index. |
Identifiers: LCCN 2018041663 (print) | LCCN 2018043006 (ebook) | ISBN 9780735223691 (ebook) | ISBN 9780735223677 (hardcover)
Subjects: LCSH: Cities and towns—History.
Classification: LCC HT111 (ebook) | LCC HT111 .S547 2019 (print) | DDC 307.76—dc23
LC record available at https://lccn.loc.gov/2018041663

Printed in the United States of America
1 3 5 7 9 10 8 6 4 2

DESIGNED BY MEIGHAN CAVANAUGH

FRONTISPIECE: World's first city map, from the Mesopotamian site of Nippur, c. 1500 B.C.

CONTENTS

The amalgamation of numerous villages creates a unified city-state, large enough to be self-sufficient or nearly so, starting from the need to survive, and continuing its existence for the sake of a comfortable lifestyle.

—ARISTOTLE

CITIES

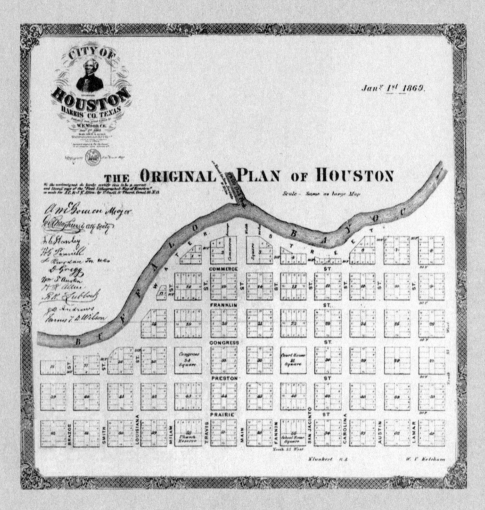

Original plan for the city of Houston, A.D. 1863

1

WHY CITIES?

As an archaeologist, my favorite place in Rome is not the Colosseum or the Forum. It's the ancient trash dump of Monte Testaccio. Right in the middle of the city, it is a giant mound of broken pottery where the ancient Romans threw away the containers used to ship wine and olive oil all around the Mediterranean. Each of those vessels was about half the height of a person and made of coarse clay that would have roughed up a stevedore's hands. Their odd shape of two handles and a pointy base made them good for packing into a ship's hold or standing upright on a sandy shoreline but very inconvenient for much else. After a cargo of them arrived at its destination on the bustling shores of the Tiber at the very heart of the Roman world, a few were reused and a few were recycled. Mostly, people poured out the contents and threw the containers away. Over the centuries, the pile of discards grew, with the result that one of the famous hills of Rome is actually not a hill at all but a human construction—a landfill, essentially. Today Monte Testaccio is topped by trendy nightclubs and has been endlessly mined for construction, but there are still the remains of twenty-five million ancient containers poking up from the vegetation of the hillside.

Now consider a very different metropolis. My favorite part of Tokyo? The backside of the Tsukiji fish market, the part that tourists don't visit. Tsukiji is enormous, and the passageways are crowded with plastic buckets and barrels teeming with every kind of creature that you can imagine from the briny deep. Crabs attempt to crawl their way out of baskets, little fish are piled up in ice buckets, and great slabs of tuna glisten under the klieg lights. The market is open to everyone, with chefs and restaurant owners jostling with homemakers for a clearer view of the day's catch. It's a world without friendly chitchat, punctuated by the dangerous darting movements of souped-up forklifts that dodge their way in and out of the building and heap up their discards out back. Behind the market is an enormous dump of plastic-foam shipping boxes used to transport the globally sourced tuna, squid, and shrimp from each morning's auctions. The pile of containers is taller than a two-story building and so large that it is continually cleared by bulldozer. Some of the cartons are trampled and broken in the process, with bits and pieces that spill farther into the passageway. In between the endless runs of machinery, merchants and their helpers come to pick through the heaps of box fragments. Sorting through the pile to find ones that aren't too broken, they carry them off to repack with fish or whatever else they're selling.

Ancient Rome and modern Tokyo are literally a world apart, but if we stand back and look at them as cities, they have identical characteristics. In addition to markets and trash, there are multistory buildings, long streets, sewer pipes, water mains, public squares, and a "downtown" zone of financial institutions and government offices. There are a thousand varieties of sounds and smells, competing with the weather and daylight that frame the skyline of the built environment. There are crowds of people—rich, poor, young, old, female, male, gay, straight, trans, abled, disabled, employed, students, jobless, residents, and visitors. Production and consumption opportunities are scaled up in cities to provide not only more things but also more things per person, a completely ironic abundance given that urban residences tend to be much smaller than their rural counterparts. In the midst of so much abundance, the only solution is to cycle through possessions faster, turning everything into trash.

It's the act of discard that provides the most telling evidence of urban activity, whether it's a broken potsherd from two thousand years ago or a fragment of a plastic crate that was shattered this morning. Once you start to look for the concentrated detritus of your own urban life, it's everywhere: in the trash cans that bear the proud logo of the downtown business improvement district; in the Dumpster parked outside a building that signals a renovation taking place inside; in the garbage truck that obstructs your commute; in the legions of sanitation workers employed to sweep the streets and subways and haul away the accumulations of discards. Trash has a familiar rhythm and concentration. Holidays bring a hangover of extra-full trash bins; parades and festivals and summer weekends in the park are witnessed through their aftermath of overflowing containers. Whether directly or by proxy, an urban obsession with trash is everywhere, and once you start to look, you won't be able to stop seeing it. Congratulations! You're an archaeologist.

Moving your gaze upward, or to the side, you might notice that it's not just trash that silently tells a story of urban life. Your own metropolis, even if it's new, has many traces that reveal its history before you moved through its streets. Maybe it's a bolt hole in the sidewalk where a telephone booth used to stand, or an out-of-use railroad track now embedded in the asphalt of a city street. Maybe it's a building that has been updated once or twice, resulting in the pastiche of a Victorian facade with mirrored glass windows, or a modernist concrete structure fronted by flowers and cheerful painted windowsills. And maybe it's a newly cut ditch in the street where you can see the layered pavements of prior years right up to the present. Buildings and streets and parks serve as a living map of variable time, a collection of structures that all exist simultaneously whether they were constructed a millennium ago, in your grandparents' time, or last week.

Your growing archaeological insights serve you well when looking not only at modern cities but also at the ancient cities that are found by the hundreds on nearly every continent, from famous ones such as Rome to not-so-famous ones with romantic names like Tikal, Tell Brak, and Xi'an. When we look beyond the rubble and ruins, what we unearth in our excavations of them rings true to the experiences that we have in our own cities: neighborhoods and streets, open plazas and grand buildings, lines of sight to the residences of the powerful, and marketplaces where people from all walks of life met their daily needs for food and fuel. When we walk through the streets of an ancient city like Pompeii, we encounter an environment where everything makes sense, from the sewer grates and the narrow passageways between apartment buildings to the food stalls and the cocky ancient graffiti scribbled on the walls. Although there's a popular impression that ancient cities were prone to collapse, the vast majority of the world's first cities are still right underfoot in the biggest metropolitan areas today: not only Rome and Xi'an, but also London, Paris, Guangzhou, Mexico City, Tokyo, Baghdad, Cuzco, Cairo, Athens, Delhi, Istanbul . . . the list goes on. And those cities became interconnected with other cities that sprang up alongside them, growing into a global phenomenon that dominates the planet. Today, more than 50 percent of the world's people live in cities, and that percentage will soon be larger. It's predicted that by 2030, more than 50 percent of Africans, 60 percent of Chinese, 87 percent of Americans, and 92 percent of the residents of the United Kingdom will live in cities.

In their layouts and constructions, ancient cities look so much like the ones we build for ourselves that it seems they should always have existed. And the growth and success of modern cities also suggest that humans thrive in urban locales. But cities are not actually the natural condition of our species, nor did we humans need to develop cities in order to survive or to successfully colonize the world. For a million years, our ancestors had lived scattered across the landscape, housed in humble huts in everyone-knows-everyone villages. By the time cities were invented six thousand years ago, our ancestors had already done a good job of filling up all of the easy places to live and many of the difficult ones, too. They had a system of pathways to get across the land, and they had developed rafts and boats to get from place to place across the trackless water. They had moved out of caves and other natural shelters into huts that they built themselves out of stone, bamboo, or brick. People had a sophisticated repertoire of language, art, music, and dance to pass the time, and they had many ways of displaying their individual identities through ornaments and tattoos and hairstyles. They already had reverence for the dead, encoded in the placement of burial goods laid to rest with the deceased. There were plenty of objects for the living, too, because people had already invented all the essentials of life. There were clothes to keep warm, plows to till the land, pottery and baskets to keep the harvest safe, and stone knives and bronze weapons to carve up food (and to keep enemies in check). There were domesticated plants for a steady supply of beer and bread, and domesticated animals as a ready source of milk, wool, transportation, and companionship. In sum, we had everything we needed for a successful life of small-scale farming that would still have allowed for population growth to cover the planet, one little village at a time.

Clearly, that simple and straightforward village life wasn't enough for our urban ancestors. Despite having everything that members of our species needed to survive, people wanted plenty of intangible things that they couldn't get out there in the countryside: the thrill of a crowd, the excitement of new inventions and novel foods, and the tantalizing allure of meeting a romantic partner from beyond the confines of the village. Before there were cities, such experiences could be found only in ritual spaces that people might visit once or twice in a lifetime. Located far away from settlements, ritual places like Stonehenge provided the only escape from village life where people from different areas could gather together for the purpose of celebrating a festival or honoring a deity. Drawn to those places by some distinctive point of topography, people often added special ritual architecture meant to be the focus of collective attention and to serve as a proof of collective action.

By bringing people together for a shared purpose, ritual places made it possible for people to develop and practice the skills of communication and interaction that enabled them to deal with so many strangers. Yet places like Stonehenge, however appealing, were only temporary: people were not meant to stay there beyond a few days of feasting and worship. Only cities could make that opportunity for intense interaction permanent and for a much greater range of purposes—social, economic, political—than could ever have been envisioned for a ritual space. Summed up in a phrase, it's "bright lights, big city" with all of the connotations of enticements and activity that we continue to experience in our own urban centers today. Cities were the homes of human creativity, manifested not only in culture, fashion, and fine arts but also in small things like clothing, ornaments, housewares, food, and hairstyles. Through the acquisition of a constantly changing array of objects, people living in cities proclaimed new alliances and new senses of self; even if they could not purchase stylish new goods regularly, they could talk about what was fashionable in a vicarious and free appropriation of urban style.

Before cities, there was only a landscape of villages in which every family was more or less the same, consisting of farmers and herders who experienced very little ethnic or social diversity. Every house was the same, too, except for the chief's house or the shaman's house, which might have been a little larger or that had a few different artifacts that enabled their occupants to do the special jobs of leadership and curing the sick. And the shamans kept their secrets to themselves: those objects weren't for everyone to touch, or see, or know about. Everyone else did the same work, day in and day out, and everyone had the same basic repertoire of food and objects. Those objects were solid and sober, with styles and decorations that had stood the test of time. Social interactions were solid and sober, too. People might have had a little fun when they were young or when they went on an occasional trip to a distant wedding or on a once-in-a-lifetime pilgrimage. The majority of their days, however, were spent in an atmosphere where they knew everyone else. In the modest farming settlements that people built all over the globe, there was very little movement in or out of the community. People spent their entire lives in the company of the same people, and almost everyone was related. New faces appeared only at the time of marriage or when itinerant peddlers came with their wares. Familiarity was the constant measure of human relations, and strangers were regarded with wariness and misgiving.

Places like Rome and Xi'an and every other ancient metropolis represent a spectacular change in the way that humans related to their environments and to one another. In urban settlements, *unfamiliarity* became the measure of human relations. The first cities were larger than the largest family-like village, and the people who moved into those settlements had to suppress a suspicion of others from the very first day. People had to adapt to densely crowded neighborhoods full of people they had never seen before; they had to negotiate ritual and political relationships with other newcomers; and they had to accept the near-constant dissonance of interacting with people representing different cultures, languages, and customs. Encounters with strangers were no longer limited to the occasional addition of a newlywed to the collective hearth, but constituted a recurring condition of daily life. People moved in and out of the city, coming and leaving as new opportunities opened up. As they worked, played, and shopped, urban residents had to constantly update their roster of relationships.

Urban social life and the entrepreneurial spirit associated with migration constituted a feedback loop that enticed more and more people who were looking to better their circumstances. Before cities, there wasn't a middle class as a group of people who have income that can support activities beyond the range of basic life and who can make some investments in housing and objects and education. Before cities, there wasn't infrastructure—all of those pipes and highways and drains that suddenly became necessary as a way to logistically connect large groups of people. And before cities, there wasn't even take-out food! All of those were invented only as cities came into existence, and they all come together: the middle class, the objects, the physical networks of connectivity, and the trash. It's as though there was a pent-up capacity for all of those things that had somehow been encoded into our collective conscious, just waiting for an opportunity to burst forth.

When scientists want to understand a phenomenon, they first have to define it. Astronomers first ask themselves "What is a planet?" as a basis for classifying not only things that they want to compare as planets but also all of the other celestial phenomena that need names too, like moons and meteors and black holes. They can't see the big bang or the birth of any individual planet, but instead extrapolate from the celestial bodies that are with us now in their quest to understand how the universe works. Biologists query themselves about what a species is and carefully scrutinize the variability that they see before they assess the way that species are related to one another in space and time, deducing the pace and effects of evolution from the staccato appearance of extinct species that are often represented only by stray fossils and fragmentary skeletons. And chemists first ask "What is an atom?" before they can identify the ways in which those atoms can be combined in novel ways to make new substances like plastics and aerogels or divided for explosive effect.

In light of how much cities mean to us today, the archaeological definition of urbanism takes on a special weight and meaning. It's only after we define what a city is that we can agree on which site can be seen as the first of its kind or that we can compare the ones that have sprung up ever since. But before we define ancient cities, we might want to look at our own urban definitions, which can be quite surprising compared with our expectations of how an "urban" place looks and feels. In Cuba today, the minimum number of people to qualify a location as a city is two thousand; in the American state of Ohio, a city is defined as any place that has five thousand or more registered voters; and in Senegal, the minimum number of inhabitants needed for a place to earn urban status is ten thousand. Those government statistics are principally related to the fact that places defined as cities can access certain types of government funding and support because of their perceived importance in the landscape.

If we can't agree on a working definition of what a city is according to an arbitrary threshold number, and even when we can see living examples right in front of us, how can we make a definition of cities that serves us for both the past and the present? Should we instead fall back on something more qualitative—like that old quip about pornography being difficult to define but that we know it when we see it? We could start our search for an urban definition with some flippant responses that nonetheless reveal the kernel of a useful approach. In the modern world, we might argue, a "real" city is one that has an Apple Store or a Mercedes-Benz dealership. This is not because people in the countryside lack the capacity to own the latest smartphone or drive an expensive automobile but because cities are the only places that have a large enough population of potential consumers to justify the expense of maintaining brick-and-mortar premises. And beyond the actual customers, there are other ways that urban consumption reflects economies of scale. Specialty stores are in cities because there are enough people to highlight the brand, like those who come into the store for the product experience in a way that affirms an item's popularity or who simply pass by the store with an acknowledgment of its presence as a marker of the status of an entire neighborhood. A physical store is the consumer tip of the iceberg that assures us there is in fact an entire diverse, vibrant economic underpinning to a densely occupied space.

Cities are not just about economic opportunities. Other potential definitions of urbanism focus on qualitative components such as the presence of government offices or significant administrative services like judicial courts or other bureaucracies. Researchers who emphasize these bureaucratic components always do so within a framework of relative population density to avoid ascribing urban status to lonely outposts or skewing a subsequent analysis among places that can't truly be compared. Thus, the anthropologist Richard Fox suggested that a city be defined as "a center of population concentration and/or a site for the performance of prestige," while the social theorist V. Gordon Childe suggested that the first cities, even if they were relatively small, were places that had "truly monumental public buildings" and that were ten times bigger than any village.

By defining what a city is through what it has in it, we can approach the archaeological record in order to answer our real question, which is "Why did cities come about at all?" Yet like all definitions, there's a little slippage between what we think we see and its realities that make it hard to be perfectly precise 100 percent of the time. We can return to the analogy of other scientific disciplines. Remember the continuing argument about Pluto and whether it's really a planet? Although schoolkids now have some interesting conversations with their grandparents about whether Pluto "counts" for their solar-system science projects, the challenge comes about not because the concept of defining things is wrong, or that scientists can't decide what to call things. In fact, the interstices of definitions are exactly where the most interesting revelations take place. When it comes to cities, we know there was a time when there weren't any cities at all. The definition of what afterward made something "urban" is a key to understanding just how different they were from everything that had come before them.

For the purposes of this book, a city is defined as a place that has some or all of the following characteristics: a dense population, multiple ethnicities, and a diverse economy with goods found in an abundance and variety beyond what is available in the surrounding rural spaces. A city's structures often include ritual buildings like temples, mosques, or churches, but there are other large buildings beyond those religious ones. In keeping with a multifunctional economy and an intensity of habitation, there is a landscape of verticality that includes residential units, courts, government offices, and schools. There are formal entertainment venues, whether a sports stadium or a theater or a racetrack or an opera house. There is an open ground that fulfills a multipurpose function: on some days it might be a market ground, on other days a venue for strolling and pickup sports. There are at least some broad avenues and thoroughfares that connect the world of wealth and privilege, contrasting with the winding streets of ordinary neighborhoods. And above all there is an interdependence of people in the city for the most fundamental human needs of water and food. In villages, people always know where their next meal is coming from because they have their fields and domestic animals firmly under their control. In cities, there's no way to keep a year's worth of grain or a herd of animals in a residence.

In all respects, the earliest cities represented an entirely different scale of human experience. Not everything was positive, of course. Crowding, pollution, noise, crime, water shortages, sewage backups, mucky streets, and a higher cost of living would have been among the disadvantages faced by the residents of the first cities, six thousand years ago, as well as those of us who live in cities today. Trade-offs were constant: there was a greater chance of communicable diseases, but also more doctors to treat them; higher food prices, but a much greater repertoire of foods and eateries to select from; more challenging conditions of work, but a higher salary and more opportunities for promotion. Then as now, challenges and risks were mitigated by the access to increasing amounts of information that enabled people to *feel* empowered about their circumstances, if not actually in charge of them. The result is that a city—however small it was at the beginning or however large it may grow to be—feels like a place in which many aspects of everyday life hold open the possibility of choice among a variety of potential actions.

My own quest to understand the process of early urbanism emanates from the sense of excitement and vexation that I feel from my own city of Los Angeles and the other metropolitan areas that I've had the privilege to live in. And as an archaeologist, I have been fortunate to get an insider's perspective on many spectacular ancient cities as well. There's certainly a romance of ruins that is interspersed with this intellectual investment, whether sites are in the open landscapes of the countryside like Mexico's Teotihuacan or buried deep under a modern metropolis like Athens, Tokyo, and London. Still, I didn't understand my own feelings about urbanism until I moved from a small college town straight to Manhattan. I had always taken cities for granted before, but once I found myself living in a city again,

I began to think about the compelling similarities not only of our own global urbanism but also of the urbanism that was on display in the many ancient cities that lived on into the present. Since then, I've pursued the story of ancient urbanism across multiple continents and through fieldwork in places as diverse as India and Bangladesh, England and Tunisia, Egypt and Turkey, and Madagascar and Italy.

I have had the good fortune to work at a number of ancient city sites, feeling the soil slip away under my fingers to reveal both the extraordinary structures and the mundane artifacts that made up those long-ago urban lives. Under the flick of a trowel that removes the dust of centuries, I have found little fragments of pottery vessels from some long-ago meal. In the shadow of the city wall, I have uncovered a bit of an ancient ornament left behind by a traveling merchant or perhaps carelessly lost by a city dweller rushing by on an errand. Looking at the wall itself, I notice the fingertips traced in lines of mortar, a moment's handiwork from thousands of years ago preserved between courses of stone. Picking at the foundations of an ordinary house, I have seen an ancient urbanite's quest for display: although the house itself was made of broken bricks, the rough edges were turned to the unseen interior, preserving the illusion of a structure created with pristine materials.

Archaeological findings both large and small are familiar in so many ways that when I am working at an ancient city, I sometimes feel as though I am excavating a dusty vestige of the present day. A house is a container for the daily routines of family life, while big buildings compel us to look beyond that intimate world to the entire community. Plazas make a physical space where multitudes of people could mingle on market days or during celebrations, but they also marked a place where an individual, walking alone, could feel a bit spooked after midnight. Little bylanes and passageways are reminiscent of the crowded apartment buildings and streetscapes of our own urban experience, where we encounter the same neighbors and do the same errands day after day. Lofty administrative buildings, whether represented by temples or fancy palaces, remind us that someone was in charge of the city's central zone and that the relationships between people and their administrators were complex ones of obedience, permission, and resistance. Throughout the city, there's an elevated sense of style, a diversity of material goods, and an urban "look" in both architecture and artifacts that distinguished urbanites from their rural compatriots.

The question I would pose to you as a reader is "Why cities?" Are they a natural step in human habitation's evolution or a response to something else? It's an exciting time in human history to ask this question. First of all, we finally have enough archaeological data from ancient cities around the world to be able to reconstruct in some detail how the first cities began and how they were sustained in a tremendous range of environments from desert oases to riverbanks to lush tropical jungles. Second, our ability to understand the development of cities as an irreversible burst of change has been paralleled in our own lifetimes by the development of another phenomenon that has seemingly sprung out of nowhere and causes a good deal of trouble, yet has become thoroughly interwoven with our lives: the internet.

Many of us experienced the internet for the first time when we were already adults. Our children experience the world much differently and already find our stories of communication limited to paper maps, landlines, and written letters to be quaint and obsolete. And a little unbelievable ("really . . . you didn't have a smartphone!"). The same response must have greeted the residents of the very first urban centers when they explained to their children and grandchildren how the great city of Tell Brak or Tikal or Xi'an didn't exist in their youth but that they had seen its beginnings and rapid growth first-hand. The old folks no doubt spun tales of the excitement and novelty of urban life and how the city had a diversity of people, food, and festivities that livened up the drudgery of routine work. How could it not be that way? the children wondered, rolling their eyes at the thought of a time without the daily marketplaces, busy thorough-fares, and year-round temples, without the rush of people, and without the tantalizing appeal of cheap trinkets and exotic aromas.

Once cities were invented, our ancestors' ability to adjust to urbanism was just as rapid as our modern adjustment to a web-connected world. Like the internet, the first cities represented both work and leisure opportunities bundled together in the same physical locale. Today, a phone or a laptop easily tacks back and forth from social media and family shenanigans to serious-looking messages from the boss. The internet gives us an autonomy of choice of inter-action: you can be connected to a vast array of friends and families and strangers, but you can be happily absorbed in a game that you play on your own. And there is plenty that is available that you can filter out. Just as you navigate the physical streets of your city by pay-ing attention to only some of the interactions and possibilities going on all around you, you navigate the internet by directing yourself along a pathway of websites according to your needs of the moment. You know that when the time comes for some new query or experi-ence, you can elicit it from the collective mass of data that resides online for every need from birth to death: homework hints, bridal salons, fertility advice, parenting tips, financial and legal counsel, dog-walking services, hearing aids, medical care, mortuary services.

For our ancient ancestors, cities were the first internet: a way to communicate and interact with an enormous range and diversity of people, to engage in new forms of work and leisure, and to constantly be in contact with others. Just as the internet provides us with the opportunity to engage in a fundamental human need for communication and display, the city form provided something so compelling that once it was invented, people couldn't imagine life without it. But as in the case of the internet, the concept of cities had many necessary preexisting components: the human capacity for language, our ancestral history of migration, the human species' uniquely intensive dependence on objects, and our collective drive to envision and build diverse types of architecture. As we'll explore in this book, each of those components was essential for the development of urban life and for its continuity in the modern world.

Historical and modern building facades

2

CITY LIFE, PAST AND PRESENT

C ities were invented only six thousand years ago but are now so widespread that we have a hard time "unseeing" them from the landscape. We have subconsciously integrated our most mundane daily experiences into the urban form, and when we travel, our home city becomes the frame of reference through which we experience a new place. Without realizing it, we have absorbed expectations that provide us with a template for our behavior. We know people don't grow their own food or keep animals in their houses, so we don't think to look for a feed store or a cattle barn in an urban place: a city means a place where food is already prepared for us to eat, whether in the form of restaurants, food stalls, or itinerant vendors. We know that people in a city get their water from a tap and not from a bucket dipped into a river, even if the river is nearby. Accordingly, we look around at the architecture to see the locales where we're most likely to get a drink, wash our hands, or use a restroom. And we know that cities are places where there is a variety of modes of transport, many of which are actually redundant but represent different levels of expenditure to achieve the same routing whether by taxi, shared-ride services, bus, trolley, subway, bike path, monorail, or electric scooter.

When you go to a new city, there's a rapid learning curve, but it's a curve that you quickly master, and it doesn't take long for you to begin to fit in. How many times have you been in a new city, and on the first day someone asks *you* for directions? Within a short time, you have already become more expert than someone else in a way that you could never be in a small town or a dispersed village where people can be hard to find and perhaps a bit reluctant to give information to a stranger. In being able to carry on in your new urban surroundings, you're just the same as the leader of a long-ago merchant caravan entering Byzantine Constantinople or the shepherd bringing a flock into market in ancient Babylon. Like them, when you enter the city, you first seek out something familiar: the marketplace, a crossroads, an eatery. While you are there, you are able to look around you, to get a sense of your surroundings, to see what others are doing and how they are dressed, to ascertain where they are coming from and where you are going next.

Proof of humans' predisposition for urban life—the reason you can walk into a strange city and begin to negotiate it almost immediately—comes from the moments in which people from one part of the world met people from another culture in which the only commonality was the urban form. Perhaps the starkest historical example is when Spanish soldier-explorers arrived as a ragtag band in the capital of the Aztecs in central Mexico in 1519, barely a generation after the first reports of a "new world" were carried back to Spain by an errant Christopher Columbus. The Spanish adventurers of that swashbuckling era included little bands of fighters, governors, and priests dispatched across the Atlantic whose conquests and colonialism ultimately created the Americas as we know them today. Made famous by Jared Diamond's *Guns, Germs, and Steel* and by other scholarly treatments of the before and after of the colonial encounter, the contact that was to have such a cataclysmic effect on our planet was initiated on a very modest scale.

In thinking of those first meetings between the representatives of two entirely different civilizations, we have to remember how the small group of Spanish men had been traveling across the world on an uncharted journey that was, for its day, much like our own explorations of outer space. What equipment should be carried along, and where would the journey end? What unexpected wonders and dangers lurked beyond the visible horizon? What were the chances of being killed en route, either going or coming back? Speculations and anxieties must have darkly entered personal thoughts and furtive conversations behind the captain's back on the long, creaky voyage by boat across the Atlantic. When they finally reached the coast of Mexico, the journey was only partially over because now a whole new strange odyssey had to be forged over land to the center of the Aztec Empire. There were unknown landscapes, unfamiliar foods, and strange animals. For those among the Spanish bearing trinkets and trade goods, there was the potential for new friends; for those bearing arms, the certainty of new enemies. Landing on the Atlantic shore, the Spanish were only would-be conquistadors and had yet to conquer anything or anyone. Like the moment when the first-stage rocket falls away and other power sources take over as a rocket ship hurtles farther into space, the voyagers only knew that they would have new experiences whose implications could not have been foreseen.

The trip in from the Mexican coast required weeks of overland travel by foot and horseback through terrain that was new to them but well known to the locals. The Spanish made use of the trails that the Aztec merchants, known as *pochteca,* had already used for centuries, slowly climbing up from the steamy jungles of the coast to the arid mountains of mid-continent. Communication along the trail was limited (how quickly could a native hinterland dweller have learned rudimentary Spanish, or the Spanish have learned any of the varied regional tongues?). Yet there were plenty of clues about the human geography as they approached the heart of the Aztecs' Triple Alliance. Making their way through the highlands, the Spanish went against the flow of empty baskets that were headed to the coast and in the slipstream of full tumplines of commerce traveling inland. Houses started to appear closer and closer together, and the pathways became wider and more worn. There were more and more people, and they were speaking a greater variety of languages and wearing a greater variety of clothes. Locals on the pathways contrasted with the heavily laden *pochteca,* acting like the equivalent of the modern commuters whom we see on the fringes of Mumbai and Madrid and Manhattan: just a day bag, and dressed with a little extra flair.

Although everything they heard and smelled was new, what the Spaniards saw as they approached the Mexican highlands was nonetheless utterly familiar. Their ability to read the landscape of population and productivity prepared them for the appearance of a city, and they were right. When they arrived at the place the locals called Tenochtitlan, they knew exactly what they were looking at and how it functioned:

We saw the aqueduct that comes from Chapultepec to supply the town with sweet water, and at intervals along the
three causeways the bridges which let the water flow from
one part of the lake to another. We saw a multitude of boats
upon the great lake, some coming with provisions, some
going off loaded with merchandise . . . and we saw the ter-
raced houses, and along the causeways the other towers and
chapels that looked like fortresses. So, having gazed at all
this and reflected upon it, we turned our eyes to the great
marketplace and the host of people down there who were
buying and selling. . . . And among us were soldiers who had
been in many parts of the world, at Constantinople, all over
Italy and at Rome; and they said they had never seen a market so well ordered, so large and so crowded with people.

What should have been an incomprehensible moment of foreign-
ness in the encounter between Old World and New, where there had
never been direct contact, instead was instantly readable. Everything that the Spaniards expected in a city—the markets, the trading,
the infrastructure—was right before their eyes. They innately understood that people had to rely on the import of food to the city in bulk
and that people did not all go out to farm from their urban households. They immediately focused on the dense monumental center of
the city with its pyramids and temples as the locus of political authority. And they marveled at the array of ornaments, decorations,
and garments worn by the inhabitants, comparing their own memories of home as inferior to the finery of the Aztec capital.

A little over a decade later, the Spanish experience was repeated at the ancient Inka capital of Cuzco in Peru, a continent away from Tenochtitlan. Cuzco is surrounded by mountains and getting there required a long trek from the Pacific coast. The ordeal was made more arduous by the steep climb up the Andes, where pathways required numerous stream crossings and backtracking. The Spanish arrived in the highlands after nearly two years of marching and conflict, in which they had immersed themselves in the fratricidal civil war of the Inka rulership along the way. Yet the capital itself had remained relatively unscathed, such that the Spanish explorer Pedro Sancho witnessed Cuzco as an intact and functioning city. He described well-built houses and fortification walls and wrote about the entire range of urban infrastructure from spacious plazas to mundane conduits with a glowing sense of admiration, concluding that

> the city of Cuzco, being the primary place where the lords
> made their residence, is so great and so beautiful and with so
> many buildings that it would be worthy to be seen in Spain.

Europeans' experiences with New World cities like Tenochtitlan and Cuzco provide the nearest thing to a laboratory condition for capturing the universality of the urban form. The Spanish were able to understand and negotiate the magnificent capitals of the Aztecs and the Inka because those cities looked exactly like what the explorers themselves had experienced back home. Yet there had been no contact between people in Europe or Asia with people in the Americas; each place had evolved its own urban centers completely independently. Shaped by cognitive opportunities and constraints in a brain that was the same the world over, people created the exact same template for crowd-based living, with neighborhoods, open spaces, monumental architecture, and housing whose sizes and styles varied according to the social status of the occupants.

The architecture of cities—including buildings and the infrastructure of water, waste, and transportation—not only diversified the types of built environments that people lived in but also expanded the repertoire of social engagements. In cities, people could suppress their tribal impulses to fight by refocusing on the density and variety of ways to satisfy desires for food, objects, and goods. The people who inhabited the first cities used economic strategies such as the division of labor in workshops, where each person efficiently made only a part of an object, with the result that many more objects could be made. Economies of scale also were achieved through the acquisition of raw materials in bulk and from many different sources. Those economies of scale in turn brought into existence new institutions like urban temples and warehouses that were a source of wealth and patronage but that also created new types of jobs for everyone from savants to sweepers. People used political strategies of taxation, contracts, insurance, and law to enforce expectations and demands, with a pooling of resources that could provide stability even when the turnover of actual people was high due to migration or urban epidemics (of which there are plenty documented in ancient sources).

As a result of filling out their social roster to include a much larger variety of casual contacts and work relationships in cities, people almost unwittingly engaged with an impulse to align with their commonalities rather than to divide according to their differences. In the first cities in the area that is now Mexico, people constructed not only ritual buildings such as pyramids and temples but also ball courts as a distinctive form of architecture in which rival teams played a soccer-like game with a hard rubber ball. Like our own sports stadiums that are located within walking distance of downtown, those ancient ball courts were located right in the heart of the city next to the temples and palaces of the elites. In the areas of South America where the Inka were later to grow their empire, the attractors to urban life included ritual sites focused on the deity known as the Staff God, depicted in majestic command on top of monumental gateways as was the case at Tiwanaku or brooding deep underground like the stone sculpture at Chavín.

The Spanish experience in the New World echoes our own recognition that wherever people make them, cities have the same component parts: streets and neighborhoods, markets and government buildings, open spaces and crowded alleyways. There are places for entertainment and places for education. The necessary connectivities of infrastructure, like water supplies and roads and bridges, are exhibits of sober engineering but also a celebration of soaring architectural achievement and even a little urban "branding." There are areas in which the wealthiest people reside, and there are slums where the poorest residents take shelter. There are merchants and bookkeepers and teachers who constitute a middle stratum of rank and wealth whose houses and possessions reflect a preoccupation with status and comfort as well as a capacity to buy the little extras of urban decor. And although the religious tradition is different from place to place, people clearly demarcated the sites of ritual activity with monumental buildings and grand surrounding spaces.

Long-ago explorers used cities as their destinations and nodes of contact, finding in them a logic and regularity that transcended cultural differences and enabled them to get what they needed as they went from place to place. When the Roman Empire began to grow, people were connected not by land but by water, and their conquests across the Mediterranean first targeted urban centers like Athens and Carthage as staging points for a growing international trade network. And when the Romans extended their networks far to the east and south through Arabian and African intermediaries, their knowledge of distant places was gleaned through the people from intervening ports of call. The most distant contacts were in India, but the Romans described the subcontinent's cities with an accuracy that has since been confirmed by indigenous texts and archaeological evidence from the subcontinent.

The Romans weren't the only ones using cities to punctuate their travels. In central Asia over two thousand years ago, merchants, pilgrims, and soldiers of fortune crossed vast expanses of desert by caravan to the oasis cities of the Silk Road. In the Middle East, people traveled a well-worn pathway of connect-the-dots from the Arabian Peninsula to the grand suqs of Cairo and then across the sands of the Sahara to Timbuktu and Mali in west Africa. In the Indian subcontinent, they followed the Ganges River along a vast network of ancient cities stretching from Afghanistan in the north to the island of Sri Lanka in the south. In China, early dynastic rulers conquered their predecessors' urban palaces and markets, enfolding the antiquity of place into a legitimation of the present. By the time Europeans engaged in the frenzy of Renaissance exploration that featured the Spanish encounter with Mexico and Peru, they were merely following a long-standing strategy of capture focused on the port cities where commodities came from the hinterlands. Using their familiarity with the mannerisms and social configurations of cities, they tapped into vast networks of trade without setting foot in the unknown terrain of the backcountry.

The Urban Map

Long before cities came into being, our ancestors had the capacity for dead reckoning and mental mapmaking. As they moved around the landscape, they made use of natural markers such as trees and stony outcrops to create cognitive maps of movements and desires for themselves. When the natural world became subordinate to the built environment, as increasingly became the case in cities, there were many more ways for people to mark the spaces of their movements from home to work to school to entertainment venues and back again. There were shops and alleyways and distinctive street angles. There were monuments of all kinds: a temple or an obelisk or a minaret. There were signs, sometimes in writing but more often symbolic, like the abstraction of barbershop poles or the display of wares through a shop window. Even things that might otherwise be characterized as mobile, like a pushcart or a homeless person or an animal tethered to a doorpost, served as tools of urban way finding.

By comparison to the dynamic way that we know people move around in a city every day, the maps we create to depict ancient cities are flat and static. Publishers usually hate to have illustrations in a book, so they try to limit authors' use of images for reasons of cost and editorial convenience. As a result, a single map often serves as the illustration for centuries of urban history: you might get just one cartographic representation of the city of Rome (or, for that matter, the entire Roman Empire). In order to be efficient, a cartographer shows the city at its maximal extent. That's fairly misleading, because the first inhabitants certainly never saw anything but the beginnings of an urban idea as they threaded their way through the frenzied building activity that was just starting to anchor their ancient downtowns. In their flow of movements through the urban sphere, they were constantly having to update their mental maps with new buildings that sprang up and the disappearance of older structures that were torn down. Temples that had been built to accommodate a few dozen people, or a few hundred, were almost instantly outgrown and enticed their followers to expand the premises upward and outward. And mighty city walls were just someone's idea yet to be made real through the sweaty labor of construction. Long after the walls had been started, they might still be just a work in progress that was short enough to walk over or truncated enough to walk around, a little bump of linear topography that was hard to take seriously as a form of protection or deterrent to warfare.

Over the long generations of urban buildup, residents would have experienced a different metropolis from one generation to the next, and few would ever have seen their city at its fullest extent the way that we look at a map of it now. It was not just the monuments and walls that underwent change in ancient cities. The first residential structures would have been thrown together in a hurry to accommodate migrants pouring into the budding metropolis. Drawn in by any of the number of things that sparked the first settlements in a particular spot—a handy place for trade, a good source of raw materials, a royal decree, or a religious vision—the first settlers might not have come with the intention of making their residences permanent. But when they mended their houses after a season or two of rain and sun, their acts of patching and upgrades served as an acknowledgment that they would be staying. Meanwhile, others in the vicinity were making the same calculation, resulting in a dense network of other houses and shops and pathways and playgrounds. Along with those fledgling neighborhoods—we probably should call them slums—were the households of wealthy patrons and the middlebrow residences of project managers and workshop owners who had come into the city to take advantage of its growing population, to make new products, and to participate in new forms of consumption in education and entertainment.

We rarely find the remains of those flimsy initial structures, in part because studies of the "ordinary people" of ancient metropolitan centers don't have quite the pizzazz (or the funding-agency appeal) of tombs and temples. But even the maps of monumental architecture are misleading because they obscure the growing pains and false starts that characterize durable structures as much as ephemeral ones. We know from textual studies that people often rebuilt major urban structures in ways that renovated the earlier buildings out of existence entirely. Just as we do today, ancient architects could enlarge structures in ways that dwarfed the original ground plan, reface or reroof buildings in ways that changed their function and style, or repurpose a building's component parts for the sake of making new constructions elsewhere. Sometimes the process was sparked by rulers proudly "improving" their predecessors' creations, and sometimes there were factors completely out of human control, like the earthquakes that frequently toppled the grand constructions of Roman and Greek cities. With so many different human and natural actions, any map would quickly become obsolete.

But perhaps we shouldn't be too hard on ourselves about the depictions we make of archaeological cities, because ancient people picked and chose what went on *their* maps of the city, too. The earliest city plan is on a portable terracotta tablet from the ancient Mesopotamian city of Nippur and dates to more than three thousand years ago. Working with the wet clay much as a sketch artist would, the mapmaker quickly incised the soft surface of the tablet with the major streets and canals of the city, along with the temple to the ancient god Enlil. The map is rather interesting for what it leaves out, such as the many ordinary residences that crowded the city but that weren't as important to the mapmaker as the religious and civic infrastructure. Among the religious sites, there was a little editing, too; the map omits some of the temples we know to have been there, like the temple to Enlil's competitor Ninurta. And it's particularly interesting to see the incidental information about the odd corners of the city that the mapmaker included, like the opening in the city wall that was labeled in tiny, neat cuneiform writing as "The Gate of the Unclean Women."

One of the most spectacular and enigmatic maps of an ancient city is the one of Rome that was made in three-dimensional form nearly two thousand years ago. Known as the Severan Marble Plan, it was carved from stone at the beginning of the third century A.D., when the city of Rome had already been in existence for nearly a thousand years. Its original size was at least sixty by forty-three feet and bigger than the side of a two-story house. The plan was attached to a wall of the temple known as the *Templum Pacis,* a structure that eventually collapsed. Unfortunately, the Severan Plan is today a jumble of about a thousand fragments, some of which remain mismatched because of missing joins. Archaeologists, who love a good jigsaw puzzle, have been working to reassemble the Severan Plan ever since the first pieces started turning up in the zeal for classical archaeological excavation that began in the sixteenth century. And because excavations are still ongoing, bits and pieces continue to turn up, eliciting considerable excitement (we must, however, lament the actions of earlier curators such as Pietro Forrier, who in 1741 sawed off irregular corners of some of the map fragments to make them match up better). Strangely enough, many fragments of the Severan Plan have been found relatively far away from the building where the complete map had once been attached, suggesting that at some point the ancient Romans found the map obsolete and discarded it much as you would throw out an outdated paper map of your own city.

To the ancient Romans, the Severan Marble Plan presented what some city planner or tax collector intended to be the "complete" picture of the living city, with depictions not only of the famous monuments of the time but also of run-of-the-mill shops and gathering places of everyday life. Yet the map's contemporary audiences also knew that there were older buildings that had since disappeared and couldn't be represented, just as they also recognized that as soon as the map was complete, parts of it were sure to have become obsolete. While the marble carvers were laboriously working on the giant plan, there were no doubt numerous conversations about what to do about a building that had been damaged by an earthquake or a fire and was surely going to be demolished or rebuilt—should it be included or not? And what about a building that was actually under construction, though not yet named or occupied? As for the act of mapmaking and the sculptor's personal thoughts about the matter, there was probably a bit of editorializing there, too. Carving the streets would have been accompanied by thoughts about the activities that took place there but couldn't be fully represented in mere physical form, no doubt prompting the sculptor's apprentice to let out a longing sigh or shake his head.

Undaunted by the specter of incompleteness and the realities of instant obsolescence, we are still attached to physical urban plans today. London, Houston, and Manhattan, among other cities, have sprouted new, attractive maps set up in public places that serve as signposts throughout the towns and provide a tangible "you are here" moment. It's interesting to watch visitors approach one of these maps as they compare the posted version with the paper map that they have in one hand and the smartphone map app that they have in another. Each of the maps is equally "true," and yet their utility comes only from the fact that they underwrite an individual's quest to go somewhere, in which there is always more than meets the eye. Embodied in our own experiences, the sign on a map reads differently to us after we visit a place on it and make it our own, compressing time in the same way as the Severan Plan. We can imagine an ancient Roman giving someone directions the way we do, drawing on past and present landmarks: "Well, you go past the place where the shoe repair used to be, until you get to the toga shop, and turn left."

Why Cities "Flow"

The whole point of maps and signposts is not to anchor us in place but to give us markers for movement. And movement is the hallmark of cities: people moving in from the countryside, visitors moving through the city on their way to somewhere else, and people moving among the city's dispersed spaces of residence, work, worship, shopping, exercise, education, and intimacy. Even within a single neighborhood, there are many diverse places and pathways, all of which provide the opportunity for people to engage with constantly updated information inputs about goods, services, and events. Just being out in the streets provides, every day, the opportunity to do things slightly differently through changes of pace and direction. We walk straight and then turn left and right, or right and left, all of which lets us end up at the desired destination by picking our way through city streets with confidence.

The social theorist Mihaly Csikszentmihalyi has suggested that our sense of well-being comes about from the mastery of our surroundings and from the confidence of knowing the constraints through which we channel our energies. He calls this concept flow, in which optimal experience and happiness are gained through focused concentration. Interestingly, people achieve flow not when they are in a completely unfettered environment but because of the opposite: constraints actually enable people to concentrate their energies, resulting in an intensely focused outcome. Examples of flow-inducing activities range from rock climbing to surgery to playing games with one's own children, in which people are "in the moment" in a way that supersedes perceptions of time and place, resulting in deep fulfillment. The fulfillment comes from negotiating mental constraints like the rules of a game, a musical score, or the logical steps of a complex operation. As Csikszentmihalyi states, "By far the overwhelming proportion of optimal experiences are reported to occur within sequences of activities that are goal-directed and bounded by rules—activities that require the investment of psychic energy, and that could not be done without the appropriate skills."

In cities, we can think of flow as something that results from the physical constraints of the streets, bridges, and subway lines that channel our forward motion. The narrowing of passageways and the greater number of people traveling through them accelerate the very physics of what it means to be alive in a city, like a conduit that increases the speed of water as the diameter narrows. Cities have as their essence a continual sense of movement, starting at the very moment of urban formation when rural people move into the metropolis. From that initial settlement, the people who come into a city are joined by other kinetic forces. Itinerant traders loop in and out of the city with fresh vegetables from close-by farms and fields, while longer-distance traders come with grain and other food staples on a seasonal basis. Haulers bring in raw materials for urban workshops and take out bulk waste and recyclables. Suburban professionals—scribes, lawyers, accountants, middle managers—come in and out of the city on a daily commute. Weaving in and out from those pulsating waves are the urban residents who move around from home to work to recreation to food sources within tightly circumscribed neighborhoods. And the people themselves create a kind of constraint that adds to the creation of flow: coming into a city, you feel the clip of urban walk-worlds as something faster than a rural gait, and you find yourself stepping up the pace.

The physical constraints of cities have a spillover effect on social interactions in other ways as well. In a village, you can pick out a pathway depending on a few simple factors: Are you on good terms with that neighbor? Do you feel "at home" crossing that other person's yard? By virtue of the village size and the fact that you had lived there for years, you're likely to know quite a bit about those neighbors (including whether there was a large unfriendly hound in the yard). By contrast, people in cities are absolved from creating face-to-face relationships through the mute abstraction of the built environment and the sheer number of people. In a city, one needs to get from points A to B without having to personally know everyone else in the vicinity or without having to remember all of the social networks sustained among all those households. That anonymity of the greater urban realm removes the necessity for sustained social inter-actions and explains why you might look up and smile at passersby on a rural lane but rarely on a city street. The physical structures of cities—their formal routes, roads, and pathways, along with the writ-ten and unwritten rules for empty spaces like parks and plazas—all provide containers that simultaneously constrain physical opportu-nities and paradoxically free people from the cognitive overload of what would otherwise be an overwhelming number of social obliga-tions just for the sake of movement.

Constricted spaces—crowded bridges, narrow streets, and nar-rower alleyways—were part of ancient cities, too. Excavations at places like Pompeii in Italy and the ancient Indus city of Mohenjo Daro in Pakistan have revealed a pedestrian cityscape that enables us to walk in the footsteps of our urban ancestors. Under the intense sun of midday, we can appreciate the shade cast by tall buildings while dodging the mad-dog blind alleys that abutted the major thor-oughfares. At the ancient Mexican city of Teotihuacan, a century of digging has revealed grand boulevards as well as intricate little by-lanes and courtyards within residential compounds. In those differ-entiated spaces, the ancient residents would have threaded their way through a maze of interconnected paths and experienced different rates and scales of flow as they moved about from day to day. Visitors today can still experience those spatial elements and retrace move-ments from the most intimate realm of the family hearth through the passageways of densely occupied neighborhoods to the massive pyramid complexes and the Avenue of the Dead.

Our understanding of the realm of motion in ancient sites comes from more than just appreciating their architecture. In moving along the pathways through neighborhoods and markets and temple plazas, ancient people left traces that we can actually see at the microscopic level. At the archaeological city of Kerkenes in Turkey, the archaeologist Scott Branting and his colleagues used an innovative sequence of techniques to show pedestrian movements. It would have taken centuries to excavate the entirety of Kerkenes, but a high-tech mapping process let them look at the layout of the buildings and streets like a geophysical "X-ray" in just a few summer months of fieldwork. The team made use of a survey method known as magnetic gradiometry, which reveals differential subsurface densities and results in a computer-generated map showing the outlines of structures in a ghostly version of the Nippur map or the Severan Marble Plan. Branting's team then conducted surgically precise excavations in some of the streets. They collected materials from vertical slices of the street deposits that showed the layering effect of dust accumulation over time and looked at samples of the layered sediments under a microscope. The more rounded the sand particles, they reasoned, the more the pathways had been traversed. Every footfall rounded the grains of sand just a little more, and the cumulative effect of all that walking enabled the team to identify which streets were more popular than others and which ones carried the most traffic.

In Kerkenes, pedestrians flowed through networks of streets that crisscrossed the urban sphere, and evidence of that flow was right there under the microscope. Similar patterns of movement can be envisioned for every ancient city, in which the impact of each individual person could, in theory, be measured at the molecular level. The collective pattern of all of those individual interactions created a personal sense of flow but also resulted in a collective pattern of movement. High-frequency streets are places where we envision the presence of shops and market stalls, while low-traffic lanes wound their way through houses and alleys where few people had the need to be moving about. People going from high traffic areas to low traffic ones and back again took in the world around them as they walked or rode from one place to another, choosing their ways from among the many combinations of streets that would lead them from their residences, through their neighborhoods, to the monumental temples, palaces, and plazas of their metropolis.

Sometimes street layouts in ancient cities were the result of powerful decree and enforced consensus. We can see this thousands of years ago, when the gridded plan of the archaeological site of Sisupalgarh in India laid out a command of place that directed the flow of movement, just as we see the evidence for planning in relatively new modern cities like Washington, D.C., Brasília, and Chandigarh. Most often, however, the layout of ancient city streets was the result of incremental growth. This was particularly true at the start of urbanism six thousand years ago where the first inhabitants arrived with only their village experiences of ad hoc juxtaposition, as though plenty of space would always be available. Even after the organizational pattern of a city's central area was well established, there was still a tendency to make new constructions with reference to the geometry of the nearest adjacent structure. The scholar Jeremy Till has called this the phenomenon of "architectural dependence," in which there are few opportunities for entire built environments to start over from zero. Instead, the patterns established at the beginning of the construction process are the ones that continue to shape the creative potential of every subsequent generation.

In cities, the notion of architectural dependence constrains the near-constant sense of motion that is an essential part of urban life. From the time of the very first city, movement was channeled by the built environment; for the purposes of making one's way through a space, a temporary building was just as much of a barrier as a permanent one. The resultant distinct flow within a city was thus neither mindless nor incidental but embedded and expressed in each architectural gesture and every pedestrian gait. In Chang'an, a great ancient capital of China that is just outside the modern metropolis of Xi'an, pathways and constructions provided not only an allowable flow but also moments of interrupted flow through structures that conveyed political authority. The palace, for example, sat athwart the traffic like a giant rock in a stream that otherwise passed to one side and the other. At Teotihuacan, the Sun Pyramid and the Feathered Serpent Pyramid were both very important structures, but their compounds were visually subordinate to the grand axis of the Moon Pyramid and the Street of the Dead. In the Roman period, it was not just in Rome but in every city around the Mediterranean that "the street became a substantive building, a public building with a sky-lighted central tube of transit and shadowed aisles, that fell into uniform bays of pause. As such, it assembled the economic life of the city in shops and offices ranked behind its porticoes, subjecting to its spatial laws another of the daily routines of living."

From the perspective of the thousands of ordinary people who took up residence in urban centers, it was those "daily routines of living" that made cities new and distinct and compelling. Compared with the dispersed landscapes of rural life and the intense family spaces of villages, the architecture of urban centers provided the opportunity for people to create close ties of their own design. Cities provided channels of movement in and around the many new types of buildings that had never before existed in permanent settlements: plazas that were larger than entire villages, and neighborhoods that mimicked the size of a village yet constituted just one tiny building block of an entire urban realm. Crowded streets of buildings and passageways provided new horizons that supplanted the natural skyline, making cities an anthropogenic maze. New verticalities of architecture, created for the first time in cities, invited people to look *up*. Just as for us the linearity of the internet has opened up an entire network of interconnected opportunities when one hyperlink leads to another, the built environment of cities resulted in a new circuitry of connections. Both the literal and the social flows of people were physically inscribed into the landscape, leaving us with the tangible remains of the past in the form of archaeological evidence.

Excavations at the Campus Martius by Jean Barbault, A.D. 1749

HOW TO DIG
AN ANCIENT CITY

There's something magical about the start of an archaeological project: after long hours in the library, and after months of planning and grant writing and finalizing permissions, you're finally ready to go. You've already checked in for the flight or put gas in the car, and you've double-checked your equipment list (don't forget the spare batteries!). You grab your last cup of departmental coffee and check your mailbox. You sign some last-minute paperwork and say thanks to the office staff for minding your business while you're gone, all the while gathering the envious glances of your co-workers. With a broad smile on your face and boots on your feet, you're "off to the field."

What skill set does it take to investigate the ancient past? You might think that it requires apprenticeship on a research team or years of advanced studies, maybe even a Ph.D. Those things are useful, of course, but the only thing you *really* need to be an archaeologist is a good sense of observation. Some of the best field-workers

I've known are people who are actually librarians, accountants, and doctors by profession who bring their steady work habits and good record-keeping skills to the patient uncovering of the ancient past. Bit by bit, and working with tools that range from hefty pickaxes to tiny paintbrushes, they uncover the buildings, burials, and trash pits of antiquity right down to the very first human activities. Once they've dug down to the bottom of the cultural layers, they often keep going in order to see what the landscape was like before people arrived.

But why do we have to dig, and where did all of that dirt come from? It certainly seems odd that something as big as an entire ancient city could have vanished under the earth. Are our own cities similarly in danger of being buried? The simple answer is . . . yes. Just think about that abandoned lot you pass by from time to time, a haven for windblown trash and weeds that trap additional trash, leaves, and dust. If no one cleared out the lot for a hundred years, there would be a foot or so of detritus and soil. Now imagine if a house had been there, abandoned, with the roof eventually collapsing and the walls caving in. Throughout the decades of decomposition, half-empty and dilapidated, the structure would harbor some scurrying rats or mice, a few birds' nests, and perhaps a transient or two whose discards would have added to the accumulation. After a couple of centuries, the house would probably be unrecognizable, flattened by weather, gravity, and people scrounging away its more usable components.

In many cases, however, ancient cities were buried not because they were abandoned but because they remained occupied. As more and more people came into the first urban areas, there was a demand for residential and mercantile space by newcomers and by residents who were already there. People were continually building to improve their conditions and to satisfy their itch for architectural novelty through renovations. The site remained vibrant and kept growing. Ancient people didn't have bulldozers to clear away old houses or outmoded temples, and it was much easier to salvage the best building materials, pull down the walls, and fill in the spaces of the old foundation with rubble to make a platform for the next phase of building. Urban structures thus became quarries for each successive phase of construction as residents modified entire neighborhoods over and over again to suit their changing tastes. During the course of time, the cycle of buildup and collapse raised the entire city, one building at a time.

Today, people working underground to create subway tunnels and building foundations in Mexico City, Athens, Rome, London, Paris, Xi'an, and Istanbul—to name just a few—are constantly encountering new evidence of their city's earliest incarnations. Amazing finds are made by happenstance when a sharp-eyed bulldozer operator cuts the engine at the first nick of an ancient stone or when electronic survey equipment detects a void in the earth that turns out to be an ancient shrine or bathhouse or grain storeroom. By the time professionals come to supervise the recovery of artifacts, the resulting excavations are quite a bit different from the romantic visions of archaeologists silhouetted by a setting sun and standing tall next to picturesque windswept ruins. Excavation under a living city involves hard hats, maneuvers with heavy equipment deep underground where light and air are scarce, and the endless technical challenges of uncovering the remains, removing the dirt, and bringing the artifacts up to the surface, where they can be displayed in museums or kept for study in research institutes.

Regardless of the circumstances of discovery, archaeological research proceeds according to a fairly standard rubric of approach. Each layer of ancient habitation has sealed off the era that came before, a phenomenon resulting in a sequence of events that is like the layering of geologic eras. Although we now have increasingly sophisticated ways of ascertaining the precise age of archaeological finds, like radiocarbon dating and its newer cousin optically stimulated luminescence dating, the positionality of archaeological layers is still our main way of telling the story of an ancient site. By recovering objects that are found together in the different layers, we can see the effects of stylistic change over time in which some plain and useful objects can stay the same for centuries while some decorative objects come onto the scene in an inspired flash of novelty. One good example of an entrepreneurial change that also provides a handy marker of time is Greek red-figure pottery that constituted both a technological innovation and a new decorative style starting around 530 B.C. in cities like Athens. Becoming instantly popular as an item for household decorating and as part of wine-drinking table sets, even a tiny sherd of such pottery found in an archaeological excavation is a marker of a watershed moment of cultural change and provides a date for the context of the other finds. The concept of stratigraphy also informs us about the array of goods and architectural types used together in different time periods and the way in which households of differential wealth, ethnicity, and size had some things in common like cookware and hairstyling tools and figurines. This resultant assemblage-based approach of research is quite different from the museum perspective on objects in which each item is sealed away in a glass case, separated from the other things that all would have been in use at the same time.

Our experiences as archaeologists are a far cry from the experiences of museumgoers in other ways as well, because we're the lucky ones who can actually put our hands on the past. Things come out of the ground and make themselves visible through our actions, and sometimes at the most unexpected moments, too (when I brief the excavation team at the beginning of every field season, I remind them that the most exciting thing that we find in an excavation could happen on the first day, or on the last day, or at a moment when we're a bit distracted by visitors, illness, or the prospect of a lunch break). In the process of archaeological recovery, we come upon myriad items that were designed to be handled and buildings that bore the brunt of actual daily life. Although we afterward aggregate the statistics of production and consumption to understand cities as a whole, it's important to remember that just as in the modern day statistics are made up of the incremental actions of real people. Whether we excavate an ancient household and its trash pile or an ancient temple and its magnificent ritual artworks, we are uncovering the outcome of decisions made on individual and collective levels.

It is ordinary people—you and I and millions of others—who make cities what they are. The most casual actions can leave a durable trace that sparks our imaginations to bridge the gap of centuries that passed between the past and today. Not long ago, I was in a classroom of sixth graders when one of them asked me what my favorite thing was that I ever found. To their surprise, I answered that it was not some precious jewel or priceless pot. Instead, my favorite find came in the moment when we were cutting through the mighty brick city wall of the ancient city of Sisupalgarh in India, recording every size and position of the layers of construction. In between two courses of bricks, we saw an ancient handprint where the mason had smeared mud mortar before laying the next course. For the ancient engineers and laborers, it was a momentary action, a routine gesture of construction that was visible for only a second until the next brick was sandwiched on top. For two thousand years, that little act lay sealed away from human eyes, until we found it. When we excavated the wall under the blazing, humid sun of the Indian coastal winter, I gingerly put my fingers next to those imprints by way of respectful comparison. It's as close as I've ever come to transporting myself to the ancient past.

In between those aha! moments of singular discovery, the process of excavation can be fast or slow depending on the context: Is it a structure with a floor made of fine clay, easily nicked by a digging tool? In that case, we had better proceed slowly. Or is it the fill of an ancient well, tumbled in with broken pottery and the infilling mud of sequential rainstorms? In that case, we can move more quickly. We don't always work with a tiny brush as you see in the movies or in documentaries: sometimes we work with a backhoe, if for example an ancient site was buried by several feet of alluvial silt from a flood that we can safely remove with heavy equipment. The sheer scale of ancient cities means that some layers of dirt can be removed expediently so that we can make sure we save enough time for the deeper portions of the dig, when work is slower and spaces more constrained. If we spend too much time in the upper layers of a site, we'll run out of time to carefully excavate the lowest, earliest levels of occupation (it's a truism that archaeologists often find something very interesting during the very last days of the field season, when we are deep down in the trench).

Being an archaeologist is a little like being a carpenter; with a standard set of tools like a pickax, a trowel, and a brush, we can go to sites anywhere and get to work peeling our way down through the layers of time. We often add to our tool kit the standard agricultural implements of the region, like hoes and mattocks. The practice of using local tools and talent isn't just a matter of wanting to save money on shipping shovels. We need to assemble all of the expertise we can muster. Many of our excavation crew members are farmers in the other seasons of the year, and by having them dig with the tools with which they are most familiar, we benefit from their skill in separating out the different types of soil that constitute the layers and activity areas of ancient life. They can easily tell the difference between a flood deposit, windborne silt, the sweepings that accumulate in the corners of abandoned buildings, and the dark and trampled soil of ancient animal pens. Archaeologists have many ways of recognizing the essential work they do, from the sponsorship of end-of-season parties to placing them front and center in archaeological publications as Sir John Marshall did in the very first page of his three-volume work on the city of Taxila in Pakistan: "Let us not forget that it is to the toil and sweat of the diggers that, first and foremost, we owe the vast majority of our archaeological treasures."

No one knows the subtleties of dirt like local farmers! Their understanding of the soils that cover ancient remains is often far greater than ours, and a humbling reminder that dialogues about work are not driven only by the experiences and education of the project directors. The best archaeological teams encompass a variety of knowledge streams: university-based faculty and students bring their perspectives of theory and interpretation, members of the regional and national government agencies bring their experience of comparative analysis, and locals bring their knowledge of the specific conditions in which we find the ancient site. The resultant project, often conducted under time pressure and challenging environmental conditions, results in a kind of pressure-cooker magic of teamwork. Given the stories, reminiscences, and insider humor that build up in those conditions, it's no wonder that archaeological projects engender a camaraderie that lasts for the lifetime of the participants. When we meet up at archaeological conferences or institute "open house" days, we grab a beer and relive the day that the project vehicle lost a wheel or the time we exposed a nest of centipedes that exploded out of the side of the excavation trench and straight into the antiquities bucket.

We excavate to answer specific research questions, like "What's the scale of production in this city's ancient workshops and warehouses?" with its implications for ancient urban economic organization, or "How healthy was the urban population?" through the study of ancient skeletons. Those broad academic questions are tailored to fit the portions of the site that are accessible relative to local logistics and permissions. Uncovering a big building, the traces of which might be seen aboveground in the form of a dilapidated wall or a telltale line of vegetation, is easy compared with the more painstaking investigations of a city's innumerable humble dwellings of thatch, wood, or mud. Perishable architectural elements would have rotted away or, more likely, been pulled apart by home owners and their descendants in an endless series of upgrades to their growing households. Representing the shanties and lean-tos of ancient migrant populations, these ephemeral structures still leave a faint yet discernible archaeological trace in the form of wall lines and postholes that are revealed only by a patient field-worker's careful clearance with a brush or trowel. Other types of discoveries take time too, whether it's the piece-by-piece recovery of a broken pottery vessel whose individual fragments are labeled to help the conservator reconstruct it or the laborious sifting of soil to retrieve tiny pieces of ornaments and manufacturing debris. Archaeologists tend to have a long-term view and a lot of patience; after all, we've been searching for the pieces of the Severan Marble Plan of Rome since 1562, and while we have a lot to work with, we still have only about 10 percent of the original.

But patience is its own reward as we dig and scrape and puzzle over the past in our excavation trenches. Even an ancient hole in the ground contains information! Working at the site of Tepe Sharafabad in Iran, the archaeologist Richard Redding was able to discern that a pit from the mid-fourth millennium B.C. had slowly filled in over several different seasons rather than all at once. The tip-off was an intact toad skeleton that was found in a layer of mud that accumulated when the pit had been left open to the elements. Redding reasoned that the only way the toad skeleton would have survived was if it had died during the course of its summer estivation, later to be covered over by windblown and waterborne silt. This gentle burial was followed by repeated layers of debris tossed in by local residents over several years in a process that gradually filled the hole. By carefully removing the contents of the ancient pit layer-wise, Redding and his colleagues were able to show that the sequential fill corresponded to summer and winter activities in the community.

As farmers and gardeners know today, summer and winter don't oscillate in an entirely regular way, and there can be a lot of variability in the seasons from one year to the next. In some years, you might get a bumper crop of zucchini that leaves you searching out lots of different recipes and willing neighbors. In other years, there might be late rains or pest invasions that leave you with only a handful of produce and nothing to share. Your compost pile and kitchen trash would show the relative quantities of discard from one year to the next as you dealt with the variable quantity and quality of the harvest. In the case of Tepe Sharafabad, the layers of trash showed the difference between good years and bad ones, marked by the relative proportion of slaughtered young sheep and goats. Although we might be tempted to interpret a spike in the number of bones as a sign of plenty and a celebration of abundance, the researchers saw something darker in the picture. Informed by the strategies of local people who today cull their herds when summer drought foretells a shortage of winter fodder, the investigators concluded that ancient people's feasts would have masked a circumstance of cutting their losses.

Redding's experience with the ancient pit is a good example of the way that nothing gets overlooked at a dig site. Soil samples taken for laboratory analysis are tested for traces of pigments from ancient manufacturing activities. Phosphates reveal the traces of ancient toilets, and the hardy eggs of parasites recovered from privies can be used to track human health. Microscopic analysis reveals the traces of ancient vegetation through phytoliths, the indestructible silica structures of plant cell walls. In addition to the little envelopes of soil that we remove for laboratory tests, we take bigger sacks of excavated soil and put them through water sieves. Through that process, we recover tiny fish and bird bones along with the seeds of crops and weeds that got carbonized when they were swept into an ancient fire and preserved from the rot that otherwise besets organic materials. We might get a fragment of a well-worn bone needle, broken long ago, or some little chips of stone that were the result of someone's making a stone knife or sharpening a blade for kitchen work. Sometimes there is a tiny little bead, a fugitive from a necklace whose string broke and whose owner would surely have spent days peering around to find until finally giving it up for lost.

When archaeologists dig, we work backward in time, starting with the site's last phases of occupation that are just below the surface. At the beginning of a project, we can climb in and out of the excavation trenches without ladders, and the structures and features that we uncover are easy for visitors to see. Deeper digs that enable us to analyze the whole evolution of an urban site are more challenging. Visitors have a harder time peering into the depths, and excavations generally get smaller in area as we go down and strategically poke around to find a place to continue digging where we don't disturb any interesting or photogenic features that the local visitors' bureau might want to turn into a tourist attraction. The ultimate goal in an excavation is to reach natural, so-called virgin, soil that represents the ground surface that existed prior to human occupation. By the time this is achieved at the end of a long, hot excavation season, the trench can be very small, sometimes only as large an area as one person working alone can dig. In those final days of the project, the crew members peer down to the lucky (unlucky?) person at the bottom, a bit apprehensive for her or his safety at such depths. Curious local children and farm animals are held back to keep them from falling in; local dogs are smarter and stay away. The lone excavator's voice, muffled by the depths, asks for things to be sent down: some water, a flashlight, a camera, a square of aluminum foil for a radiocarbon sample. The collective hope is that the sample can be dated to reveal the chronology of the earliest habitation at the site.

But is this seemingly random approach the best way to find out about urban origins? It might stand to reason that if you wanted to find the oldest cities, it would be logical to find the biggest site around, under the assumption that cities grow in a linear, incremental process analogous to the way that the oldest trees have a girth that matches their age. In that case, it should be easy to start at the apex and drill all the way down. But what if the site itself was just *too large* to contemplate? If you can imagine how difficult it would be to try to excavate a site as big as New York City or Tokyo in the sticky heat of summer, you'll sympathize with Max Mallowan upon his first encounter with the remains of the ancient site of Tell Brak in northern Syria:

> I saw the great mound of Brak for the first time on a hot af-ternoon in November, 1934, when, together with my wife and Mr. Macartney, I was examining the ancient sites in the Khabur and Jaghjagha valleys of northern Syria. As we walked up the steep slopes of the *tall* we kicked aside count-less fragments of potsherds and other ancient debris, and parched as we were it seemed tedious to speculate on what periods of history lay buried within.... I noted that this was a magnificent site which would be well worth digging, pro-vided that sufficient funds were available for the purpose. But before attempting to come to grips with so formidable a mound it was obviously desirable to find out more about the general sequence of stratification elsewhere in the district. We therefore continued to look for a smaller site which would yield results more quickly.

Mallowan's cautionary tale is just one of many about the costs, risks, and relative value of digging in the biggest sites compared with sites of more manageable size. The challenges of digging deep come with logistical risks as well. In countries with strong occupational safety laws, or when sediments risk collapsing into deep trenches, archaeologists put up shoring as they descend. Sometimes the downward excavations are further complicated by a water table that has risen since ancient times due to local waterlogging, agricultural irrigation, or modern dam construction that has altered the configuration of the entire region's groundwater. Our team experienced this phenomenon in Sisupalgarh in India, where the only solution was to dig while using electric pumps to remove the seeping water from the deepening trench. The local men who were our field-workers included several who were well diggers by profession, a convenient combination of our needs and their expertise. The resultant collaboration involved a devil-may-care approach to long electric wires snaking across open fields made soggy by the backwash of the trench, but our field-workers' insights did lead to new and useful innovations. The next year we dug a similar trench in another location and took their advice to make the trench round instead of square so that the sidewalls would better withstand the pressure. This worked out well, although we did have to continually explain to visiting colleagues and students the rationale for our decidedly unorthodox approach and that, no, it was not some newfangled type of excavation strategy from America.

Archaeologists working all over the world have recognized the challenges of digging through tens of feet of deposits to reach the very first levels of ancient urban occupation. The fact that some of the best sites for research are the ones whose beginnings are hidden beneath the most debris means that knowledge about the origins of urban life is frustratingly elusive. The scholarly game of ping-pong known as "my site is older than your site" (and the more serious question of "why did people first settle here?") is continually updated by the stamina and luck of teams that have probed sites over and over again to find the earliest deposits. A good example is the ancient city of Harappa, which is part of the ancient Indus culture, where it took Mark Kenoyer and his joint U.S.-Pakistani team more than twenty years of painstaking work to identify the small area under a massive site that represented the earliest settlement. Quickly outgrown by subsequent habitations, the initial phase was quite literally hiding under the massive quantity of structural debris that represented the city's subsequent successful growth over time.

Another way of thinking about the challenges of finding urban origins is to imagine an ancient city as an enormous king cake, in which there is a tiny token figure baked into the batter and invisible from the surface. Only one slice of the cake contains the figure, and the cake can be vast, meaning that most slices have nothing at all. Now imagine that instead of taking a whole slice that represents some sizable portion of the cake, such as an eighth or a twelfth that would at least give some reasonable odds that you would recover a token, you take a much smaller initial cut. Not only that, but your tiny fraction gets smaller and smaller as you dig down from the frosting and layers at the top, so that the exposed surface diminishes toward the bottom of the cake. By the time you reach the part that touches the plate, your excavations have the dimensions the width of a toothpick. Under those conditions, how many dig sessions, each representing an entire year's worth of effort, might you have to undertake before finding the token of the earliest occupation? How many times would you probe the cake before concluding that there was no such token to be found?

Despite the intellectual and logistical challenges associated with deep digs, the process of discovery itself continually results in new ways of thinking, new data, and new labels for the ancient urban works that we have discovered. A constant process of revision is encompassed in the structure of research and incumbent on archaeologists' background, funding, and taste for long-term commitment. Max Mallowan dealt with the massive archaeological site of Tell Brak by initially turning away from it, in favor of pursuing a smaller site where he could test out techniques of investigation and interpretation. Other investigators have plunged right into their massive sites, like the German archaeologist Robert Koldewey, who writes crisply that his excavations at Babylon "commenced on March 26, 1899, on the east side of the Kasr to the north of the Ishtar Gate." Yet the interpretations of the site were not so easily marshaled. By the time he finished his excavation project thirteen years later, he admitted that "my view of the purpose of the various buildings has altered during the course of the excavations, especially in relation to the literary sources. This is the natural result of gradual progress in research, never working with conclusive material."

When we are successful in reaching an ancient city's first levels, those moments of deep discovery lead to both elation and doubt. We are relieved that we have finally reached the bottom of the occupational deposits and that we can turn our attention to the other pressing business of the season's end such as data recording, taking final photographs of the excavation, labeling the trunks of artifacts to be shipped to labs, packing away the equipment, and getting the students to their trains and planes on time so that they can return to their classes. As we celebrate a layer in which no artifacts are found, suggesting that we have reached the earliest levels—the "year 0" of urban occupation, there's nonetheless a nagging sense of uncertainty. What do we really know about the beginnings of site occupation? What if this just happened to be an empty patch of someone's house compound, and there is a structure just a few yards away that is itself on top of an older layer that remains undiscovered? Did that radiocarbon sample, collected in the cool dim depths of the trench on the next-to-last day of the project season, come from an intentional act of ancient house construction or cooking activity? Or was it blown in by the wind from a brush fire that long predated settlements, or dropped down a rodent hole from a time period many centuries later?

The beginnings of cities are hard to interpret, even when we find more than fragmentary potsherds or enigmatic bits of charcoal, and even when we can convince ourselves and our colleagues that we've truly reached the bottom. Early occupational phases were often ephemeral, like the shantytowns that spring up at the edges of modern cities and are quickly demolished as residents get a leg up in the urban economy. If anything does remain from those first occupational eras, it's often just a few courses of building foundations that require a great deal of imagination to render into a picture of ancient lifeways. Yet despite all this, the exposure of early levels is often supported by local tourism boards eager to make the most of their city's claims of historical longevity. The remains of ancient York can be seen through a glass floor in the basement of the Jorvik Viking Centre located in the heart of town. In Osaka, Japan, the Museum of History has a subterranean view of the archaeological remains that were found by happenstance in the construction process. For eight euros—about the price of a sandwich—tourists can see some building foundations of the ancient Gallo-Roman town of Lutetia in the "archaeological crypt" of the Cathedral of Notre Dame in Paris. Visitors' puzzled glances reveal the unspoken question "why are we looking at these bits and pieces?" The answer is: because that's all that's left.

What If You Can't Dig?

Although archaeologists are famously associated with digging, that's not our only mode of investigation. In the case of studying ancient cities, that's a good thing, because the size and complexity of urban centers are so great that the most ambitious excavation projects can uncover only a tiny fraction of them. To address ancient cities at a scale commensurate with their complexities, archaeologists often use a landscape approach. This enables us to incorporate the study of an ancient city's charismatic core and its monuments, temples, and palaces with the surrounding halos of settlement and the extensions of those settlements out into the countrysides that supplied cities with food and raw materials. Known as archaeological survey, these research programs have the same goals of knowledge capture as surveys in biology, botany, and geology that allow for data collection and the analysis of complex interactions on a large spatial scale.

There are many urban sites that aren't buried by modern ones— Tell Brak itself, for example, as well as sites like Chang'an in China, Teotihuacan in Mexico, and Leptiminus in Tunisia. For sites such as these, one of the simplest nonexcavation approaches consists of a technique called field walking. It means just what it sounds like: the act of walking across the surface and looking for fragmentary archaeological remains. We assemble a team of three to six people who walk across the site in straight lines ten to thirty feet apart, guided by a compass bearing to ensure uniform coverage of the area. With clipboards or iPads in hand, each person keeps up a steady pace with the others while looking down at the ground to the left and right.

The field walkers note and record the traces of anything archaeo-logical underfoot, including artifacts, architectural elements, and production debris such as beads, pottery, slag, bricks, and little chips of stone. At the end of the day, the researchers return to base camp to compare notes and compile the data. Little by little, the survey's re-sults are added to the project map, resulting in a depiction of ancient urban residents' patterns of production and consumption as revealed by surface remains across the vast spaces of the ancient city.

Whether overgrown by jungle, scoured clear of vegetation by des-ert winds, or plowed by modern farmers, the surfaces of ancient cities are still littered with the debris of both monumental and everyday life. While some artifacts are on the surface because they were used during the last periods of occupation, the continual upward cycling of debris enables us to also capture the story of the city's earlier occupa-tions. Some early materials end up on the surface because ancient people didn't just build up their cities into mounds through hermeti-cally sealed layers. Instead, they actively burrowed into lower depos-its while retrieving usable building materials, constructing house foundations, and digging wells, all of which brought older stuff up to the living surface. The process is analogous to the way in which a maintenance ditch or a deep sewer pipe replacement on your own city streets might go through several layers of pavement before it gets to the century-old pipe down below. When the workers put the dirt from the trench back in, the older materials simply get mixed into the re-filling of the trench, such that there's just as much chance that a coin from this year could be down at the bottom of the trench and that the uppermost artifact will now be an antique glass bottle fragment.

In addition to the unintentional mixing of older deposits with newer layers, ancient people sometimes kept old things on purpose.

Just as we own heirlooms as a reminder of our heritage, ancient people had a fascination with the objects that came from still older times. In Mesopotamia, they routinely recycled venerable ritual items into new sanctuaries, like the priest Enannatum, who paid homage to centuries-old cuneiform inscriptions at Ur by enshrining them in a new temple room. For ordinary people as well, there were plenty of opportunities to integrate something old into their repertoire of objects: an old bead took its place on a necklace along with newly made ornaments, an ancient potsherd became a handy feeding dish for an animal, an old-style pestle was cleaned up and put back into service in the kitchen or used as a doorstop. For an archaeologist investigating the mixed chronologies of ancient use contexts, the interpretation is a little like a mystery novel: How do the parts fit together into a single moment of use-time, and how were those old objects meaningful? You can experience this yourself the next time you walk into an elderly person's house and see a display of items that date not only from his life span but also from his parents' and grandparents' time, all on the same countertop with a smartphone or a new appliance. Or you can think of your own trash, in which you might have discarded, in the same day, a banana peel from breakfast, last week's theater ticket, and the broken fragments of a piece of your grandmother's china.

The artifacts that we find, however fragmentary, do more than answer questions: they can sometimes prompt whole new lines of inquiry and interpretations. In Sisupalgarh, I initiated three sequential years of surface survey, carried out by painstaking hands-and-knees collection of regularly spaced sample units across the site (I once overheard the local villagers asking each other what crime I had committed in my country that I would be sentenced to come so far and look for tiny bits of broken things). Our investigations showed that some wealth indicators such as metal fragments tended to be concentrated in some part of the site and not others, an outcome that was expected given our understanding that different neighborhoods would have been inhabited by people of varied socioeconomic status. The survey also unexpectedly revealed that some items that might otherwise be interpreted as signs of wealth, such as fragments of polished pottery, were quite widespread throughout the site. This observation provided two epiphanies about ancient urban life. First, the presence of identical goods suggested there was an appreciation of a shared "style" that permeated the urban milieu and cut across socioeconomic lines. Second, even low-income households in a city have the equivalent of "good teacups" that marked them as urban(e) residents in ways that they might not have been able to afford in the countryside.

In addition to surveys focused on low-tech walking and collecting, archaeologists make use of a vast array of emerging technologies in their study of ancient cities. High-tech approaches, ranging from noninvasive subsurface probing to aerial and satellite imagery, constitute an increasingly essential part of the modern archaeological tool kit. Among the most rewarding techniques are remote sensing capacities that enable us to identify the buried remains of structures, wells, and kilns where ancient production took place or that reveal the entire streetscape by detecting the differences between solid structures and the empty spaces between them. Magnetic gradiometry is a technique that records the ambient variable magnetism of subsurface deposits through an instrument that a human operator carries while walking back and forth across an ancient site. Other types of instrumentation capture signals sent out by the operator that bounce back from differential subsurface remnants: resistivity reads the returning arc of a mild electric current to assess the density of underground deposits, while ground-penetrating radar assesses density through radar waves that can pick up the traces of subsurface remains fifteen feet or more in depth and showing multiple phases of ancient constructions.

A more high-tech approach known as LIDAR—an acronym for "Light Detection and Ranging"—has revolutionized studies of ancient urbanism in areas covered by jungle such as the Yucatán Peninsula and Southeast Asia. The technique makes use of an airplane-mounted laser scanner flown above the treetops to produce a map of the ground's surface. Remarkably, the LIDAR process can see through vegetation, revealing an entire landscape of small mounds, ditches, reservoirs, and roads that were previously invisible to researchers. Like other high-tech approaches, LIDAR has provided new data, but more important, the technique also has prompted new ways of thinking and new frameworks for interpretation. When archaeologists first investigated the Maya cities of the Yucatán and adjacent Central America by slashing a pathway through the jungle, practically the only things that were visible through the thick foliage were the tall remains of pyramids and temples. These dramatic structures were interpreted as the commanding icons of crushing royal-ritual power, simply because nothing else could be seen around them! Thanks to LIDAR, we now know that the pyramids and temples of Maya cities were equivalent to a downtown area, and that a monumental central zone was surrounded by vast "suburbs" linked to the urban core by an extensive network of pathways.

LIDAR and other aerial technologies have also enabled the study of ancient cities that can't be accessed for other reasons. The French-Cambodian team working at the ancient medieval city of Angkor have used ultralight planes, LIDAR, and satellite imagery for the simple reason that field walking is impossible in a country that is still full of land mines. In the Near East, the prevalence of warfare and civil unrest has resulted in an entire generation of archaeologists who have had little opportunity to physically travel to the regions that they study. In a remarkable example of the scholarly equivalent of "when life gives you lemons, make lemonade," Jason Ur, now a Harvard professor, conducted research on ancient Mesopotamian cities while still a graduate student. He used declassified 1960s U.S. government satellite photographs to search for known sites and to examine the surrounding landscape for patterns of connectivity. The black-and-white images, which preserve a record of the terrain from before the time of the modern population boom in the region, have in that way actually proven to be better for seeking out ancient features than today's digital images. From the bird's-eye view, he was able to conclude that hinterland fields and pasturelands were linked to ancient cities by radial pathways, not unlike the massive networks of roads that form the neural ganglia of cities like Chicago and London today.

Thanks to archaeologists' creative use of both surveys and excavations, the evidence for urbanism is both intensive and extensive. Even if any particular site has had only a little investigation, we can glean enough information from nearby areas to form a comparative data set to address not only what people did in cities but why cities came about at all. The question is so compelling that it inspires archaeologists to put in years of effort to tackle the largest sites in search of answers. Max Mallowan eventually reconciled himself to digging at Brak, thus discovering what has subsequently been acknowledged as the world's first city. But he wasn't alone in his quest: the wife whom he mentioned was the mystery novelist Agatha Christie, who often accompanied him to the field and whom he thanked in his publications for being his general helpmate and site photographer (she had other interests too; Joan Oates, a more recent excavator at Brak, has shared with me stories of Christie's coming along to the site and saying, "Let's go for a picnic!"). Archaeology and detective work were, in this case, literal bedfellows, and both Christie and Mallowan were deeply engaged in a life's pursuit of whodunit. Enticing their readers to look sharply for clues that revealed past events, they spun out tales in which hypotheses and interpretations put casual assumptions in check from one turn of the page to the next. Among the biggest mysteries was this: Why did cities happen at all, and what came before them?

Alabaster eye idol from Tell Brak

4

BEFORE CITIES, THERE WAS . . .

Perhaps we're wrong to assume that the best place to look for the archaeological evidence of urban beginnings is under the actual ancient cities themselves. Maybe in order to find out the reason for urbanism, we need to look at someplace that *isn't* a city. After all, even when we excavate, we have a hard time getting much of a view of the earliest residents of an ancient metropolis. The specific reason for why people came to a particular locale is likely to elude us in the tiny hole that we manage to poke all the way through an ancient site's many layers of habitation. A city that might initially have been established because it was a convenient place for trade or mining or the mustering of troops might have grown within a generation or two—a blink of an eye in archaeological chronologies—to become a place that was attractive for other reasons, such as the growth of a particular manufacturing industry, the emergence of educational institutions, or the seat of a government. The activities of newcomers would quickly have obscured or renovated the first constructions, leaving us with no discoverable answers about what happened at the beginning.

So where can we look to figure out what people did before cities existed as dynamic, multipurpose places? For the million-plus years of our human existence, the only form of residence was small villages dispersed across the landscape. But deep in our ancestral past, there were places that brought people into groups much larger than the population of any village and that served as the blueprints for the eventual development of urban spaces. Sometimes it was a summer-bright mountain pass that provided seasonal opportunities for people to meet and marry. Sometimes it was a place where rivers met, blending the convenience of trade routes with the potential for bumper crops. And sometimes it was a forbidding cave or sacred forest that drew people together for a journey of shared purpose. Pilgrimages of both secular and sacred forms took place during the nicer seasons of the year, when people could camp out with light clothing and just a few belongings. They went with light hearts as well, anticipating the opportunities for trade or love affairs in the mingling crowds.

Our ancestors' forays to those temporary gatherings entailed some inconveniences and uncertainties. New arrivals would need help figuring out where to sleep and where to get food and water. They would have to ask others about the agreed-upon location for bathing and toileting and whether there was an established schedule for getting together and worshipping. Along with solemn ritual activities or serious trade negotiations, there would be meals and libations ladled out by enterprising cooks who set up shop to feed the hungry masses. Feasts might draw in human hangers-on, a few stray dogs, and a host of other pests like flies and rats. There were times of inconvenience, of being muddy, thirsty, or uncomfortably hot. After a few days of feasting, the trampled ground around the campsites would be smelly and unpleasant, but people didn't seem to mind, and in any case they would soon be going home and leaving the trash behind. Returning to their villages, those who had gone on the trek probably embellished their tales of travel with the details of minor hardships and awkward mishaps that provided proof of their participation. Like a prehistoric Woodstock, a personal recollection of discomfort lent authenticity and humor to the stories told afterward.

Of all the ritual sites that show this incipient tolerance of crowded conditions and community engagement, the most remarkable is Göbekli Tepe, located in the hot, dry plains of southern Turkey. Hard by the Syrian border, the region easily reaches 120 degrees Fahrenheit in the summer (I have done archaeological fieldwork in the nearby province of Diyarbakir, where the project director, Tim Matney, candidly told us that the weather was so hot that "any decision that you make after 10:00 in the morning is probably not a good decision"). Although the environment was likely to have been just as uncompromising ten thousand years ago, the builders of Göbekli Tepe were probably wise enough to avoid the heat of the summer days. They focused their energies instead on the spring and fall, when they could hunt and gather while they consecrated some of their time to community life, with the most distinct marker of their devotion manifested in the form of towering stone pillars. Set up in a circle, those pillars constitute what we now recognize as the world's earliest ritual structure, what Charles Mann has poetically termed "the first structure human beings put together that was bigger and more complicated than a hut."

The stones of Göbekli Tepe weren't just simple monoliths dragged from a nearby hillside quarry, although that act alone would have been impressive. More than being big rocks, the pillars were carefully shaped after they were quarried in a process of stone working that added countless hours to the actions of moving and emplacing the uprights. The pillars' decorators then added even more work by carving primitive, haunting representations of animals in low relief, an entire zoology of local wild animals, including vultures, scorpions, gazelles, boars, snakes, and foxes. The remarkable preservation of artistic skill illustrates the types of things that we are often missing in the archaeological record, given that similar carvings would probably have been represented in perishable materials such as wood, if such things survived the passage of time (they usually don't). Numerous people contributed to the decoration of Göbekli Tepe's stone columns, as evidenced by the slightly different styles of animals and birds, revealing the presence of multiple sculptural "hands." The effect is reminiscent of other, more recent ritual constructions, like European cathedrals that also were the product of many dozens of specialists working with many hundreds of laborers over many years, with similar idiosyncrasies of style and form.

The result of all of that collaborative effort is one of the most beautiful and enigmatic ancient religious sites in the world. Yet the most amazing thing about Göbekli Tepe is not that it constitutes the earliest known record of human community architecture, or that it was built by people who created it entirely through the energy of human hands without any help from domestic animals or mechanical devices. It is the fact that once the imposing circular monument was constructed and consecrated, it was *intentionally buried* by the people who had built it. Having constructed their phenomenal place, they then committed what would seem to be the entirely illogical act of deliberately obscuring it and starting over. And they buried and

restarted the monument not just once but several times! Archaeologists have now found at least four iterations of circular column structures at Göbekli Tepe, and further excavations will surely reveal
more. For the site's ancient sculptors and artisans, it seems that it
was the act of constructing, and not just the construction itself, that
was the key activity. Even after the monuments were constructed,
their users viewed them as "works in progress," in which an apparent physical wholeness was not enough. A visitor could not step into
the same Göbekli Tepe twice; for each generation, it had to be completed and put away so that new things could happen.

Stonehenge, more familiar to us perhaps than Göbekli Tepe, presents a similar landscape of continued renewal and physical activities
of construction. Although we tend to envision Stonehenge as an
iconic, singular place out on the windswept Salisbury Plain, archaeological research illustrates how the upright circlet at Stonehenge was
part of a much larger ritual landscape that evolved over fifteen hundred years of active use. Stonehenge was surrounded by other ritual
features, including the Aubrey holes, Woodhenge, Silbury Hill, and
Avebury across twenty miles of landscape—an entire day's travel by
foot. The research team headed by the University College London
professor Mike Parker Pearson has taken a landscape-scale approach
utilizing remote sensing and geophysical survey to make new discoveries about connectivity among the sites. The team's research is
informed not only by high-tech tests but also by a rethinking of sacred
landscapes in which each generation constructed and used Stonehenge
anew amid a living landscape of secular village life. Ancient pilgrims'
ongoing processes of placement and landscape learning stretched out
over hundreds of years, throughout which time dozens of generations
of people came to Stonehenge for periodic memory-making feasts, the

commemoration of the dead, and participation in the creation of the sacred surroundings.

Stonehenge was located on a flat, grassy plain in the middle of nowhere; even today, there is no nearby city. From time immemorial, there has been no natural crag or cave that served as the awe-inspiring initiation of worship. In every way, Stonehenge is a human-led creation, the result of people's taking ritual matters into their own hands. Through their communications and planning activities, they created distinctive, labor-intensive mediations between the human world and the divine realm. The pillars became the fixed points for the comings and goings of pilgrimage and served a map-making function, with each generation augmenting and aggrandizing the "here" part of "you are here." Given the evidence of continual remodeling, it is clear that the act of creation was as important as the finished product, enabling each generation to contribute something new to the ensemble. In the course of undertaking those physical activities, people engaged with other pilgrims, many of whom would have been strangers. In deference to a shared religious vision, they worked together to make something beyond what any village could make for itself.

But it wasn't just the muscle of hundreds of people working together that enabled the development of new human-selected focal points of pilgrimage at places like Göbekli Tepe and Stonehenge. Stone circles and the ritual spaces that followed them, like temples (and much later, cathedrals, monasteries, and mosques), were the tangible results of conversations among a variety of specialists. Engineers, architects, and artisans had to reach a consensus about form and function in the initial design stages as well as through every subsequent episode of augmentation, maintenance, and use. Throughout each of the stages of construction, from the hewing of the stones to their transport and placement, members of the team conferred. Should they start with a small-diameter circle or a big one? Which angle of stone or decorative animal was most appropriate to be seen in the raking light of the rising sun or the harsh overhead brightness of high noon? Should they drag the massive stones or roll them? Was a ramp or a wedge or a rope the best way to lever the stones upright?

Once the design of the monument was agreed upon, someone appointed to be the leader then had to supervise the different activities. Who could develop the expertise to carve great monoliths from a quarry, when the sum total of all prior individual experience was limited to working on stones that could be held in one hand? Who would be able to move the stones across the landscape, overcoming the inevitable challenges of broken ropes, hummocky ground, and bad turns of weather? Would the same crew be responsible for placing the stones, or would their hard slog across the landscape be eclipsed by a different group selected (or self-selected) to earn the glories of emplacement? Beyond the construction of the monument itself, other groups were needed in addition to those who worked with the stones. Some people would have been charged with hunting or gathering or growing enough food to feed those engaged in the construction work. Others might have been dedicated to caring for the young, the infirm, and the elderly members of the group, putting them to work at simple tasks or keeping them out of harm's way. And cooking the big feasts of reward and celebration required management expertise, too. Fuel had to be gathered, cooking pots had to be stirred, and camp dogs had to be kept away until after the meal was eaten.

When the leader of the project died before the project was finished (and this was almost certain to be the case given the length of time that small groups would have needed to make a place like Stonehenge or Göbekli Tepe), who would take over? How much could the design be modified? When could the project be declared "finished" enough for formal inauguration and use? All of these factors would have resulted in conversations well beyond the leader to the organizers of different activity teams. Discussions about the sacred landscape might initially have focused entirely on the ritual structure itself, but that initial conversation implied subtle signs of directionality and emplacement within a larger landscape. Once the pathway was established, it was easier to walk down that route than to pioneer an alternative pathway across the uneven terrain, where a stumble or a fall would be a bad omen. Once the collective hearths were established, it was clear that they were places for some people to go and for others, such as small children, to avoid. Once the burial ground was established, it was understood that all subsequent funerals would take place there. Trash was not scattered everywhere but concentrated in pits and dumps that in their accumulation would have drawn people's attention to expected patterns of behavior.

Ritual places dissipated the tensions of tribalism and the isolation of village life by calling upon the higher authority of a deity or the powerful forces of nature. The festival-like atmosphere provided the opportunity to exchange goods and services and to acquire new practical knowledge about tools and medicines and hunting strategies. The gatherings of young people provided the welcome chance to branch out beyond their own villages' dating pool. And ritual spaces, by being temporary places of residence, avoided the long-term consequences of having people living in one place: people could carry their own provisions for a few days, and by the time the pilgrimage site became truly messy with trash and human waste, it was time for people to go home. It would seem that ritual spaces would have thus provided everything we needed as a species, so why is the world today filled with hundreds of cities, and not with hundreds of Göbekli Tepes and Stonehenges?

As good as they were for serving social and economic needs, pilgrimage sites had two big disadvantages: First of all, they were not designed to be permanent, so the promising initiations of convivial achievement, social interaction, and lively contacts with strangers were ruptured by the process of returning to dispersed villages. Visitors were meant to move along back home, whether to be replaced by a new crowd of pilgrims or simply to leave the place alone for the good cleaning it would get from the seasonal cycle of wind and rain. Second, religious activity couldn't sustain everyone; people had to do something for a living, and there were few jobs available for people other than priestesses and shamans. Regardless of how awe-inspiring a ritual place might be, most people didn't want to give up a secular life with its pleasures and rewards of the here and now. Cities became the "sweet spot" for human interactions that melded both individual opportunity and a permanence of place.

The First City

Like other scientists, archaeologists sometimes like to play the game of "first" and "oldest." We argue about which site is the earliest to display all the characteristics of urbanism, such as a dense population, a diverse economy, secular architecture, and differential social classes. The evidence for such characteristics is scarce because, as we've already seen, the initial settlements of ancient cities are buried deeply under layers of subsequent habitations. As a result, we place a great deal of interpretive weight on a fragment of an ancient vessel or the radiocarbon date of a tiny bit of charcoal or a few stray seeds retrieved from the lowest depths of an excavation trench. As with other phenomena whose inceptions we can see only after the fact or by proxy (like supernovas or the beginnings of life on earth), we can be more successful in understanding the beginnings of cities by looking at what they set in motion. And because the development of urbanism was something that occurred as the result of a process shared by many people, rather than a single aha! moment of change, the search for a single first is something more like a fun parlor game than a serious academic question.

But for the sake of argument, if we had to pick a "first," the best candidate we currently have is Tell Brak, the site that Max Mallowan approached with a certain reluctance and to which he eventually put his spade. Spread out over nearly a mile, Tell Brak's ancient grandeur is seen in the excavated traces of temples, houses, and passageways occupied six thousand years ago on the dusty plains of northern Syria. As a site with the oldest recognizable urban characteristics in the famed "cradle of civilization" that is Mesopotamia, Tell Brak's long history of investigation lets us tell the story of a daring transition to the permanence of city life. Its inhabitants—all hailing from local villages, farmers and herders by trade—were pioneers in creating a new form of community as they moved in one by one. By doing so, they created the brand-new dichotomy of "urban" and "rural," with all of the implied distinctions of those two realms that are still with us today. And that moment of urban creation was something that was not a matter of anonymous or collective statistics, but a face-to-face encounter with others and a deeply individualized and purposeful change in the structure of daily life. For the first time in human history, people lived among strangers, rather than among familiar faces they had known their whole lives. For the first time, people did not have all of their food supply directly under their control, because space was too valuable to keep a whole herd or an entire grain harvest within their homes. And for the first time, there were opportunities for upward mobility through work that did not depend on the ownership of land but instead relied on individual entrepreneurship.

What was the tipping point that suddenly made it attractive for Brak's first residents to accept the seemingly illogical prospect of living in a hot, dusty place with too many neighbors and without a homegrown supply of food right under the roof with them? With a distant memory of Göbekli Tepe, people were captivated by the opportunity to make a permanent festival atmosphere. And once they made their sense of place permanent, the people who lived at Brak in some respects locked themselves into new social and economic patterns, becoming much busier than they had ever been in the countryside. Their activities included not only new forms of entrepreneurship and new strategies of living close to strangers in neighborhoods but also staggering new projects of religious architecture right in the city. Among the most startling of the new urban religious edifices was the Eye Temple, which Mallowan started excavating in 1937. It's named the Eye Temple because of all the . . . eyes. Digging deep in the temple's long-buried rubble, Mallowan uncovered thousands of little carved figurines staring up at him from the dirt, with oversized, eerie eyes on an otherwise abstract geometric body. Some of the figurines were of a single being, while others were in pairs or groups. Sometimes there were smaller individuals inscribed on the same slab as though they were couples or families. Whether singly or in groups, they always had those blank, staring eyes looking straight out. We can only speculate on their meaning. Were they meant to be gods watching over people? Or people watchful of the gods? Or maybe people watching out for each other, their wide-eyed stares a mixture of devotion and diligence and maybe a little suspicion?

Writing of another time and place, the archaeologist Mark Kenoyer has observed that stylized eyes, encoded into talismans, were invented by urbanites because watchfulness by proxy suddenly became a highly useful characteristic. In a village, the only eyes that you needed were your own and those of your family. After all, you had known your neighbors all your life, and they had known you, too. They knew how much wealth you had, because they had seen the grains you harvested from the fields, and they had counted the birth of the calves or llamas or piglets that showed your skills and luck in animal husbandry. They knew every ornament you owned, because they had seen you barter for it at your doorstep with the itinerant peddler who made the village rounds, or watched as you glowingly accepted the bauble on your wedding day. And you knew that if one of your ornaments went missing, it couldn't suddenly turn up on your neighbor's neck without inviting retaliation that would last for generations. Every kind of information, good and bad, was out in the open, and hiding one's assets was an impossible task.

In a city, by contrast, it was impossible to know everyone. Not only were there too many people to keep track of, but there was also a rapid turnover and a continual stream of new migrants. Assets were now likely to be small, portable items like money, ornaments, or precious metals. Small and easily pocketed, your urban wealth could be much more easily stolen from you than a bulky sack of grain or a grunting, unwilling animal pulled from a farmyard. No wonder that the people of Brak guaranteed their safety through the concentration of eyes in the temple as a way of affirming their watchfulness. Eyes proliferated in other urban centers too, most often in the shape of dotted beads that mimicked a human eye. For people who couldn't afford the more expensive stone version, there were cheap knockoffs in painted clay, steatite, and faience. Keeping away the "evil eye," those beads were worn and displayed so that everyone could see them, a way of silently advertising what you believed in and to whom you entrusted your well-being. Even today, eyes are your sharpest sense in the city. Your ears become used to the noise, you get used to the feeling of being bumped by passersby, and your senses of taste and smell are dulled by dust and smoke. But sight is something else altogether, facilitating an ancestral caution about strangers that we revive every time we look through the peephole of our front door.

Max Mallowan's discovery of so many eye idols at Tell Brak and archaeologists' recovery of so many eye beads at other sites suggest that people were not shying away from the challenges of urbanism. Instead of running away from cities' new dangers and annoyances, people stuck tight to their newly emergent settlements while also developing entrepreneurial forms of coping. Those coping mechanisms included not only the portable ornaments or votive offerings that people made to feel more assured in their surroundings but also a number of practical innovations in addition to symbolic ones. People developed infrastructure that brought in water and siphoned away waste. They developed fortification walls to enclose themselves within the safety of an urban space. They developed street patterns that enabled the flow of movement among houses, shops, and the many specialized ritual and government buildings within that space.

Moreover, cities as human creations were not limited to a single type of topography: people built them in deserts and on seashores, mountains and river deltas, oases and altiplanos. Their creativity superseded the limitations of any particular environment, subsuming the natural world in ways that we see continued today as we see cities take over the landscape through the proliferation of buildings and pavements and parkways. Once the idea of a city sprang up in one place, it was quickly joined by the development of other cities in the same region. We can return to the story of Tell Brak to see that the earliest configuration of an entire urban network happened in Mesopotamia, where the dawn of urbanism was accompanied by the simultaneous emergence of other cities that shared the same language and culture. At the moment when Brak was becoming a year-round place of residence for people in the north, people also developed cities like Ur and Uruk in southern Mesopotamia down where the Tigris and Euphrates rivers met the Persian Gulf. Those rivers, giant and sinuous in their meanderings down the central plains of what is now the country of Iraq, provided a handy transport link among the cities along their banks. They also served as the source of irrigation water that enabled the people of the surrounding villages to support urban centers through the production of wheat and barley, cattle and goats, and flax and wool.

Unlike Brak, Ur needed no process of rediscovery; its enormous central ritual structure, the great ziggurat, still stood tall at the center of the site and beckoned archaeologists from far and wide. The subsequent study of Ur is a classic example of the magnificence and scope of early twentieth-century research, when scholars were scrambling to claim archaeological prizes for their respective countries and nations. The British archaeologist Leonard Woolley, fresh from his excavations at the city of Amarna along the Egyptian Nile, started excavations at Ur in 1922 with a consortium of researchers from the British Museum and the University of Pennsylvania. It was already a bumper year for big digs focused on the great civilizations of the Near East: Franz Cumont started work at the ancient classical city of Dura-Europos in Syria, and Howard Carter discovered King Tut's tomb. Even with this competition for media coverage and research funds, Ur was special in its size and scope. The site captivated Woolley for more than a dozen years of fieldwork and earned him a British knighthood in the process.

Woolley's publications on his excavations at Ur include not only the exhaustive academic tomes that typically result from archaeological research but also a book for a general audience that was so popular that within a month of its release in 1929 it went into a second printing. Still a delightful read despite (or perhaps because of) its slightly old-fashioned prose, his *Ur of the Chaldees* gives us an intimate firsthand view of the excavations. He repeatedly ties the site to the biblical history of the region through its identification as the "City of Abraham," weaving in his observations about the temples and palaces of the site with some refreshingly frank assessments of the realities of excavation that still resonate today, such as his description of unearthing the temple of the goddess Ningal. Measuring an impressive 240 feet on a side, the temple had been the target of marauding Elamites around 1885 B.C. and subsequently rebuilt. As a result of the multiple constructions:

> The inner court and the sanctuary had been terribly ruined, but enough remained of them to show the place of the great altar of sacrifice in the court and inside the sanctuary. . . .

[E]xcavation was made difficult by the presence of later walls whose foundations went down nearly as deep as the old work, while in some places the old floor-level had actually been re-used and the new walls simply set on the existing brick pavement. It was no easy matter to unravel the tangle of ruinous brickwork and to assign each fragment to its proper period, but when this was done the early plan was found to be remarkably regular and what had seemed mere confusion took on a very definite character.

In addition to their painstaking work at the temple and in other buildings, Woolley's team excavated the more modest houses of the middle class and the winding roads, open spaces, and courtyards that were interspersed between the crowded dwellings of the poor. As a result of the extended focus on the site, Ur is one of the few ancient cities in the world where entire neighborhoods have been revealed through archaeological excavation. And Ur also had something else: lavish, cruel royal burials that provided evidence of the existence of an upper echelon of rulers. Among them was the elaborate and well-appointed tomb of Queen Puabi, whose servants and animals had been killed so that they could follow their mistress unto death.

Uruk—another famous Mesopotamian site—was just forty miles away from Ur and a day's easy sail down the Euphrates in ancient times. Researchers from the German Oriental Society plunged their spades into its sprawling expanse starting in 1912 and found that its earliest residents were focused not only on solving the practical problems of everyday urban life, such as keeping their belongings safe and constructing the world's first indoor toilet, but also on gracing the city with ritual buildings. One of the mounds at Uruk revealed a temple of the goddess Inanna, with multiple construction phases that attested to its residents' devotion to the same cult over time through increasingly sophisticated temple architecture. Uruk's ancient construction crews had been busy elsewhere too: the inhabitants had built a city wall that was so substantial it is still visible from space. The same satellite imagery also reveals that the city was at the center of a vast network of ancient canals that would have provided irrigation water to farmers and drinking water to the city's inhabitants. Tens of thousands of people would have been needed to build the city's infrastructure, and hundreds of people would have been in charge of running it. Someone had to organize the laborers to make mud bricks from the plentiful local clay, to bring in timbers for roofing, and to make sure that structural engineering was sound as the constructions reached skyward. In return, those middle managers enjoyed a little extra prestige and a little larger paycheck.

There were many cities up and down the Mesopotamian heartland in addition to Brak, Ur, and Uruk—a host of romantically named places like Lagash, Mari, Urkesh, and Babylon. Within this realm of thriving metropolitan diversity, the city of Uruk retained a special cachet. Even today there's a competition among places that are equally sophisticated but defer to Paris and New York as leading icons of modern urban life, with their instantly recognizable "brand" emblazoned on everything from fancy furniture to souvenir coffee mugs. In ancient times, vessels were the equivalent of handbags and T-shirts, providing everyday items made of stone and clay that linked people together in a network of urban style. Uruk pottery was handsomely decorated with naturalistic motifs such as birds and ibex interspersed between graceful lines. By the fourth millennium B.C., the pottery was shipped all over Mesopotamia and as far east as Iran and is the basis upon which archaeologists define an entire era of Meso-potamian civilization. In addition to helping us learn something about ancient Mesopotamian cities, the appeal of Uruk's culture puts the modern world of the Near East into context as a place where so-cial continuities have long superseded national boundaries. Fron-tiers currently drawn as dotted lines between countries such as Iran, Iraq, and Syria are only the most recent manifestation of artificial lines drawn in and around entire civilizations.

The challenges of nation-making aren't the only enigma in the re-gion of the ancient Near East. Many years ago, researchers investi-gating the flowering of the earliest urbanism in Mesopotamia made a strong tie between the fact that the region had been the location of the earliest domestication of some of the world's most important plants and animals such as wheat and barley, and cattle, sheep, and goats starting several thousand years before the development of cit-ies. Archaeologists like James Henry Breasted enthusiastically called the region along the curve of the Zagros Mountains the "Fertile Crescent," reading human success from static maps of topography and rain shadows. Yet the theoretical abundance of the region had always been at odds with researchers' own experiences in a place that was infamously difficult for archaeological fieldwork (remember Max Mallowan hardly caring how old the site was by the time he reached the top of Brak under a parching sun, or Tim Matney's ad-vice about decisions after 10:00 a.m.?). The realities of Mesopotamia are quite a bit harsher than might logically have been anticipated for putting in the hard work of making a city; after all, if urbanism re-sulted in more people doing more things, it would stand to reason that the first cities should have sprung up in paradisiacal locales.

Instead, cities like Brak, Ur, and Uruk developed in places that didn't seem to have much going for them. In northern Mesopotamia around the area of Brak, the land was hot and dry, with farming that failed on an unpredictable basis from place to place and from year to year. The residents of cities like Ur and Uruk in southern Mesopotamia suffered from occasional floods and had other quotidian struggles. Not only were the lower reaches of the Tigris and Euphrates rivers marshy and humid, but there was no local source of stone. Every single piece of rock that people used, whether for construction or beads or millstones, had to be brought from distant mountains. And some stones, like the carnelian beads found in Puabi's tomb at Ur, came from as far away as India. Similar challenges of agriculture, water, and daily-use goods held true for the dozens of other cities in the heart of Mesopotamia.

As we saw in the story about the hole at Tepe Sharafabad where Richard Redding revealed the evidence for cyclical stresses that led to the culling of herds, good seasons of agricultural productivity were followed unpredictably by bad ones. To archaeologists working in the region, it was increasingly obvious that the concept of the "Fertile Crescent" didn't make much sense. Researchers suddenly snapped to attention when they realized that they had been thinking of the Mesopotamian environment as though it were easy, when all of their own personal experiences had revealed it to be exactly the opposite. In a flash of inspiration, the archaeologist Tony Wilkinson and his colleagues rechristened the area the "Fragile Crescent." This change of perspective not only acknowledged the impact of the fickle local climate on urban beginnings but also brought in a fascinating follow-up idea. Perhaps Mesopotamia was famous as the heartland of cities not because it was inherently wealthy but because it was inherently vulnerable: in order for people to be successful, they had to be much more entrepreneurial, creative, and interdependent.

Mihaly Csikszentmihalyi's examination of "flow" as the product of constraints enables us to appreciate the ways in which ancient urban residents benefited from their challenging environments. Connectivity was key to making any individual metropolis successful, enabling each city to be sustainable and environmentally resilient because of its link to other places. The situation at first glance seems like a giant Ponzi scheme, with each new city bringing more into the network than it could draw out. Yet the benefit of an interconnected urban landscape is not merely what one city can deliver to another but the way in which each city engages tightly with its own local environment to draw in food, goods, and people to work in the city's burgeoning enterprises. Jason Ur's satellite-image maps of ancient Mesopotamian cities revealed not just one or two roads coming in and out of those ancient sites but dozens of roads emanating from the ancient city cores like the spokes of a wheel, with each spoke connecting outlying communities. As a result, a city could always get food from somewhere. If any particular link was broken because of a supply disruption brought about by localized crop failure or warfare or stubborn noncompliance, there were plenty of other links that could still supply the city from some other direction. Urban expansions thus not only changed their own specific local ecologies but leveraged changes in entire regions with a cascade effect that often supported the spawn of other cities both nearby and far away. Each of those cities provided the ongoing support network for an urban expansion in a way that was different from a simple mass gathering.

This is why there's only one Göbekli Tepe but many cities in the subsequent evolution of Mesopotamia.

Mesopotamia was not the only place where cities were started not as singular entities but as parts of interconnected networks of urban places. Economic, social, and ritual interactions joined the cities of the Maya realm a thousand years ago, often literally traced across the landscape through formal raised roads that led from one site to the next through the jungle. LIDAR survey has revealed an amazing crisscross of pathways all across southern Mexico and Central America, with the longest roads reaching more than fifty miles—truly an ancient superhighway network that for its day rivaled the interstate travel network of the United States or the *routes nationales* of France. In the Indian subcontinent, the earliest cities of the first millennium B.C. formed a constellation of more than a hundred urban centers connected by a combination of land pathways and networks. And the Romans linked their dozens of cities by water transport, turning the Mediterranean into *mare nostrum* as an expression of their political network: "our sea," they called it, with an easy and confident sense of ownership.

Giovanni Maggi map of Rome, A.D. 1625

URBAN BUILDING BLOCKS

I n the beginning, Tell Brak was an unremarkable little spot along the flanks of the Mesopotamian hills. Tikal was a simple cross-roads deep in the Maya jungle. Teotihuacan had a cave, sacred and close in the darkness of the underground. Xi'an had a nearby river winding its way through endless landscapes of hills and agricultural land. What enabled people to transform these places into cities starting six thousand years ago was not the geology or topography itself but the fact that a physical place became an anchor for settlement. In looking around them, people found that there was some aspect that seemed "just right." Maybe it was a convenient river crossing, or maybe an unusually prominent rock that a previous generation had ascribed with spiritual meaning. Maybe it was a place that had a good spring where travelers could rest, or a rich and productive hinterland for agriculture, or a variety of topographies that enabled herders, farmers, and fisherfolk to trade their wares in proximity. But maybe there was nothing particularly obvious about the place, making it a bit of a mystery as to why any particular city came into being.

As we've seen for Mesopotamia, when there is a synergy of willingness and intrigue, people can turn the most unlikely places into thriving metropolitan areas. Nearly every city, past and present, has subsequently had both occasional and ongoing obstacles through which their residents suffered. Ancient Romans fell prey to malaria because of the surrounding swampy lands and sluggish waterways. Modern Mumbai's sprawl is impossibly hampered by the narrow neck of the peninsula on which the city's port sits. Beyond the factors of daily grind and risk, there are occasional catastrophic events, like the tropical storms that have historically hit New Orleans, Houston, and Manila and the earthquakes that have wreaked havoc deep inland in cities such as Bam as well as all along the Pacific's Ring of Fire. And, of course, there were catastrophes in which cities were deliberately targeted, such as acts of war, siege, and internal aggression. Yet just as was the case for the Fragile Crescent of Mesopotamia, the vulnerability of cities was countered with a creative resilience that grew out of the networks of provisioning and communication.

What made cities persevere is also what enabled them to come into existence in the first place. We can identify four ancestral elements that were essential precursors to the creation and sustaining of metropolitan life: the use of language to envision scenarios before they happen; the human propensity for migration that continually enables our species to adapt to new circumstances; our dependence on objects for both practical and symbolic purposes; and the use of architecture as creative place making. The combination of these factors not only made cities the only viable form of concentrated human population but also enabled cities to be incubators for other new phenomena, including massive economies of production and consumption, the development of infrastructure (such as roads, bridges, and water conduits) as the physical mechanism of connectivity, and the emergence of the middle class as the essential managers and consumers of urban life.

Our Talkative Ancestors

The seed of our collective urge to mobilize is found in our most ancient relatives, the australopithecines of 4.2 million years ago. Represented most famously by the little skeleton of Lucy, found in Ethiopia in 1974, the australopithecine physique invoked something altogether new in the mammalian repertoire in the form of the first habitually bipedal primate genus. The division of corporeal labor between feet for walking and hands for carrying provided the physical capacities of multitasking that eventually enabled their descendants—us—to become increasingly sophisticated planners and doers. Yet australopithecines appeared to be cautious homebodies, and their many variant species never migrated beyond the southern and eastern Africa plains of their genesis. Though they had the legs to wander the world, they perhaps lacked the will, or the courage, or the need.

By a million years ago, the australopithecine physique was crowned by a more sophisticated and adventurous brain. With that big brain, the physical capacity of multitasking that was inherent in prior walk-and-carry strategies was augmented by an increasingly sophisticated language capacity. The anthropologist Robin Dunbar has one compelling word to describe the impetus of ancient language development: "gossip"! In his book *Grooming, Gossip, and the*

Evolution of Language, Dunbar has evaluated the ways in which language replaced physical contact as the most efficient way for individuals to interact with other individuals. Language as a mode of communication is an efficient way of making use of the breathing apparatus (which an individual is using anyway) to make a social impact. Spoken language is enhanced by subtle glances or bold-handed gestures to reinforce a point or to frame a story, making the speaker a physical presence. The listeners are part of the performance of language, and they respond, keep silent, or gesture in turn. For humans as a brainy but vulnerable primate, individual survival was not just about communicating facts but about communicating desires, requests, and commands in ways that enhanced survival and well-being. Through words as well as pointed silence, every person participated in the formation of a community.

The word "grammar" usually makes us groan, associated as it is with schools and rules that seemed arbitrary and restrictive no matter what language we grew up with. Yet grammar is a positive force for communication; without grammar it would be difficult to efficiently understand a speaker's intent and to build on that intent through subsequent dialogue of back-and-forth communication. Words can't be strung together in random order in any language, because the result is an ambiguous phrasing that leaves the possibility for misinterpretation. When headed to a particular destination, you might tell your family or roommate: "I am going to the store." People would still understand what you meant if you said "Going to the store I am," but it would take them a little longer to process the message, and they would expect an explanation for the joke. Grammar is like a shock absorber for the real work of language, which is to enable the speaker to persuade, teach, warn, or compliment the listener. Standardized grammar is essential to save the energy of higher-order cognitive processing for the interesting parts of language, such as nuance and intent. By having a shared grammar, and a shared expectation of the structure of language, our human ancestors could focus their communication energy on the development of ideas, the initiation of plans, and the coordination of activities. Individuals need not have formal education to absorb grammar and make use of it in their communications; in many parts of the world today, there are individuals who grow up without classroom education yet speak in the same standardized grammatical structure as ministers and presidents.

Now let's think about the power of two other aspects of speech that became essential in the development of our species' capacity to interact in larger and larger groups: the past tense and the future tense. The very existence of the past tense would seem to be something of a paradox for a forward-looking species. Why would there be any need to revisit the past, to share information about it, or to dwell on it? If memory is important in guiding present actions, it should be sufficient to merely remember the past while invoking commands in the present. A person remembering the effects of a close call with a predator, or an injury caused by a fire, could well convey to others a forceful "Don't do that!" without articulating the circumstances of a specific prior experience. Or the very fact that an older, experienced individual made the command could have been sufficient, if our ancestors were primed to simply take the silverback's word for everything.

The use of a past tense opens up the social realm of speaking, enabling everyone to demonstrate a legitimacy of direct experience. Through the use of a past tense, the power of linguistic performance is not limited to the oldest or most physically imposing member of the group: any individual can effectively use language to cajole, declare, explain, or demand (as we can experience with children or elders who repeat phrases in ways that capture our attention). Adding a lilt or rhythm turns words into songs as another compelling mechanism by which the disenfranchised can make their voices heard. Even when stating simple "facts," a speaker can convey legitimacy and authority through the selection among the range and frequency of past experiences, enabling the listener to ascertain both the believability of the utterances and the credibility of the person uttering them. Every individual has her or his own experience of an event, but sharing those memories makes it possible to achieve a collective sense of the past, of history, and of intents that make future connections possible.

The future tense is the "flip side" of the past. The past is a matter of record that can be confirmed by consulting other people, but the actions of the future are entirely hypothetical because they haven't happened yet. Why did the human brain and its cognitive mechanisms develop to accommodate a fictional construct? Pointing and gesturing would have been perfectly adequate for our migratory ancestors to convey the direction of their next move. But the ability to think about the future, and the ability to conceptualize as-yet-unseen circumstances along different lengths of time (a day, a week, a year, or indefinitely), gave every individual the potential of control over knowledge, planning, and action in a way that eventually contributed to the development of group-level projects.

Closely linked to the future tense is the conditional tense. An "if . . . then" phrasing structure enables people to imagine outcomes before they occur, enabling them to combine both a memory of the past and a prediction for the future. Through the use of the conditional tense, language facilitated an efficient conceptualization of strategies to share with other people. Although many species other than our own have a capacity for stimulus and response that is instinctually coded and individually experienced, what is distinct about humans is our capacity to convert individual experience into collective knowledge. Projected into the public realm through language, the conditional tense is a powerful tool. "If . . . then" phrasings marked our ancestors' first deliberations about variable courses of action and their likely outcomes. Incorporated into the urban realm, those conditional phrases became essential to ideas of barter, contracts, agreements, and reciprocal interactions, in which promises were committed to memory and actions projected to the future.

A Restless Species

Like us, our ancient ancestors had a greater sense of ease in some places compared with others. And long before people started building structures or making monuments, and certainly long before cities, they "read" the physical landscape as places of invitation or foreboding and gravitated toward certain places that would have been socially valued not only for their raw materials but also as places of authority, healing, and community. Yet there remained an ebb and flow to our ancestral movements, a factor that both complicates and energizes research on early human migrations. One of the most challenging and interesting aspects of human DNA studies is the revelation that our ancestors did not radiate outward from an African homeland in a single, directional wave but had many moments of changed direction and backtracking. Bold moves, as well as long-held hesitations, would have been the continuous stuff of conversations and exhortations, blending language with footfalls across a big and diverse world.

Our species, *Homo sapiens,* undertook migrations long before the development of cities, and even before the development of villages. They followed animals and gathered plants, selecting foods from a seasonally changing repertoire. They had relatively few needs other than food, but they did depend on good-quality stone from which all of their tools and weapons were made. In a remarkable study of the way that people solved this resource-acquisition problem, the archaeologist Marcy Rockman utilized landscape-scale geographic analysis to evaluate why our ancestors migrated where they did. Focusing on the interstices of the great ice ages tens of thousands of years ago that sequentially opened up and then closed off vast swaths of the European continent to human settlement, Rockman evaluated patterns of reoccupation to see where people went and what they were seeking in their quest. Her work revealed that far from being a mechanical search-and-find operation, there were many social and cognitive aspects to our ancestors' ancient tool quest.

One particularly nice place to live—then as now—was the region of Paris, where the gentle topography provided a sense of open space and a refuge from the glaciation that had completely iced over the more northerly latitudes. When Britain finally thawed out about thirteen thousand years ago, people migrated across from France across what was, at the time, dry land in the Channel, and went seeking their fortunes to the north. Rockman found that although people did look for flint as a particularly desirable stone for toolmaking, they didn't necessarily settle for the first outcrops they found. Instead of stopping in southeast England, they went much farther inland to the area of the Salisbury Plain. Why did people bypass an apparently good spot? Rockman suggests that there was more to the journey than just a search for a particular kind of raw material and that the attraction of the Salisbury Plain was the presence of a whole landscape that greatly resembled the geology, topography, and "feel" of the Paris basin, where people had lived in the long frozen interim.

Rockman's study showed how the mechanics of landscape learning involves both spatial and temporal knowledge. Locations have fixed-place elements that can be learned relatively easily, such as the outcrops that would have contained flint and other stones good for toolmaking, or the shallow stream crossings used by herds of migratory animals. These landmarks could be observed and reported by anyone, whether a first-time entrant to a given environmental system or a long-term resident. A second component of landscape learning is longitudinal, what Rockman calls the "limitation" knowledge of places. Limitation knowledge is variable and conditional and relies on both individual experiences and the memories encoded through the speech of others. When does the snow cover that high-mountain stone outcrop? When in the spring do migratory animals cross the stream? Acquiring and sharing limitation knowledge not only makes use of memory and the future tense to capture and convey information but also requires observations about minute variations in what is typical for a region as well as the most recent environmental events. Those longitudinal appreciations enable people to discern what is unusual and anomalous, compared with what is routine, typical, and likely to be experienced in the future.

The propensity to seek out novelty within the context of routines also made it possible for people to inhabit urban spaces. Locational information in today's cities (where is the best place to get bagels/ *pupusas*/fish and chips?) can be acquired by individuals by trial and error, but you can also talk to people who live there and gather opinions that way. Similarly, longitudinal information can be amassed over seasons and years as residents learn about weather patterns and routine holiday closures. But there are shortcuts to achieving limitational knowledge when we talk to other people about our needs and communicate our own observations to help them along. As urban dwellers, we can "read" our landscapes on the basis of our prior experiences and can satisfy our ancestral urges to migrate by the global travels through our city's diverse neighborhoods while still being able to return to our own bed at night. And with the urban experiences of places from which we have come, we seek out a vertical and a horizontal configuration that feels comfortable and in which we can acquire the things that we've identified as needs.

Moving into a new neighborhood as an urban migrant means moving into an environment that is full of strangers and contains many more points of contact than any village. Those contacts aren't just a way of getting needed things; they are also a way of getting needed information. The sociologist Mark Granovetter coined a term for the way in which daily transactions with cashiers and mail carriers and your favorite barista provide the opportunity for information that can be activated with very little cost to you. He calls these "weak ties" because you don't really owe anything to those people, but you can use them for information when you need it and they represent a network that is much wider than your "strong ties" of family. If you're looking for employment, for example, your actual family might not have very many leads. But if you can tack on a question about "who's hiring?" with all of the other people you meet on a daily basis as part of the casual chitchat of encounter, you're likely to reap a much bigger amount of information. More all-purpose than ritual centers, cities facilitate many more weak ties across and within social groups compared with a rural setting, where all the ties are strong (in some cases suffocatingly so).

Our human migrations—starting a million years ago, spurred by the environmental changes that made some places suddenly livable, and continuing through today—show how our species evolved with a remarkable capacity to adapt to new circumstances. As individuals, we embody powerful capacities for communication that include a grammar of memory (the past tense) and an articulation of planning (the future tense). The ability to remember and communicate past events and the ability to describe and communicate multiple potential outcomes to others were essential parts of the migratory process. The ability to make use of new places and to deal with new circumstances provided individuals with confidence that something suitable could be elicited from any environment, no matter how challenging.

People and Things

There are many animals that collect things and squirrel them away, including pack rats, crows, and of course squirrels. Among all of the creatures on earth, however, humans are the only species that has so much "stuff" and so much diversity of stuff. We're the only species that values a diversity of objects, and we're the only species that continually uses objects throughout our lifetimes (and not just in the mating season; actually, humans don't have a "mating season," which means that the all-important business of procreation is part of a year-round calendar of other social and economic activities). Everything that we acquire, collect, display, and discard in the modern world—and the impulse for our entire human history of trash making—can be traced to the first deliberate transformation of natural raw materials into human-modified artifacts starting more than two million years ago. That's the time when our ancestors began to modify and make things rather than just using any old stick or stone within reach. It's also the time when they started to pick and choose the best source of raw materials for a particular use, sometimes focusing on technical qualities such as the ability of a stone to keep a sharp edge and sometimes focusing on aesthetic aspects like color.

Our species' first real social and practical artifact was the stone tool known as a hand ax. It is about the size of your two hands flattened palm to palm, made in a variety of materials yet always having the same teardrop shape. They're widely distributed in all of the areas of our human ancestors' migrations in the Old World, from Africa to the Arabian Peninsula to the Indian subcontinent, and through Europe to the British Isles. The distribution of identical objects certainly wasn't the result of a single individual walking all that distance showing others how to make them, like a Paleolithic Johnny Appleseed. Instead, the concept of a hand ax as a physical and social object seems to have been perpetuated by a thousand subsequent generations who enacted it in a variety of materials and in a variety of places. They made the same shape over and over again, secure in their prowess of manufacturing while using the stone to demonstrate their skill and savoir faire (one theory about them is that they were a good social calling card that demonstrated their maker's intelligence and ability to carry a complex task through to completion: "Hey, baby, look at my hand ax!").

Through our own continual experiments with even the most basic functional objects, we have inherited our ancestors' willingness to spend time making things more elaborate than what mere utility would require. We cannot imagine a life without objects, and today we hardly use anything in its natural state without some modification. If we use wood for a campfire, we first cut it with a saw. If we collect something, like a shell from the seashore, we put it in a pocket or a glass jar or on a string as an impromptu necklace. Flower arrangements usually come not from wild blooms but from plants that have been tamed and cultivated to be aesthetically pleasing. Nearly all of the foods we eat come from plants and animals that are domesticated, each species having passed through cycles of human modification that have changed their size, their nutritional value, and their taste. Our bodies are rarely in their natural state of nakedness; from morning until night, and from birth until death, we are almost always covered by something, whether a blanket, some clothing, or a condom.

Right from the beginning, people created objects from every kind of material available to them, from stones and feathers to wood and animal skins. They modified natural objects to be more suited for human use: a little sharper, a little shinier, a little more colorful. There was a concern for form as well as function, and an intersection between practical use and communication. The resultant "style" is still encoded in all of our most practical tools today, from pens and pencils to clothing, computers, and cars. Style took a special hold on things that had no semblance of practical use at all, like ornaments. The story of jewelry goes back long before urbanism, and long before settled village life, when our ancestors were still in their initial explorations of the world. Covering the landscape in small bands as hunter-gatherers and living off the land, they came into contact with other little groups on an occasional basis. Was the solution to make love or to make war? And how could the wishes for either love or war be communicated without making the wrong first move? About 100,000 years ago, a dramatic breakthrough in communication came in the form of something so small that it's easy to miss in an archaeological dig: beads.

Like a hand ax, a bead is a created artifact that requires deliberation in its manufacture and a vision of how a piece of natural material can be fashioned into something that has use only for a fellow member of the species. The vision of creation is one that constantly oscillates between having something that is distinct and having something that is recognizably similar enough that it conveys meaning to someone else. In her study of the natural environments that surround the sites where the earliest shell beads have been found, the archaeologist Mary Stiner has noted that people weren't just picking up random shells but instead collecting a consistent range of shapes and sizes. She uses the concept of "bandwidth" to explain why people selected a particular shape and color among all of the available types of shells. As a concept made familiar by radio and television today, bandwidth is the development of a common signal within which there is intelligibility on the part of both the sender and the recipient. A recognition of a shared spectrum makes communication possible, in the same way that grammar structures speech in a manner that can be quickly coded and decoded by participants in a conversation.

Beads are just one way in which communication is "materialized"— rendered into something physical and tangible that serves as a frame of reference for subsequent interactions, even among strangers. As the first ornaments, beads allowed people both to blend in by participating in expected forms of display and to stand out through the idiosyncratic ways that they strung the beads or put the strings on their bodies. As a form of communication, beads are much more efficient than hand axes because they grace the body while leaving the hands free for other activities (it's a combination of bodily decoration and authority that perfectly complements our species' migratory instincts, the precursor of the three-piece suit). Stiner also makes the point that beads allow for the communication of amplitude, making the statement "louder" through the accumulation of multiples. A person wearing one bead signals participation in a group or an idea. A person with a whole string of beads is communicating something beyond the basics of belonging to make a statement about a particular strength, authority, or level of experience.

Our ancestors' use of beads as a form of display was accompanied by an understanding of the appeal of selective revelation, made possible by the near-simultaneous development of another important human artifact: clothing. Clothing, because it is relatively easy to put on and remove, allows for spontaneous acts of communication through the fluid motions of bodily interaction (compare the rapidity with which you can pull off a T-shirt with the more precise fine-motor skills required to remove a necklace). Items of clothing can easily be layered for social effects beyond their practical use, of which the modern examples are neckties and fashion scarves. And finally, clothing can be an artful way to strategically hide one's assets by drawing fabric over something that would otherwise have powerful communication potential, like a necklace or a tattoo. With the advent of clothing, the concept of *inconspicuous* consumption came into existence, allowing yet another complex, subtle way for individuals to engage in social signaling and identity making, moving the capacity for secrecy in possessions from the realm of the shaman to the realm of the everyday.

Objects, particularly small ones like beads, had other social and economic functions. They could be shared, gifted, bought, traded, and stolen. The use of portable objects in transactions creates obligations of both reciprocity and dependence, a topic extensively plumbed by social scientists in their analysis of human social dynamics. Among the most famous of these treatments is the book-length essay *The Gift* by Marcel Mauss, which describes the way that the things we give to others implies control on the part of the givers and the acceptance of sometimes-awkward obligations by the recipient. As we have experienced ourselves at both special-purpose occasions and in daily life, gift giving is a tricky business that sometimes encompasses genuine pleasure and sometimes results in embarrassing moments of excessive generosity or underwhelming presentations that strain rather than improve relationships. Despite that potential awkwardness, physical objects are the most visible and tangible way to create and demonstrate social bonds. Whether we offer someone a gift as costly as a piece of jewelry or as mundane and ephemeral as a cup of coffee, we are materializing our words of connectivity with something that can be seen, handled, and witnessed by others.

Making Space(s)

Long back in our human ancestry, the use of portable objects enabled individuals to identify themselves within a group and to advertise their social and intellectual capacities to others. The objects that people carried with them, wore, and traded with others were signals of prowess in the social realm. But there were only so many things that people could carry around at once, with possessions limited to lightweight, handheld items that were not very visible beyond a small group of people. Passing them around meant a risk of theft or damage, and the show-and-tell part of an object's story required the time-consuming use of language to make the point to the audience. You might have received a particular bead from an old relative or a new trading partner, but you had to explain it every single time by encoding it into words. What was needed was a way to scale up portable material culture, to make it speak "louder" than just the cumulative effect of a pile of hand axes or a fulsome string of beads.

To overcome the challenges of communicating with portable objects, our ancestors turned to architecture, first as an augmentation of natural places and afterward in the form of stand-alone constructions. Our ancestors had long been accustomed to seeking particular kinds of spaces, whether in the form of whole landscapes as in the case of Marcy Rockman's study of the Paris basin or in places with specific types of trees, plants, or animals. Those landscapes, whether large and open or small and encompassing, were encoded with meaning as well as having practical functions. Caves are the prime example of this interweaving of the practical and the symbolic, and the reason why caves the world over are found to have not only human occupation but also enhancements such as rock art as an embellishment for places that were already powerful in the human imagination. Because not every habitable part of the planet is geologically endowed with caves, humans filled the niche by creating structures from other materials such as wood, bamboo, thatch, and brick.

By building things that were bigger than artifacts, people created markers of sociality that were fixed beyond the boundaries of a single encounter. Architectural spaces not only represented a conversation that became "louder" as structures proliferated but also were a manifestation of something else: cooperation in the process of construction. To make an artifact requires only one pair of hands at a time, an intimate process that required patience and practice. That artisanship might still require some communication with others, perhaps in the learning process through some help from a teacher to get it just right, perhaps in the sharing of the finished piece to explain its importance and design. Architecture, however, required something beyond that. By definition, architecture is created out in the open, a collective activity where there could be lots of shouting and physical effort. Physical buildings increasingly became the place in which there was visible evidence of cooperation and collective action that brought people together to create spaces and not merely to fill them.

The networks of interaction that people enjoyed in the earliest ritual spheres became permanently ensconced in the architecture of urban places, where individuals could make a pilgrimage with lasting economic effect and a pulsating idealism that is still with us today. Consider the words of one young modern-day urban migrant:

> The idea to come here was from me. My family was in difficult circumstances. My father was sick, and my mother is very old, and my family is poor, with very difficult living conditions. So I came with my cousin to the city. I was happy to come here as I could get money to support the family. The reason to come to the city is for financial problems, and also I want to earn money to keep for my future.

The young woman in question was speaking of her move to Phnom Penh, but the same sentiments are reported around the world, over and over again. Mexican migrants moving into Mexicali explain their move as a process of *"buscar la vida,"* to seek life. Vietnamese urban migrants philosophize that "when you are of working age, you should live in cities." And women who had moved into colonial-era Lourenço

Marques in mid-century Mozambique recalled their migration experiences with a fierce first-person narrative of accomplishment:

> I did not know where Xilunguine [Lourenço Marques] was. I got in the train and said I wanted to go to the city. I paid 15 *escudos*. I got off in Micoquene and followed the flow toward Ximpanminine. I found some people from Xinavane. A man let me go to live with him. In the house where he lived somebody else worked at Tarana, so I got a job at Tarana. I really did not know what money was. I just got used to this.

The language of urban migration is often empowering and optimistic, particularly among young people, whose memories of the past and plans for the future mask the objectively difficult conditions that they often find upon urban arrival.

The migrant experience in the world's contemporary cities gives us a spark of insight about the way in which cities are continually created by real people seeking something that they could not achieve in a rural village environment. In cities, collective activities happen in collective spaces: not only inside buildings but also in the spaces between them like marketplaces and plazas, bylanes and alleyways, jetties and bridges and crossroads. Over time, people built up and combined the four propensities of language, migration, objects, and architecture to result in the scaffolding for urban life. In part, each propensity scaled up from singular incidents to an amplitude of expression and capacity because of the greater number of people concentrated in a single place. Language can be made "louder" through repeated transmissions and through sharing among larger and larger groups of people. Migration can be undertaken by one person at a time, but it results in a mass phenomenon that involves thousands, or hundreds of thousands, or millions of people moving together from one region to another whether by force or by enticement. Objects also are easily scaled up to massive and abundant quantities; even our Paleolithic ancestors, with their modest repertoire of skills, sensed the power of making hand axes beyond the number needed for daily tasks. The capacity to make, use, and discard large quantities of items became the resultant hallmark of city life from the very beginning of urbanism, an experience and expectation of abundance that enabled people to see beyond the challenges of city life.

The Discourse of Slums

Today, Shanghai is a paragon of modern global urbanism. Its waterfront gleams with tall buildings, and its shopping centers are full of well-heeled residents seeking the latest fashions. Yet that urbane polish that we take for granted and expect in a place like Shanghai is a far cry from the city's initial beginnings. For many of its early twentieth-century residents, Shanghai was . . . awful.

Located at the banks of the Huangpu River in southern China, by the late nineteenth century Shanghai drew in thousands of people from the surrounding countryside with an easy link to the commerce of the Pacific Ocean. The watery substrate of Shanghai life was never very far below the surface, and as new people came rushing into town via the Grand Canal, they often took up residence in the very same boats they had used to arrive in the city. Worse conditions were still to come: "When a boat became too decrepit to stay afloat, the family that lived aboard would steer the leaking craft onto the river bank, thus beginning the second stage of their residence in Shanghai. They would either live in the grounded boat, or, sometimes when the boat was simply too far gone to serve as shelter, they would use material from the old boat's roof to set up a hut on the muddy ground of the bank." Squatters might hope to eventually make a more permanent shack of straw and bamboo, wedging themselves in among the neighbors' existing shacks in an ad hoc constraint of architectural dependency. Bit by bit, migrants addressed their housing problems through their own efforts, although many other challenges remained, among which the lack of any kind of infrastructure meant that the same creeks served both as a dump for sewage and as a source of bathing and drinking water.

Like Shanghai, many of our modern cosmopolitan realms hide the secret of a slummy past. New York had its infamous Five Points neighborhood, whose convenient location in the middle of the island of Manhattan—not unlike the centrality of the infamous slum of Dharavi in Mumbai—made it an attractive place of settlement even as it became more crowded and dangerous, "a slum in the very center of a city." Paris had rough neighborhoods that were hotbeds of unrest that survived the upheaval of gentrification in the nineteenth century by simply moving from one physical locale to another and often out to the suburban *banlieues.* Those outlying areas "had no infrastructure to speak of, lagged far behind the original city in development, and became a dumping ground for the poor driven out of Paris by Haussmann's demolitions and his disinterest in building affordable housing." And London had plenty of low-income areas in places that have long since become fashionable: Bermondsey, today within sight of the City of London and its Tower Bridge, was once known as Jacob's Island, where houses were built on piles over a sewage-laden swamp that also provided the inhabitants' drinking and bath water.

The histories of today's most glamorous cities suggest that slums are part and parcel of the urban growth trajectory. Far from being an accidental, unfortunate by-product of urban life, slums may well be an essential component of both modern and ancient cities. By "essential," I mean foundational and inescapable, places where marginalized migrants gain a foothold in the urban experience even if that experience is extremely unpleasant in many respects. Coming into the city for work, education, or medical care, individuals give little thought to the niceties of city life, never confusing urban for urbane as they get a foothold in ways that seem impossible for many of us to envision. They sleep many individuals to a room, eat at opportunistic times and places, work a multitude of odd jobs at odd times of the day, and literally lean on their neighbors through the architecture of shacks that are too weak to stand on their own. Slums continue not only as transition zones for migrants but also as permanent settlement concepts in their own right, popping up in opportune places as urban growth continues.

Archaeologists, spurred by the recognition of the way in which modern cities are growing, have started to deploy their picks and paintbrushes in search of the slums of the past. It's certainly harder to find the casual, ephemeral evidence of makeshift housing than it is to find the sturdy walls and nice mosaic floors of the elite. The challenges of decomposition that the residents of Shanghai faced in the twentieth century would have been faced by the ancient residents of riverside Ur and Mohenjo Daro as well, and little would have survived the natural decomposition processes of organic materials. Not only were many residences made of wood, straw, and other flimsy materials that decomposed in place and left little trace of their existence, but the process of structural recycling also removed some of that material before it had a chance to rot. What the Shanghai migrants did with their boats was what urban migrants did in shanty-towns worldwide, making it that much harder to find evidence of the squatter settlements that were the first stop for many urban residents.

When we look carefully, however, we can see the remains of temporary and handcrafted housing amid the archaeological ruins. Maybe it's a row of fist-sized pieces of mud with reed impressions that show the disintegration of an ancient lean-to. Sometimes it's a few broken bricks that anchored a post that in turn would have anchored a piece of canvas or tarp. Or perhaps it's a row of nails that fell into the mud and couldn't be retrieved by the owners as the only remaining evidence that a discarded boat hull fragment once served as a bulwark against the winter wind. Yet we still have a lot of work to do to legitimize the search for informal housing, because our grants' structure and popular appeal are still for the big monuments, awe-inspiring temples, and fancy tombs that constitute the "great discoveries" of archaeological research. With a few exceptions, the archaeology of the disenfranchised has yet to make much of a mark. It's high time that we tried, because those committed urban dwellers of the past provide a great opportunity to make the past relevant to the present and to the future.

Slums, as concentrations of many untitled land users in the same place, weren't the only ways in which low-income individuals were incorporated into ancient cities. The Peruvian desert city of Chan Chan had nine enormous formal compounds, called *ciudadelas,* that housed palace-like residences of the elite and powerful. Within each walled *ciudadela* was a tremendous variety of structural types that included large-sized residences as well as cluster upon cluster of small rooms that were close to or physically abutted the higher-quality architecture. The small rooms had specific purposes and were, for example, the only places within the compounds where craft-making debris was found. Each of the nine giant compounds was like a neighborhood—or a small city—unto itself. Yet it was not completely independent, and remained thoroughly networked with the other compounds and spaces of the ancient city. Archaeologists have also looked around the edges of these enormous compounds to examine the interstices of the built environment and the constructions that would have been part of the street life in and around the compounds. They found little houses and shacks built on the exterior of the walls, made of reeds and plastered with mud. The residents of those outside quarters might have been staff or servants; slaves would most likely have been housed inside the compounds, where they could be watched.

The inhabitants of Teotihuacan in Mexico lived in walled compounds, which archaeologists have often called "apartments" to emphasize the ways in which they are similar to today's dense urban housing units. Each apartment compound had similar features, including domestic residential areas as well as shared courtyards and patios. In the courtyards, there were small temples that were the places of daily worship. Older people and new mothers who might not have ventured out from their own compounds to the grand pyramids in the city center could conduct their rituals at home, while those who did go forth into the swirling crowds of the Avenue of the Dead could supplement their civic prayers with private ones. In many compounds, there was evidence for crafts such as cloth production or the manufacturing of blades from the region's plentiful obsidian volcanic glass, and residents were clearly quite aware of each other's possessions, lifestyle, and mode of life. In many cases, interior rooms can accessed only be by passing through outer rooms that themselves abut onto the courtyard; one can imagine that kids and dogs were probably romping through other families' quarters all the time within a tight-knit community.

The city of Rome has been extensively excavated both by design and by happenstance as the modern city has grown. In the course of nearly four hundred years of digging, archaeologists have revealed every type of construction, from public baths and amphitheaters to luxurious private houses to multistory tenement buildings. All of these were connected with a veritable web of infrastructure that served the entire range of inhabitants, from the highest elites to the middle class to the poor. Piecing together data from numerous different research projects, the archaeologist Andrew Wallace-Hadrill concluded that the city had a cell-like articulation of neighborhoods in which grand houses, simple flats, and shops all constituted social and economic subunits. As the city grew, new cells replicated themselves to fill up a larger and larger area around the anchor of the Tiber, creating neighborhoods that formed the backbone of social, economic, and political life through an interweaving of different class groups. Crowded, damp, and cacophonous slums were interwoven with grand houses and the tidy homes of the middle class, all linked by the same aqueducts, sewer pipes, and streets.

A Springboard for Everything

In cities, people transformed their prior capacities into new inventions designed to make urban life easier and faster. Entrepreneurs supercharged architecture by creating new types of spaces, supercharged the economy by creating new strategies of production, and supercharged language through changes in the technology of expression, among which the most striking was the invention of writing. It was in Mesopotamia, the home of the world's earliest cities, that we have evidence for the first writing in the form of clay tablets with tiny, wedge-shaped cuneiform impressions. The first scribes used their invention to keep accounts, augmented with a healthy dose of divine oversight. ("You owe me one sheep, and may the Gods smite you if it dies".) People immediately put writing to use keeping track of commerce, as well as keeping track of workers and wages. Everyday commodities moved around in massive quantities, all tracked by the written documents that specified quantities and destinations: wheat and barley to be made into flour and beer, and sheep and goats and cattle used for meat, fiber, and milk. The advent of writing made it possible for people to communicate reliably at a distance and with an assurance that the message could be read as the sender had intended. No longer could a shepherd deliver a flock and claim ignorance about the ones lost (or eaten) along the way: now there was a bill of lading that showed how many a distant supplier had sent.

The whole concept of migration also changed and diversified once urbanism emerged. For one thing, the city as a distinct fixed point in the landscape exerted a gravitational pull on its surrounding hinterlands: food and raw materials and most of all the people who constituted the labor force of the nascent metropolis. Although ritual places had been a focus of travel for tens of thousands of years, each visit was of limited duration: almost no one expected to live at a ritual center like Stonehenge for months or years on end. The fact that cities can and do serve as year-round places of habitation in dense populations made it possible for individuals to time their movements according to a number of autonomous factors rather than the demarcations of a specific season or time of year. And people chose their moments to leave the city, too. We might assume on the basis of modern experience that migration consists exclusively of people from rural places who come to cities for schooling, medical care, employment, or pleasure. But sometimes people from cities migrate outward for agricultural work, as has been documented in places as diverse as ancient Mesopotamia and India as well as very recent Europe (Margaret Grieco, in a wonderful study of low-income London neighborhoods in the early twentieth century, showed how women were the driving force of negotiating work picking hops and peas and set up entire temporary neighborhoods out in the countryside).

Cities' many different entrepreneurial niches gave people more ways to acquire goods as well as more goods to acquire. Thousands of years before Adam Smith wrote *The Wealth of Nations* and extolled the virtues of the division of labor in factories, managers already knew that production costs could be reduced if workers each made only part of an object and combined their efforts rather than making items from start to finish on their own. In cities, artisans also reduced costs by making goods that looked the same as high-end products but were composed of less-expensive materials, such as copying costly stone beads in clay or substituting glass for laboriously hand-carved stone bowls and chalices. The result was the birth of the cheap knock-off as a concept that suited the needs of both innovative designers and object-seeking consumers. Producers also sought efficiencies in manufacturing to keep costs down. New and rapid production technologies such as molding enabled workshops to make large quantities of identical goods cheaply and quickly. Molds made use of liquid or semiliquid forms of raw materials, which meant that large batches (of metal, clay, or glass) could be prepared and doled out. Skilled labor was required for only a portion of the assembly line: once a master artisan had made the mold, less skilled employees (who could be compensated at a lower rate) could churn out perfectly executed copies. Molds made of stone or other durable materials could be used repeatedly, meaning that the initial "cost" of the mold was amortized over many iterations of manufacture.

Finally, architectural changes in cities were about having not only more structures but also more *types* of structures. Urban architecture isn't like a beehive or a wasp's nest with its repetitive accretions of identical modules. Instead, urban architecture scales up in both size and complexity, resulting in an increasingly dense array and variety of houses, shops, offices, and places of worship that are seen in the very earliest cities. There are more new types of architecture that fulfill social needs and make new building forms that rural dwellers never needed (like massive warehouses, transport hubs, and heavy-cargo docks). And cities had many new types of institutions such as schools and recreational facilities with spaces made to be distinct from houses, workshops, and administrative offices. Even the types of buildings that addressed long-standing human needs, like temples, underwent a transformation in cities. Inhabitants and civic leaders, working together, dedicated some of their energies to houses of worship that they often placed right in the heart of the metropolis. In Mesopotamia, the early cities of Brak and Ur had a temple in their very center, an impulse of architectural investment that can be found repeated over and over: cathedrals in European cities, pyramids in Maya cities, towering mosques in North Africa and the Middle East and central Asia, temples in the Indian subcontinent and Southeast Asia and China.

The idea of collective engagement in urban environments goes well beyond the existence of religious structures. There are plazas and parks, streets and riverfronts, and secular buildings like shopping centers, bazaars, courthouses, and government offices. Like religious sites, all of those venues can become places of public performance and individual activity that constitute new forms of "ritual" that expand the term beyond its religious connotations. The routine activities and movements among urban places—we should call them pilgrimages—become part of a person's worldview and regular urban experience, whether it is a park for recreation and exercise, an educational institution with expectations of regular attendance, or a pub or teahouse or hammam for social interaction and personal well-being. There are venues for special-occasion yet regularly scheduled activities such as sporting events and concerts, open places for fairs and farmers' markets and *Christkindlmarkt*. Whereas ritual places have religious activity as their primary reason for existence, cities have secular activities as their primary reason for existence, and that multiplicity of capacities provides a vastly expanded repertoire of opportunities for individuals and households.

The desire for community and the individual motivation to participate in the new economic and social opportunities of the city weren't enough for cities to magically appear or to keep them going. After all, places like Göbekli Tepe and Stonehenge didn't become cities. Urbanism required much more curation and investment than the episodic encampments at ritual sites like Göbekli Tepe and Stonehenge, and cities reflect that investment from everyone who lives in them. In order to keep going, cities required an ongoing commitment by ordinary people, marked by three things that we can analyze archaeologically: infrastructure, social stratification, and an intense upswing in consumption.

The Holborn Viaduct under construction, A.D. 1867

INFRASTRUCTURE
HOLDS THINGS UP

A s year-round settlements, cities were places where people experienced the excitement of ritual pilgrimages scaled up into much larger areas and with a permanence of place. Yet like any other kind of social network, virtual or not, urbanism came with a cost. The crowded spaces of permanent habitation could quickly descend into physical chaos, and the residents of the first ancient cities almost immediately needed to find a way out of the muck and mud on a more sustained basis. The idea of having to take responsibility for the built environment, rather than just carrying on in the same idiosyncratic way as villagers, or trusting that a place of habitation would just clean itself once the crowds were gone, was probably an unexpected surprise for those initial urban dwellers. After all, they were already busy doing more work in cities than they ever had in the countryside as they engaged in new entrepreneurial activities of manufacturing, navigated new urban spaces of intensive architecture, and made contacts in dispersed spaces of work, residence, and leisure.

From Rome and Xi'an to Tikal and Cuzco, ancient people actively shaped their growing urban environments through the building of structures and the creation of public spaces like plazas and ports. But some of their most significant acts of urban construction were done in the form of infrastructure—a term that literally means "below the structures." As busy as they were building the grand monumental buildings of the very first cities, ancient people were also busy building the connections that ran from one place to the next. They linked plazas with streets that increased in size and grandeur to carry residents and visitors closer to the centers of ritual and authority. They built bridges for pedestrian traffic across canals and rivers that served as waterborne paths of commerce. And they built conduits and aqueducts to bring the essential basics like water and food right into the heart of the urban environment.

How did the concept of urban infrastructure get started, if it had never been made before? Once again, ritual places provided the social blueprint for collective practical action. As the scene of temporary gatherings, ritual places like Göbekli Tepe and Stonehenge might not have had much in the way of infrastructure in the form of water pipes or wastewater conduits, but they did provide a venue in which people had to adhere to some kind of directed planning. Excavations reveal that the people who gathered there quickly got used to doing things in a systematic way. We find features like cooking places and waste dumps clustered together as evidence that people agreed among themselves about the places where different activities should happen. Once patterns were set, new people who came to the pilgrimage site would have been directed to follow suit. In cities, both the ritual and the secular activities of collective engagement coalesced into a large, interconnected venue where everyone was busy and where space was used for multiple purposes. The sooner that practical problems were solved, the sooner everyone could go about making a better living than they had experienced in the countryside.

Designing the City Limits

One of the biggest, and earliest, expressions of ancient urban infrastructure was in the form of city walls made of earth, stone, or brick. We think of city walls as keeping people out, but they also kept residents in and defined the metropolis as a distinct place with distinct rules. Walls also were a way of signaling to outsiders that they were entering into a different realm and should mind their manners. Walls were used for practical purposes, too, including the scrutiny of goods coming in and what could be taxed or confiscated. And archaeologists who are military-minded immediately see city walls as evidence for strategic defense against warfare. But the construction of a wall would take a long time before it could be effective as a defense or a deterrent; for months or years, the wall might be an outline just a few feet high that was easy to walk over or an unfinished perimeter that was easy to walk around. City walls were not something that could be put up overnight or when the enemy was sighted on the horizon; they had to be constructed well in advance of the potential for conflict. Before and after any enemy encounter, those massive constructions would exist as permanent emplacements of urban identity and civic governance. In other words, a wall might serve for a few days or a few months as an instrument of defense, but it served as a marker of *urbanitas* each and every day.

One of the best examples of the construction and effects of ancient city walls comes from the archaeological site of Co Loa in Vietnam, a city of the late first centuries B.C. Tucked into the countryside just outside the modern-day city of Hanoi, Co Loa has an encircling rampart whose engineering premise at first appears astoundingly simple, consisting of nothing more formidable than an earthen angle of repose. Yet the amount of work invested in them reveals that the walls could only have been built by the coordinated actions of thousands of people, resulting in massive lines of heaped-up earth that are still so distinctive they can be seen in satellite images. The layout and configuration of the walls were not the result of one day's work, or one year's work, or even one decade's work. The number of people who would have been required would have drained an entire countryside of able-bodied people (leaving rural farmers in a dilemma: how to feed all of those people in the city given that the workforce had just been enticed to the metropolis?). The layout and construction of the wall were just one of the ways in which the nascent city restructured landscapes into a sharp dichotomy of urban and rural places. Not only did the physical work of the walls show a long-term dedication to fulfilling an architectural design, but the existence of the wall is proof that someone had the capacity of persuasion sufficient to make the most audacious engineering dreams a reality.

City walls like the ones around Co Loa were the first secular expressions of monumentality, taking the zeal and stick-to-itiveness that were previously directed only to ritual life. All over the world, the idea of encircling cities was a seemingly simple exercise that encoded urban aspirations into a physical container that we can see over and over again: Babylon, Rome, Jerusalem, Xi'an, Aguateca, Aleppo, Samarkand, Paris, York, Harar, Nanjing, Tughluqabad . . . and many others. A city wall, even before it was built, echoed the conversations that had been held at ritual places but were now directed to secular concerns. Should the encirclement be round or square, oblong or trapezoidal? How high should the walls be, and what building materials should be used? Was the wall to fit snugly around the current habitation or with optimistic expectations of growth? If larger than currently necessary, how much larger should it be? And how would laborers be convinced or coerced to make something so much larger than could serve for any practical use until it was finished?

Whether at Co Loa or Babylon or anywhere else, walls were the physical evidence of urban dialogue, a back-and-forth conversation between inhabitants and planners. There were philosophical considerations of lofty urban aspirations and very practical considerations of the ordinary needs of the city's inhabitants. The dialogue also contained a fundamental conundrum about design and use, because walls had to be both porous and solid. A city wall could not be a total enclosure, because then it would be a useless construction in which no one could get in or out. Walls needed gates, a simple fact that encompasses a duality of purpose that has plagued the discussion of borders and boundaries ever since. Yet gateways as a necessary punctuation brought up an entirely new range of decisions and implications. How many gateways should there be? More gateways made for easy access by inhabitants and merchants, but it increased the possibility that invaders and smugglers would give inspectors the slip by seeking the most lenient entrance. And how should the gates themselves be fashioned? Should they be strong barricades to physically keep people out, or should they be merely ornamental archways to mark the grandeur of the urban realm that people were entering? Should gates be designed to be watched continuously, with a built-in guard shack or watchtower as an integral part of the design? Should the gates be put under lock and key or subjected to a password, in which case to whom would the codes be revealed, and who would watch the watchers to ensure security and compliance?

The walls of Rome provide a good example of the decision-making process associated with every urban barricade. The first settlement in Rome seems to have hummed along without walls for the first hundred years of its existence, until the middle of the fifth century B.C., when a large earthen rampart was constructed precisely in the same style as Co Loa: a bank and ditch, in which the ditch on the outside served as a borrow pit for the earth that was heaped up to form the perimeter. Almost as soon as this rampart was constructed, however, it was subjected to an upgrade and cut into for the insertion of a more formal stone wall in some areas, although the complete circle of the wall hadn't been finished. Not surprisingly, the city remained vulnerable and in some ways called attention to itself as a tempting target when it embarked on the project of wall construction. Warrior Celts obliged by invading in 386 B.C. Uninterested in governance so far from home, they were content to get a ransom and headed back north.

After the Celts, a pressing clamor for defense resulted in the construction of a six-mile stone wall around the settlement. It provided a marker of identity as well as a sense of security and stood firm for centuries, but a construction that large was always subject to scrutiny and "improvement," including the cutting of new ditches and the emplacement of catapults in the first century B.C. (remember that all of this took place *before* the time of Julius Caesar and the subsequent development of the Roman Empire). After Caesar and Augustus and Claudius and a few dozen other emperors had occupied the city and graced it with all of the constructions that we associate with imperial Rome, like the Forum, the Colosseum, triumphal arches, and the numerous baths, civic attention pivoted back to the wall in the third century A.D. Aurelian, emperor at the time, looked far afield to realize that the perimeter of the empire was weak and embarked on a decade-long project of city wall construction to thwart the next generation of ransom-seeking Celts (the fact that a perception of danger had persisted for six hundred years after the last event suggests something about the longevity of fear in a metropolitan context, one that resonates with the specific urban concerns for fire in London, or earthquakes in Tokyo and San Francisco). Under Aurelian, the walls were completed and for the first time Rome had a complete enclosure. That wall still stands today and compared with the other ancient architecture almost escapes our notice, even though it is more than sixty feet high in some places.

Most ancient cities lack the detailed documentary traditions that we're lucky to have for Rome. As we know from contemporary metropolitan planning, even when we do have texts, they don't necessarily tell the whole story of how structures were built. As a result, we rely on archaeology to provide clues about the layout and functioning of city walls to learn exactly what was meant and how those designs were implemented and used. At places like Co Loa and Benin City and Zincirli Höyük in Turkey, the walls themselves are visible from space, showing up as dark lines that encircle the ancient urban centers in a variety of geometric shapes: sometimes perfectly square, sometimes perfectly round, and sometimes a sinuous enclosure that hugs the local topography or a nearby river. However impressive they may be from the air, those traces in the landscape still tell only part of the story. The orientation and structure of gateways, for example, can be a little elusive to the archaeologist working at the ground level. Walls can be breached by incremental erosion and flood blowouts that can make places look like ancient gateways that are not; more rarely, actual gateways can be completely blocked by subsequent closures and infill that make it appear as though that particular spot had always been impenetrable.

Excavating an ancient rampart or gateway is not an easy undertaking. While the excavations of households, markets, temples, and palaces are predicated on the fact that the layers of cultural deposits are generally horizontal and that people habitually lived on surfaces that were more or less flat, the structure of city ramparts made of dirt or heaped-up rubble provides a distinctly different orientation of cultural deposits (one might imagine it as the difference between slicing through a layer cake with its orderly layers, compared with a chunky fruitcake with its inclusions all at odd angles). At ancient walled settlements where I've worked, like Sisupalgarh in India and Mahasthangarh in Bangladesh, months of work were required just to make a thin slice through the rampart wall. Those trenches, running straight through the ancient rampart, were just wide enough for us to pass through and document the decades of purposeful additions that resulted in a triangular profile. The sides of the trench revealed the successive heaps of dirt, debris, and plain old garbage that ancient people used that resulted in the formation and augmentation of the rampart. Just as "fill dirt" used in modern construction can contain bits of materials that are transferred from the original location to the building site, so too did the exhortation to build and maintain the city rampart result in a convenient solution to two problems at once: by discarding trash, houses got cleaned and the rampart got higher.

As archaeologists, when we do find a solid wall or platform or gateway that is part of an ancient wall's structure, we confront the meeting of fine-scaled architecture with the weighty mass of undifferentiated construction fill. Sometimes walls were cut to receive new gateways, and sometimes gateways themselves were built and rebuilt over time: narrower when the city experienced turmoil, or wider when the countryside was pacified and people were eager to move in and out of the metropolis more easily. When we excavate an ancient gateway, we look for the integral part of the construction by getting down on our hands and knees and looking carefully at the joints of the architecture. If the courses of a watchtower's foundation are bonded with the upper courses of the wall, then we can conclude that it was part and parcel of the initial construction and design. But sometimes in an excavation we can see that there has been a little wear and tear on the wall under the foundations of the watchtower, or that there was accumulated dust and dirt that suggest a long period of exposure prior to the construction of the new feature. Those little details of weathering enable us to interpret whether a watchtower was something added years or decades after the encirclement was first constructed.

Modifications of city walls would surely have prompted conversations among a city's inhabitants that were just as intense as the ones that accompanied the initial construction, or maybe *more* intense, because the existing wall could be brought into the conversation. Was the additional construction really needed, or was it a make-work project promoted by city leaders who wanted to attach their own names to the grandeur of the original builders? How was the work to be done, and who would pay for it? Would new materials be quarried or manufactured for the construction, and if so, how would they be transported to the construction site? How would the style of the structure be integrated with the style of the existing wall? We might think that the ancients viewed "style" to be a superfluous component of wall making, until we remember the magnificent multicolored Ishtar Gate of Babylon. It was built in the sixth century B.C. by the ruler Nebuchadnezzar, incorporating in its dazzling blue facade a delightful artistic display of fantastic animals. Archaeologists were so charmed by this piece of architecture that after they excavated it in 1899, they removed 30,000 of its bricks to Europe and reconstructed the gateway in the Pergamon Museum in Berlin.

Babylon was already at least two thousand years old when the Ishtar Gate was installed as a new portal to the city. Residents and city managers who had seen their city networked with other Mesopotamian settlements for centuries might well have debated the necessity of a flashy new civic addition. Some of Babylon's residents might have scoffed at the whole concept of walls and gates or mused aloud at the thought of a future time in which the wall itself might be dismantled, unwittingly foreshadowing the fate of partitions in the Ishtar Gate's eventual home of Berlin. And as the managers were organizing the construction of walls, there were demands for engineers, construction managers, and workers for other projects related to practical needs such as water, waste, and transportation. If for no other reason than a limited supply of labor, the priorities for construction had to be recalculated every time the city's residential constituency proclaimed a new need or a new desire. There might have been a phalanx of people scheduled to work on a fancy new gateway, but what if an influx of new migrants caused the city managers and neighborhood leaders to relocate the work brigade for the construction of an aqueduct or access canal? There might have been a fund dedicated by a prominent business or political leader, but what if those resources were redirected toward refurbishing a river dock after a damaging flood?

The timing, size, and intent of any piece of urban infrastructure, even something as stalwart and basic as a city wall, were the subject of ongoing discussions. Infrastructure constituted a materialized dialogue, a physical entity that encapsulated conversations about form and function and meaning and that served as a reminder to residents and visitors alike that a city was much bigger than a village. Every conversation was studded with the memory of the past that had already been rendered in physical form: The wall is already *there,* so what shall we do with it? The wall's existence structured subsequent conversations of use and desire, just as we have inherited the subways, bridges, and boulevards of the nineteenth century as an armature that we subsequently bend to our contemporary needs. In the course of own urban conversations today, we debate the relative priorities of expenditure for transportation infrastructure (roads versus rail, bridges versus tunnels) within a context in which city budgets also have to address other issues related to the provisioning of daily life, including access to food and water.

Water

Water is certainly a welcome and pleasant sight when it flows placidly in rivers and streams, when it provides a refreshing drink, or when it serves as a handy, efficient transportation route. Water is much less welcome when it falls as torrential rain that causes roofs to leak, overwhelms infrastructure, or sweeps people and animals helplessly away in the currents. By turns benign and threatening, water is nonetheless absolutely essential. A person can survive for several days without food, but a single day without water can be a death sentence. It is no surprise that people focus so much on water not only for its life-sustaining properties but also for its rejuvenating aesthetics. Those urgencies were made even more direct in cities, where people had to rely on others for their daily water just as much as for food and other essentials.

Despite its elemental characteristics and humans' daily engagement with water all over the world, archaeologists have been slow to conceptualize the many ways that water was brought into urban households and the many strategies that would have supplemented or replaced villagers' do-it-yourself approach to water provisioning. That's not surprising given that water is one of the most undervalued commodities in the world today; at least in developed countries, we rarely have to worry about whether there is enough water or whether it is of good quality and safe to drink. And in parts of the world where water infrastructure is weak, there are enough work-arounds, like private delivery services, to address the slow slide of water from a freely available entity to one whose access is conditioned by wealth and class. Yet insights from our colleagues in urban planning help to address the many ways in which people get water in cities, enabling us to evaluate the ways that basic human needs came with a cost and were often loaded with social meaning, in ancient cities much as now.

In the watery equivalent of the expansion of walls in Roman cities, the leaders of ancient Chinese cities grew networks of canals that reached across the countryside and led into the heart of urban settlements. One particularly well-studied case comes from the city of Chang'an, the ancestral city that lies to the north of the modern metropolis of Xi'an. At first glance, the construction of canals would hardly have seemed necessary given that the city was known as "surrounded by eight rivers." But the presence of a natural abundance of water still required management; rivers are capricious, with the capacity to cut their channels or overflow their banks in disastrous floods. And as the city of Chang'an grew, the water infrastructure that had been sufficient for one era was inadequate for the next one, prompting a continual cycle of reservoir and canal construction to link water sources across the city's hinterlands and to regulate the seasonal variations in water in order to provide a steady urban supply.

Ancient urban inhabitants also made it very clear that they understood the logistics and implications of water purity. In the ancient Indus culture of what is today Pakistan and India, cities like Mohenjo Daro and Harappa were located right along the mighty Indus River. This riverbank location wasn't enough to fulfill their psychological desires for water, although there was plenty of it for everyday use. In addition to river water, residents dug wells throughout the site as a way to provide access to clean water (they made provisions for dirty water, too, by building drains that enabled the flow of effluent from households to collective sumps that would have been periodically cleaned out). The exacting treatment of both clean and dirty water indicates that water was more than just something to drink or something to wash with. Out on the dusty plains of the Indus valley, water was a divine intervention in a hot, parched world and a preoccupation that led the German archaeologist Michael Jansen to coin the unctuous term *Wasserluxus* to describe the ancient Indus peoples' obsession for the stuff.

The sense of splendor, fascination, and desire for water beyond the biology of need extended not only to the creation of daily-use wells and drains but also to the creation of an enormous urban reservoir called the Great Bath, the largest monumental structure at the city of Mohenjo Daro. Imagine the Great Bath as a large, brick-lined reservoir, right on the tallest mound of the city. At the pinnacle of visibility, the act of impounding water and domesticating it through the construction of an urban pool would have been a powerful symbolic expression of the triumph of culture over nature. The Great Bath was a remarkable feat of engineering, brought into existence through the tripartite division of urban work-worlds: visionaries who created the idea of the Great Bath, middle managers who took charge of the laborers and executed the plans for its completion, and the workers who baked the bricks and then set them expertly in the reservoir and courtyard. Mohenjo Daro benefited from traders and entrepreneurs, too, essential for the transportation of the bitumen that made the Great Bath waterproof.

Wasserluxus as a transformation of a common natural element into a compelling social trope can be seen in other cities as well. In ancient Rome, just as in present-day Los Angeles or thirsty Dubai, access to abundant fresh water was a marker of social status. The development of Rome's aqueduct had to satisfy the regular consumers of water in recognition of the necessity of water for all life while also enabling people to access more water for showing off their fountains and gardens if they were able to afford them. It was a tricky balance, and there was always a debate about water access and who had the moral authority to claim a greater share. One way to provide visibly progressive water distribution was to multiply the venues of delivery in ways that could be accessed by a larger number of people, which the Romans did through the provision of baths. The city of Rome had 865 baths of varying sizes, from imperial constructions to smaller, privately owned establishments.

Baths as an expression of watery largesse were present not only in

Rome itself but also in the other cities of its network. Rome's suburban port of Ostia has been extensively excavated and provides for the visitor today a remarkably vibrant atmosphere of Roman tenement housing. Yet modest as it was, Ostia had at least fourteen public baths, an indication of the extent to which the Roman ethos permeated the most workaday of its urban settlements (you can imagine the effect of such density if you picture a typical metropolitan neighborhood today with fourteen bowling alleys, fourteen night markets, or fourteen public swimming pools). For the ancient Ostians, the circulation of people outside their homes would have been a welcome relief to domestic life otherwise carried out in cramped, stifling living quarters. The public baths were only one of the communal spaces that provided a contrast to residents; there were also year-round places for dining out, theater performances, and gladiator games. By creating these different spaces for leisure that were fully integrated into the urban infrastructure of water and transportation, the ancient Romans proved that infrastructure unifies social spaces.

Waste

If walls remained incomplete, there might be other ways to defend the city or other ways to ensure personal safety, including fleeing to the countryside when warfare loomed. If water systems were not installed, there were other ways of getting water, including going down to the nearest well or river with a vessel and carrying it home. The disposal of waste was a little more pressing, given that a pileup of trash and food waste and other kinds of discards could be seen (and smelled!) every day. Do-it-yourself provisioning had greater implications for trash than it did for other components of urban life. If you ran away from the city under siege, or if you collected water from the river yourself, there was little effect on your neighbors. But if you discarded your waste in your neighbor's yard, you were only shifting the problem rather than solving it. And you risked an escalation of any tensions that you might already have had with the people next door. Waste was smelly and attracted stray dogs and vermin. No wonder that indiscriminate waste was often regarded as both morally and physically out of place.

An urban dweller's heightened appreciation of waste infrastructure begins with something as simple as . . . a toilet. Every person, every day, eliminates waste. In our ultrasanitized modern world, we're accustomed to flushing away that simple fact of humanity. In ancient cities, and to some extent today in many parts of the world, the by-products of life were not so easily forgotten. There are a limited number of ways to deal with human waste, and when plumbing is inadequate or unavailable, solutions to the problem of daily excreta are fairly limited. When there are civic means to support alternative arrangements, portable sanitation stations can be brought in; when there's no money for a rent-a-loo, the only options are cesspits and open defecation. For many of us, this is so far removed from our experiences that we are only conscious of toilet infrastructure when we encounter the displeasure of being at a fair or a festival where there's no lavatory in sight.

Urban settlements of the past were undoubtedly much smellier and messier than our contemporary ones, as evidenced by the writings of those who came long before us. Two thousand years ago, the Roman author Juvenal grumbled about the likelihood of walking down the street, minding one's own business, only to receive a chamber pot of waste tossed out from an upper-story window. For the direct approach, you can't beat the famous twelve-seater toilet in the Roman city of Dougga, thoughtfully arranged in a semicircle to let friends keep chatting away while tending to nature's call. In other parts of the world, toilet facilities were indoors. Sometimes waste was collected in an elaborate underground sump, but just as often the effluent trickled right out of the house to the common ground between dwellings, much to the dismay of the neighbors. Initiatives against antisocial toilet behavior included attempts to frighten people as well as to shame them. In Mesopotamia, there was a toilet demon called Shulak who lurked in dark places and was blamed for illnesses. In the ninth century A.D. in Japan, officials of the capital at Nara sniffed at toilet scofflaws, sternly noting in the Decrees of Council of Administration that "untreated discharge of fouled sewage to the outside of residences shall be prohibited."

Just like fresh water that can be seen running in through a pipe or an aqueduct, dirty water obeys the law of gravity, too. When we walk down the sidewalks in a rainstorm, we notice that the water and everything that it carries rushes down into the gutter. How does that happen? No household makes its own gutter, and no apartment grades the street in order to make the visible effluent of storm water and the invisible effluent of sewage obey the law of gravity in a particular direction. Choices in the implementation of infrastructure can, for generations afterward, affect the way that people live in an urban landscape. Every gradient has a down-the-line effect on the neighbors, a fact that leaders ever since the beginnings of cities have tried to sort out by imposing rules of behavior. Not shying away from the subject, the Japanese officials at Nara had plenty more to say about sewage, warning that they had noticed that "many of the residences facing a gutter had a sluice gate in order to intentionally dam up a flow. This leads to damage to the foundations of local walls, thence causing muddiness on streets."

We have few textual records about water and waste from the very earliest cities like Brak and Teotihuacan, because writing was invented after those cities had already been in existence for some time. As in the case of the study of city walls, archaeological research is often the only way to learn about the infrastructure of urban beginnings when the first pipes or drains or wells would have been cut into the sediments underfoot. The site of Uruk in Mesopotamia had its first toilet in a religious building in 3200 B.C. (where presumably the officiants could counteract the looming specter of Shulak). The concept of the pit toilet was retained in the region for thousands of years, with the sump pits sometimes reinforced by purpose-made pottery rings.

Even when we do have documents in hand, archaeologists can benefit from an approach that combines history with science. The modern investigators at Nara noted it was not the first capital in the region and was preceded by an earlier settlement at Fujiwara that was certainly intended to be large with a layout made in the late seventh century that measured three by three miles. However, the elaborate engineering of Fujiwara's waterways contained a significant flaw. The placement of the palace to the north, in accordance with cultural concepts of directional respect for the emperor, left the structure too low relative to the location of lower-class housing, whose effluent then flowed toward the elite quarters. As a result, Fujiwara was occupied for only about sixteen years before the capital was moved to Nara. Looking at the situation from the lens of history, it's clear that the great concern of the Nara decrees reflected local memories of all that had gone wrong at the previous incarnation of the capital.

One can imagine a significant amount of "I told you so" emerging in the dialogue about water, sewage, and waste at Fujiwara, with fingers pointing in every direction. Were the original settlers to blame for overlooking the topography of the landscape, or were the later settlers to blame for overloading the natural gradients of discharge? In a whisper, some critic might have suggested that perhaps the layout of the city should not have been quite so rigid about the cardinal directions, and considered whether the emperor's palace might have been better located upstream from the flow of sewage regardless of whether that was on the northern side of the settlement. Or that there should have been better attention to maintenance (the decrees talk about that too, again with memories of recent debacles fresh in their minds: "The government office shall direct prisoners to sweep the outside of the Palace every six days, and clean up sewage in the Palace and the gutters of toilets on the day after a rainy day").

Sewage infrastructure requires the implementation of physical pipes, channels, and conduits that serve as pathways for discard, and modifications can only be made within the parameters established by previous generations' choices and preferences. Just as today Manhattan's toilets must debouch into a sewer system that is more than a century old, the infrastructure of yore in any ancient city forever afterward constrained the flow of sewage and structured any subsequent conversations, just like a grammatical structure into which new words ebb and flow. Nor is the mere existence of culverts and pipelines enough, because there is also conversation to be had about what, exactly, constitutes sewage. In the 1850s, the citizens of Paris actually argued about whether putting human waste into sewers was a good idea or whether the sewers should only be for storm water runoff. Gradually, the sentiment *"tout à l'égout!"* prevailed, and everything went down the drain from that point onward. We can imagine that similar conversations would have taken place at Mohenjo Daro and Nara, in which skeptical newcomers were persuaded, one by one, to adopt the city dwellers' habit of putting human waste—and everything else—down the drain.

In Paris, the process that we credit to a single moment of Haussmannization was actually a long one of dialogue and recurrence of conversation. Baron Haussmann was certainly a charismatic initiator of the dramatic projects of boulevard clearance and sewer construction in the mid-nineteenth century, but he was not alone. The historian Matthew Gandy points out that "the flow of water in Paris did not become modern, in the sense that we would now recognize, until after the fall of the Second Empire, with new legislative developments in the 1890s in response to rising water usage and the continuing threat of cholera." The flow of waste water in Paris was the result of hundreds of thousands of daily decisions about water use, including more frequent bath taking as notions of hygiene evolved. Those hidden actions—another kind of inconspicuous consumption, if you will—underlay the public performance of self in things like clothes, shoes, hats, and ornaments (this was, for example, the era that formed the backdrop for Guy de Maupassant's "The Necklace," published in 1884 and featuring a woman of modest means who borrows a diamond necklace to disastrous effect). Consumption was the key factor in the changing perceptions of infrastructure use, and the increased use of physical entities like water came along with the acquisition of new concepts, like the scientific knowledge about disease that became part of an urban, middle-class education.

People came to terms with sewage in London over a long time period, too. For many centuries during the medieval and Renaissance periods, the elegant system of piped water that flowed into London was kept separate from effluent, and waste was collected from local cesspools and carried out to the countryside as fertilizer. All of that changed in 1815, when house waste was allowed to flow to the Thames via sewers. That's when the trouble started, because the river was unable to absorb the magnitude of untreated sewage flowing into it. By 1858, the stench from the Thames was so bad during the summer that the river became known as the "great stink," but it wasn't until the newly rebuilt Houses of Parliament were convened along the river's edge that there was any government movement toward addressing the problem, which involved taking the sludge out to surrounding agricultural fields. Today, the gleaming Parliament complex and the tourist-tamed central district seem distinctly sanitized from their nineteenth-century circumstances. Yet the distribution of waste out to the countryside kept going all throughout the intervening time. By 1886, there was more sewage sludge generated by London than could be absorbed by rural farmers, and the overflow was trucked out to be dumped at sea—a practice that continued until 1998!

As in Paris and London, a similar evolution in thought about waste and water took place during the growth of Los Angeles, although geographic conditions were radically different from the temperate and rainy climate of Europe. In the American West, rivers run much less predictably than the Seine or the Thames, with a dramatic drought-to-flood oscillation that makes them unreliable for the steady demands of commercial transport or power generation. By the latter decades of the nineteenth century, conversations about the Los Angeles River focused primarily on fears of its unpredictable nature. The river was prone to flash floods and was perceived to be useless except as a dumping ground. With the growth of the city, the need for some kind of formal sewer system became pressing, and dialogues about waste water took on a parallel function to the much more heated debates about water supply in what was essentially a desert environment. Public opinion and an 1889 editorial in the *Los Angeles Times* proclaimed that compared with the expense of building a sewer, the river provided a cheap and easy "natural route" for waste disposal. Three years later, voters approved a plan to construct a sewer, but the river remained—in some senses, to this day—a conduit for waste.

People and Pathways

When you walk along a city street, you make it your own not in the sense of building it but in the sense of using it. It doesn't matter who planned the pathway, or how long ago, or what they were thinking at the time. The city's roads and bridges and sidewalks as they exist today enable you to do the things that *you* want to do: to get the goods and services you want, to travel to work or school, and to connect with family and friends. Even if you use mass transit or taxis or your own vehicle to move around the city, there are moments in which you are there on the ground, self-propelled, from a shop to work to the coffeehouse to the gym. You are surrounded by strangers; some of them are moving in your same direction, or coming out the door when you are going in, or bumping up against you in a crowded passageway, or abruptly darting in front of you. It's all part of urban life, and a validation that whatever you're doing and wherever you're going, it's important enough to be something that many other people want to be doing it, too.

History certainly plays a role in the urban pathways we use, and our roads and streets are the result of some long-ago conversation that's now underfoot. At some point, there was a vigorous debate about the size of the street or the width of the sidewalk (or whether there is any sidewalk at all, as a way of prioritizing vehicular traffic and keeping out infiltration by pedestrians). There was some talk, too, of how the streets were to be paved, and who was to do the work, and how they were to be paid. Some pathways are cumulative and transcend the technological shifts of time, like the broad avenues of our own cities that were designed for horse-and-buggy traffic yet now carry cars and buses with ease. Single-technology pathways like rail lines can sprout new junctures and spur lines to grow the network; on the tracks themselves, locomotive technologies keep changing, from coal to diesel to electric. And when rail lines are completely disused by trains, their traces still make a straight pathway through the city that can be converted to walkways and jogging tracks. New technologies prompt new conversations: bicycles, invented only about a century ago, are already disappearing from the landscapes of Asian cities at the same time that they are increasingly ubiquitous in Euro-American ones. In response to their presence, which socially encodes not only transportation efficiencies but also moral messages of health and environmental benefits, engineers are now inserting bike lanes and special parking spaces into spaces that used to be prioritized for cars. Most recently, electric scooters and uniwheels have continued to prompt new conversations (and controversies): Are they to be treated as vehicles or an enhanced form of pedestrian locomotion, and do they therefore belong in the street or on the sidewalk?

Although people in the past didn't have motorized transport, they still had the challenge of creating pathways for multiple agents of motion, including pedestrians, people bearing head loads of goods, herds of animals walking themselves to market, donkeys and horses and llamas carrying bags and bundles, and wheeled carts that all jostled with each other to move around the urban sphere. Pathways from the countryside to the city also were essential. As Jason Ur's lemonade-from-lemons research approach to ancient Mesopotamia showed, cities employed a hub-and-spoke approach that radiated locomotion into the surrounding countryside. It is difficult for us today to imagine the world of ancient transportation, when everything was brought into cities by human labor, the backs of animals, or boats. What would seem to us to be a profound limitation, however, hardly seemed to bother ancient people. And it certainly didn't diminish the amount of goods that came into ancient sites. Cuneiform texts from Mesopotamian cities tally hundreds of thousands of sheep and goats coming to market, while Chinese documents recorded the presence of enormous quantities of luxury goods brought in by sea from Southeast Asia, including tortoiseshell, elephant tusks, and coral.

Some of the most densely occupied, market-oriented urban cultures in the ancient world were in the areas of Mexico and Central America and had no beasts of burden at all! The Spanish chroniclers who arrived in those cities describe a dazzling display of consumer wares, and the archaeological record of actual marketplaces shows the traces of broken goods and stains in the dirt that constitute the remnants of cooking practices and manufacturing activities that demonstrate the variety of goods offered to consumers. Yet in those realms of the New World, the biggest domesticated animal was the dog. For some reason, the llamas and alpacas that provided the transportation staples of Andean South America were never brought northward (although we do know that there was contact among these regions, because maize made its way from its original location of domestication in Mexico to become a very important and prestigious staple in the Andes). In Mexico itself, the city of Teotihuacan with its massive pyramid complex was built and provisioned entirely by people; in the entire Maya and Aztec civilizations, every single object, from seashells to cooking pots to the agave that was distilled into pungent pulque, moved around on human backs.

One thing that the Maya, the Aztecs, and the Teotihuacanos did do, however, was to modify their rural landscapes to make travel as straightforward as possible. There were many ways to cross the swamps and highlands and jungles, but making a formal pathway was something that made the directionality of transit clear. If you've ever been backpacking in the wilderness and gone across country, you know the relief you feel when you find the trail again. Underfoot, you feel the smoothness of the intended pathway: *here* is where you are supposed to be; *here* is the route that you can follow to get to your destination. Someone in the past created the trail intending that it would be used by some unknown person in the future such as you. Compared with picking your way left and right around trees and boulders, following the trail is easy and enables you to concentrate your energy to get you, and your backpack, to your intended destination. Now imagine the extra relief you might feel using an elevated causeway to cross a tropical swampland full of poisonous snakes with a thirty-pound sack of cotton or salt or maize, and you can appreciate the extent to which a built trail became an essential part of the economic and social network.

In the hot, humid Yucatán Peninsula more than a thousand years ago, the ancient Maya people constructed a type of raised road called a *sacbe* that crisscrossed urban areas, linked the main plazas to the outer suburbs, and connected cities to their countrysides. The devotion of labor to the creation of pathways (and remember, this is labor that would have been diverted from other big construction projects, like building city walls or digging urban reservoirs) was something that became part and parcel of the urban configuration. In the Andes of South America, the Inka and their predecessors the Wari peoples constructed pathways up and down the mountains and right to the heart of the cities that made up their empires. And the Romans developed roads across every type of terrain to the nearest metropolis, whether across the sands of North Africa, through the damp forests of the British Isles, or along the sunny, rocky shores of the French coast, where today people find the stones of the Roman road in their backyards.

Pathways not only link people to places they already knew that they wanted to go; they also direct people toward prescribed destinations. Maya *sacbes* didn't result in a web of evenly distributed access, but instead led in particular directions to preferentially link some areas of the city and the countryside. Inka roads don't just blindly follow the paths of their predecessors, but sometimes veer off to emphasize some communities over others within the imperial territorial orbit. Today, we see how streets and freeways link communities differentially; even in a city with a strict grid pattern, some roadways are wider than others. Conversations about transportation planning always create haves and have-nots, encompassed in seemingly simple decisions about whether a particular subdivision gets a freeway on-ramp or not. The extension of a metro line legitimizes urban growth in a particular direction, and those extensions often spark an entire domino effect, starting with the planning stages. Property values go up in the vicinity of the planned stations, and new commercial and residential projects are entrepreneurially envisioned to take advantage of the area's connectivity to the city center.

A Little Planning

In contrast to the development of ritual monumental architecture that was focused on just one construction at a time—a Göbekli Tepe or a Stonehenge—the design of cities and their hinterlands required an ongoing labor investment in right-sizing projects to a social and physical landscape that was always changing. Roads and canals were designed to have their linearity expanded, and elements like city walls and gateways that appear to have been "finished" were always subject to renewals and augmentations. Urban centers almost always grow in size as populations flow in to create and inhabit new social and economic opportunities. Even when cities start with a tidy, rectilinear urban core, that kernel is soon dwarfed by a dynamically straggling extended network of settlements and pathways that extend in all directions out to the countryside. When farmers built new fields for cultivation, they also built new canals, and those new canals needed bridges if the roads were going to cross them. And when people crossed those bridges to come into cities, they in turn upped the ante for the rural dwellers they left behind to increase their productivity through more intensification of farming practices.

Mother Nature interferes with human plans as well, forcing people to reckon with environmental changes that are not of their own making. The initial settlement of Houston, Texas, serves as a great example of the decision-making processes encompassed in the birth of a city in a challenging environment, with the benefit of historical records that enable us to get a close-up view of the decision-making process. In the nineteenth century, the initial settlement of Euro-American populations in the Gulf Coast area focused on the shore-line itself, but those areas were prone to frequent hurricanes. Merchants and cattle barons looked a little farther inland to find a new place for settlement that was still within reach of the coast yet in a more protected natural environment. They made the new settle-ment of Houston on the banks of the Buffalo Bayou, one of the natu-ral watery links out to the Gulf of Mexico. The bayou itself was a meandering channel that would have been subjected to all of the variabilities of moving water: rising and speeding with rainfall, and sluggish in times of drought. It provided a ragged edge to the earliest settlers' concepts of order, in which there was a forced meeting of culture and nature: straight streets met the sinuous boundaries of the bayou, and the city of Houston was born.

If you look again at the map, Houston has other evidence of what gets laid out in the planning process. Within the grid of straight streets that truncated themselves awkwardly at the water's edge, there were blocks designated for schools, public squares, and places of worship. Each space was determined according to the cultural standards of the time, with the blocks reserved for religious establishments specifically designated as places for a "church" rather than for the house of wor-ship of some other faith. The importance of education was encoded in a distinct space that put schools within reach of every household. Each of these placements would have been the subject of conversations about taming the surrounding environment within a context of settle-ment and economic growth, a conversation that simultaneously was congratulatory about the wisdom of the founders and speculative about the direction of the next stage of growth. When you fly over

Houston today, the reach of the city into the surrounding countryside is astounding, with rural farms interspersed with pockets of suburbs that all are drawn into the urban orbit by the neural ganglia of freeways. And despite the forethought about the site's location relative to the coast, Mother Nature still has the upper hand: downtown Houston still occasionally suffers from the overflow of Buffalo Bayou when hurricanes crash inland from the sea.

An archaeological eye lets us read the traces of plans that made the urban world before we inhabited it, whether in Houston or in any other city. For cities that lacked the concept of "planning," there is still some evidence of a visionary authority: a Grand Trunk Road or a Grand Canal that anchors the urban space and provides a line of sight across the city. Once that linear spike of access has been laid out, the remainder often is incrementally filled in by people moving into the urban spaces, with perpendicular bylanes extended bit by bit, and often not quite straight, and each pathway extending a little farther into the surrounding countryside as new residences were built. In the urban core, the structures of a bygone era remain from one generation to the next, anchoring the landscape as a three-dimensional phenomenon. Old technologies leave a curious palimpsest, like the thick fractured purple glass prisms that used to be the only way that light could penetrate the dim reaches of shopkeepers' basements. Today we walk over these amethyst squares without a thought, just another type of pavement that disguises the lively world of infrastructure underfoot.

Some installments, like fixed-line telephones, become obsolete right before our eyes. Most of us have already forgotten about the constraints of communication that we used to experience, until we see the odd shell of a phone booth stuck on the side of a building or the quaint profile of a rotary dial phone that serves as an icon of connectivity (just as the three-and-a-half-inch disk still serves as the icon for "save" in word processors, although the disks themselves have long since become obsolete). In cities today, mobile communications have replaced any remaining plans for increasing the coverage of landlines, simply because landlines are more expensive to install per household served. We can think of mobile phone technology as the virtual equivalent of the ad hoc expansion of physical pathways. Left to their own devices, people make up networks of their own, incrementally putting together a pattern of connectivity that stems from thousands of individual actions.

As our own experiences with telephones show, the follow-on effects to a single shift in infrastructure result in a cascade of other changes. It's not only rotary phones that have been eclipsed by new technologies; fax machines are slowly gathering dust, too, as they are replaced by cellphone scanning software and internet-linked photocopiers. Those changes are the result of an ongoing back-and-forth among all of the constituents of the system, including the people who design the infrastructure, those with the authority to create and control hardware and software, and those who actually use the technologies and therefore validate their continued existence. Regulatory agents at the government level place conditions on where cell towers are established and the radio frequencies that they can use; entrepreneurs continually develop new phones and apps; and end users create a market by accepting or declining the features of new models based on perceptions of utility, style, and safety. Those devices in turn provide opportunities for consumers of technology to develop new behaviors, as seen in the way that mobile phones have prompted new social practices of conversation. Because mobile phones often lack good reception through walls, people now preferentially exit their buildings for the types of conversations that used to take place behind closed doors. As a result, our most private moments are shared against the background of city noise, with snippets of intimate revelations forming part of the humming streetscape. Over time, these practices will probably shift again, now that mobile communications are increasingly supported by in-building wi-fi networks.

Infrastructure is a design component that is implemented at the landscape level but actualized on the human scale of everyday life. Through the pipes and conduits and roads and walls, infrastructure is, as archaeologist Kurt Anschuetz and his colleagues have noted, an "arena for all of a community's activities. . . . Through their daily activities, beliefs, and values, communities transform physical spaces into meaningful places." But infrastructure is not just an incidental configuration of space. By its existence, infrastructure *deliberately* enables something to happen in ways that have a social impact. Canals have a beginning and an end, with a final delivery that favors those who get what they would otherwise be unable to access. Roads similarly go from place to place with a directionality that silently confirms who has the most direct access to resources. Walls define who is meant to be inside and who is meant to be outside, signaling social endorsements of some people and groups more than others. And cell towers, with their differential coverage in different parts of a city, create a map of favored and disfavored zones that sometimes matches the physical topography of hills and valleys and sometimes matches social topographies of wealth and privilege.

Ancient pottery vessels

THE HARMONY OF CONSUMPTION

I n archaeological museums, nearly everything we see is beautiful. Greek vases are stunning, even in fragments. Little statu-
ettes, preserved only as a face or a hand, bring up a wealth of
emotions. We imagine ourselves as kindred spirits with the people
who made and owned those objects, and share the lament of breaking
that vase or losing that glittering object that now finds itself isolated
in the museum display case. The Roman lady who watched her ring
fall off her slippery finger and down the drain of the public bath must
have felt a pang of remorse, as we do today when a favorite piece of
jewelry falls into the airport sink or sidewalk grate never to be retrieved. And how was that bronze dagger lost—in a battle when the
owner valiantly sank to the ground and relinquished it only in death?
Was it dropped in the midst of a rout, and lost in the chaos of retreat?
Perhaps it was placed in an old man's grave in respectful tribute to his
glory days. Or maybe . . . the owner's child took it into the woods to
play with and lost it among the leaves and twigs of the forest floor.

When we wander through museums, we can imagine a story for each object now sealed away by the aseptic glass of the case. And there are many more stories than what we can see. For every item on display, there are thousands that linger in storerooms behind the scenes. Some of them are as lovely as what you see on display but many are not. There are millions of artifacts that are unwieldy, ugly, or inappropriate for a family museum (if you've ever wondered what's on the *other* side of some of those Greek vases, just let your imagination run wild: the pornographic scenes are turned to the wall). Objects in storage, even the whole ones, are sometimes rejected from display because they disappoint our expectations of ancient aesthetics somehow being more elevated than ours. We simply don't want to see unattractive stuff from the past, and museum curators tacitly agree to keep homely objects out of public view. Yet when we highlight only the beautiful artifacts, and that, too, one at a time, we obscure something very important about ancient life, particularly ancient city life: that people made, used, and threw away enormous quantities of ordinary goods.

As an archaeologist, I can assure you that there are plenty of ugly artifacts. Among the ugliest of all is the bevel-rim bowl of ancient Mesopotamia. Known affectionately as the BRB, the bevel-rim bowl is about the size of a big cereal bowl and has a thick rim and a flat bottom, like a common flowerpot. The slightly thick rim makes it easy to pick up with one hand even if the bowl is greasy or wet, and the vessel can be set down without tipping over. It is the ancient equivalent of a polystyrene cup, manufactured by the millions, made to be used maybe once or twice and then discarded en masse. It was sometimes handmade and sometimes made in a mold, always coarse and lumpy, made of clay that had barely been prepared enough to hold together, and fired at a low temperature. It not only looked cheap; it *was* cheap. At the University of Michigan, where I went to graduate school, the museum's collection of bevel-rim bowls routinely won the "ugly artifact" contest at the annual Curators' Ball.

Yet the sheer ugliness of the Mesopotamian BRB holds some inner beauty in revealing the truth about the role of production, consumption, and waste in urban environments. Like the modern foam cup, the bowl was to serve as a container for food, in this case food that was distributed to workers in the earliest cities of Mesopotamia starting in the late fourth millennium B.C. It was an economy of massive quantities of transactions upheld by barter, because there was not yet any coined money. In fact, urbanism preceded money by more than three thousand years, so there were many thriving urban economies that relied on barter, credit, delayed reciprocity, and social ties among producers, distributors, and consumers. The receipt of food in disposable bowls solved one of the challenges of craft specialization, namely that if people were making textiles or constructing buildings all day, they had no time to also tend farms and grow food. We face the same challenges today: if we are working in an office or a factory, we are making a living, but we are not growing food directly. In order to turn our work into food, we need an intermediate proxy like a market or an institution that gives us what we need to eat when we're ready to go home and feed ourselves and our families.

For ancient Mesopotamians, the intermediate proxy was the urban temple. Featured in the center of town, often with a massive pyramidal ziggurat along with a sprawling complex of storerooms and officiants' quarters, the temple was one of the central institutions of ancient cities like Brak and Babylon. The temple was an all-purpose institution, not only devoted to a religious deity but also serving as a practical economic repository to which rulers made donations. Temples then redistributed the offtake of fields and flocks to temple workers, including the large number of women employed making textiles. Reflecting the number of people involved in those institutions, the number of discarded bevel-rim bowls in ancient sites was prodigious, on a par with the trash dumps of our most densely populated areas today. At the site of Chogha Mish in Iran, archaeologists recovered a quarter million bevel-rim bowls in just two seasons of excavation. Keeping in mind that even the grandest excavations remove an amount of dirt that isn't half the size of a competition-level swimming pool, one can only imagine how the researchers despaired of getting through all of the artifacts from just a fraction of the ancient site.

Another great example of urban discard comes from the excavations at the ancient Maya capital of Tikal in Guatemala. The city is so large and complex, with so many pyramids and palaces, that one would think archaeologists would always focus on the dramatic monuments for which the site is famous. However, it is the routine and seemingly mundane that can provide the most telling insights on ancient urban lifeways. Thanks to the work of the archaeologist Vivian Broman, we have as much detail on ancient dumps as we do on the loftiest of ritual structures. Her excavations of a deep trash deposit, consisting of ancient sweepings of the plaza, included a whole variety of discarded market items and ritual paraphernalia such as large pottery jar sherds and figurine heads. The result is the same as what we see tucked behind boarded-up buildings, abandoned in alleys, and tossed onto the periphery of public spaces in our own cities: a groaning weight of trash that is a relentless reminder of the scale of production, commerce, and consumption in urban sites.

Chogha Mish and Tikal are hardly unique. Every urban center that I've ever excavated, visited, or read about has a similarly stupefying quantity of artifacts. I've worked with piles of discarded amphorae at the ancient Roman city of Leptiminus in Tunisia and heaps of discarded food bowls at the site of Sisupalgarh. I've commiserated with my colleagues whose publication plans for their excavations are stalled, sometimes for years, until they can finish counting and classifying the tons of materials that they have unearthed. I've stood by the side of the trench explaining to local workers and students that, yes, we do want to pick up each and every potsherd we find in order to tally the full effects of ancient manufacturing and use. Often there are more sherds than dirt in an urban excavation unit, and sometimes it takes us so much time to pick out the pottery from the surrounding soil that we have abandoned an excavation trench and moved our operations to another part of the site. No matter what ancient city we investigate, we find that people couldn't make things fast enough to throw them away.

The idea of a disposable culture seems counterintuitive. If life in an urban center is expensive compared with the do-it-yourself rural world, and if every manufactured item represented some transportation costs in either raw materials or finished products at a time when people were already busier than ever before just bringing food into the city and engaging in new types of employment, what was the logic in manufacturing things designed to be disposable? As we've already seen in our earliest ancestors' interest in making perfectly good hand axes in quantities beyond the practical, or in manufacturing and wearing beads in ways that enabled their social communication to get "louder" through the addition of more and more beads on a string, there is something about abundance that long predated urbanism. The desire to acquire and display objects wasn't invented in cities, but it was certainly accelerated by the scaled-up and speeded-up manufacturing capacities of urban places.

Trash also meant something social, in that it proclaimed the status of the household. Just think about the way you read your neighbors' trash today: a recycling bin full of bottles is a sign that they had a big party. Trash is an affirming badge of affluence, a sure sign that the person throwing something away has been able to consume the contents of a container or has been able to replace a worn-out item with something new. It's not surprising that people in Mesopotamia would have wanted *more* bowls, even if they already had a lot of them, and they certainly wanted more of the food that would have been carried in those bowls. And the only way to participate in the fast-fashion turnover of style is to just get rid of some things, for which the easiest solution is simply to throw them away, whether straight into the trash or by donating them to an individual or an institution that wants our castoffs. In sum, the idea of "too much" trash is not a *modern* problem but an *urban* condition.

A considerable amount of trash results from the manufacturing process itself, although savvy manufacturers do try to recoup their investments in raw materials whenever possible. Trimmings from the production of metal objects or glass or plastic can be recycled into the next batch. Trimmings of vegetables and fruits can be turned into new products (our own "baby carrot" phenomenon is a good example). Other forms of waste can be converted or up-cycled into different yet useful products, like food waste into compost or cooking oil into biofuel, although these usages of waste require a whole separate infrastructure to collect and consolidate the discards. Other types of manufacturing face challenges in managing waste. Wood and leather scraps, for example, can't be reconstituted in the same way as remelted metal, and they are too bulky to be of much use to a compost pile or a hungry animal. Production trash also includes things like failed exemplars, unsellable "seconds," and experiments gone awry. Ancient entrepreneurs were constantly working on new inventions. Then as now, not all of those innovations worked, leading to discarded beta versions.

Industrial waste also includes things that are broken in the course of transport, display, marketing, and delivery. Pottery—the manufacturer's dream commodity because it frequently breaks and needs to be replaced—becomes a nightmare when it is broken in transit or on the shop floor before it reaches the consumer. One bump of a donkey or a clumsy apprentice could suddenly render a carefully crafted clay pot useless, not to mention the hazards of having customers handle merchandise prior to paying for it (one wonders if there were ancient equivalents of the common store sign "you break it, you buy it" in the crowded bazaars of ancient cities). One thing that is clear is that the volume of unsalable merchandise must have been considerable in the past, as it is in the present.

We got an inkling of the fickleness of consumption at the site of Sisupalgarh in India, where trash was both ubiquitous and voluminous. Among the most intriguing discards were the many different styles of terracotta ornaments in the form of bangles, beads, pendants, rings, and ear studs. Made of molded clay, they represented an extremely cheap form of manufacture: once a master carver had made a mold, a relatively untutored (and underpaid) apprentice could just fill the molds over and over again. The molding process in turned facilitated a rapid turnover of design, and the ornaments we found were sometimes in pristine condition, suggesting they had been discarded for reasons of fashion long before they were worn out. One could imagine a manufacturer who had been proud of a bumper production of floral-design ear studs and brought them to market in the city, only to learn that fashions had changed to a preference for geometric patterns. At that point, there was no choice but to deeply discount the goods or simply throw them away rather than carry them back to the shop. Just as one can't really repurpose an automotive tail fin, a poodle skirt, or a videocassette player, ancient manufacturers also had to deal with shifts in consumer demand that rendered some items obsolete and destined for the trash heap even if they were brand-new.

And trash isn't merely an afterthought of consumption. In some cases, objects were deliberately made to be used up and thrown away. In the ancient Maya world, figurines are found primarily in the trash, broken. It wasn't because people were clumsy or lacked reverence for the figurines that were part of ritual activities. In fact, it was just the opposite, because figurines were made to be broken, as seen by the fact that archaeologists find the greatest proportion of figurines not in a use context like a temple or an altar but in the refuse heaps of rich and poor households alike. Even today, deliberate breakage is very different from the accidental kind. To christen a ship, we break a bottle of Champagne on the bow. As part of a family holiday tradition, we break a turkey or chicken wishbone "for luck." Jewish weddings include the act of breaking a glass or other object to symbolize the Romans' destruction of the Temple in Jerusalem two thousand years ago and to introduce a solemnity that tempers the joyousness of the occasion. Chinese funerals and Ghost Festivals involve the burning of paper money, including both facsimiles and real currency.

Recovered by sharp-eyed archaeologists trudging across the landscape, even the tiniest fragments of ancient, broken artifacts reveal clues about ancient economic and social interactions and the cumulative outcome of individual and household activities. A flake of stone that could only have been quarried from a distant mountain is proof of long-distance contact with a wider world brokered through networks of hinterland suppliers and local vendors. A scrap of a metal tool is a testament to an entire supply chain of raw materials, manufacturing expertise, and distribution networks that funneled the item from a specialized producer with technical knowledge to an end user, often through an itinerant merchant, a periodic market, or an intermediate town. Pottery fragments are the archaeologist's best friend: they are virtually indestructible, and a tiny fragment can reveal whether the vessel was a cheaply made container or a carefully crafted serving vessel. If the fragment preserves the lip of a cup or the base of a big jar, we can begin to reconstruct systems of transportation, food storage, and cuisine through the analysis of the form, decoration, and manufacturing technique of the vessel shards.

Every city produces a mind-boggling quantity of artifacts, a factor of abundance that means that urban excavations tend to be relatively slow no matter how many people are working on the dig team. Imagine the hopelessness of trying to excavate at Monte Testaccio in Rome with its twenty-five million ancient containers (considering that most of them are fragmentary, that means nearly a billion potsherds). In our excavations at the ancient city of Sisupalgarh in India, we weighed the gunnysacks of pottery that came from the excavation trenches, in part as a managerial strategy and in part to help understand the different activity areas within the settlement. Each evening, the whole team would sit down together and report on their findings, and the day's tally of pottery became a standard comparison. Around the table, the students would report from their day's work: 200 pounds of pottery, or 240 pounds, or 300 pounds. Then one student might say, "I don't know what's going on in my trench. I got only 100 pounds." We all laughed at the thought of "only" 100 pounds of anything coming in from a day's work in the trenches.

The amount of pottery coming from the excavations of an ancient city is astounding compared with excavations of the earliest farming settlements, where an entire field season's worth of artifacts might easily fit in a single box. While today the ecologically minded among us cringe at the quantity of trash that we seem to generate even when we attempt to adhere to a reduce-reuse-recycle mantra, we should instead view trash not as an embarrassment but as a celebration. Trash is the marker of the way in which we've made cities places for the ultimate expression of individual autonomy and household aspirations, often achieved through mass-produced and relatively cheap objects. A new T-shirt proclaims our participation in a marathon or a charity event; a hat signals a link to a university or a club. And the wear and tear on our belongings indicates the way in which we used them or the meaning that they hold. A beloved alumni sweatshirt that's a little frayed proclaims that it's a connection we hold dear long past the time when we might have thrown away a different item of clothing. A coffee cup with a child's cheerful drawing reminds us of the days when our teenage offspring were much more dependent on us. And the mountains of take-out containers (our modern equivalent of the BRB!) that tumble out of the cupboard remind us that our connections to the rural world of farming are manifested through networks of transportation and intermediaries of restaurants, delis, and take-out shops.

Where Can I Put This Stuff?

It is ironic that consumption becomes so important in urban life, given that people living in cities tend to have much less space than those living in the countryside. Crowding is a universal aspect of cities, with people crammed into spaces at higher and higher densities. One way to get more consumption into your repertoire of activities is just to get more stuff and then throw it away. But there are other creative ways to enjoy more stuff without having the burden or cost of it. Hanging around stores and checking out displays enables you to be knowledgeable about fashion trends even if you don't buy anything. A large sack emblazoned with a fancy store logo gives everyone around you the impression of having been somewhere and purchased something, and no one has to know if the bag is full of things you've already owned for quite a while. Another creative solution to consumption, especially on a budget, is to share items. If you buy a fancy scarf and your friend buys a different one, you can swap and enjoy the access to two different designs. It's a common strategy among young people, so much so that the anthropologist Suzanne Scheld has described this form of consumption as "youth cosmopolitanism."

The effectiveness of consumption by proxy illustrates that in an urban environment, there are many ways to "consume" things without actually possessing them permanently. Another space-saving form of consumption is to focus on things that disappear, like food and beverages, or things that don't have any physical form at all, like the experiences of movies, theater, live performances, and sporting events. Consumption of those items through participation, even as a spectator, is a matter of identity and belonging, with memories that you can insert into conversations. The venue, the crowd, and the cost of the ticket provide a way for you to position yourself in a social group and display your urban bona fides. Even if you're on a very tight budget and engage in mostly free activities such as public parks, an afternoon out usually involves some minor splurge like a snack from a vendor or a balloon for the kids. Those little acts of consumption are part and parcel of what it means to be an urban dweller, where every day is an opportunity for letting money loose for the acquisition of some tangible or intangible thing that enhances the diverse experiences of the city or livens up an otherwise stressful day.

The desire to seek out experiences was essential in of ancient city life, too. In Pompeii, graffiti led people to the best places for food and drink. One inscription reads,

> You can get a drink here for only one *aes*. You can drink better wine for two *aeres*. You can drink premium Falernian wine for four *aeres*.

The lowest-priced drink, relative to the salary of a laborer, suggests an affordable evening out in the first century A.D. Although Roman city dwellers had plenty of enticements built into their homes, as we know from well-appointed living rooms and lively mosaic floors, there was something irresistible about going "out on the town." Urban centers had so many publicly available forms of entertainment that people had to keep up with what was fashionable and where there was entertainment to be had. In Rome, there were discussions about new plays that had the same function as the art and film reviews of our own times, and travelers wrote about their experiences as a pointer to the best excursions. Among the most famous of those writings was that by Pausanias, whose guidebook became a bestseller. Written in Greek as the lingua franca that retained an intellectual hold on educated people long after the Roman conquest of Greece itself, the book catered to a cosmopolitan crowd living in the connected cities of the Mediterranean. Pausanias took the guesswork out of being a traveler, assuring people that they wouldn't waste their time and would arrive back home having seen all of the "famous sites" that their friends would ask them about (in the days before selfies, people relied on souvenirs and their language skills to convince others that they had actually been somewhere).

The impulse for show-and-tell sprang up in urban networks elsewhere as well. When people first built Tokyo—then known as Edo—in the early seventeenth century, the new city played a cultural second fiddle to the old capital of Kyoto located on the other side of the island. Local boosters sought out cultural legitimacy through new forms of entertainment and tourism, which for educated travelers also included pilgrimages to Buddhist and Shintō shrines. Tourist circuits, entirely aimed at a Japanese audience, were promoted in guidebooks that looked exactly like their modern counterparts. The writers of the guidebooks extolled the virtues and uniqueness of Edo's many different temples, and the texts were accompanied by colorful wood-block illustrations that quickly became a distinctive art form depicting the city's natural surroundings, like Mount Fuji, and the city's many secular delights, like acrobats and geishas. Guidebooks also spiced up their descriptions with events calendars and details about local heroes and touted the urban temples as all-purpose destinations where visitors could go for health and healing, bird-watching, and gazing at the moon amid the cool breezes.

In Edo, guidebooks and new constructions constituted a frenzied feedback loop. New temples sprang up, secure in the knowledge that they, too, would become famous thanks to the new technologies of printing that enabled the rapid, cheap dissemination of information. Enticed by the volumes of description and the growth of new information about places to visit, people came in droves. The result was a supercharged urban cultural pedigree: within fifty years, there were over six hundred new religious sites in the city. In a single lifetime, then, the residents of early Edo who had moved there as children would have witnessed a profoundly changed world of horizons and verticality that channeled the spaces of urban experiences. And the development of new temples had a particularly liberating effect on women across the socioeconomic spectrum. Religious spaces were socially approved locales for female activities of work and leisure, resulting in altogether new conditions of visibility and circulation of women in the urban sphere.

The rush to visit Edo, and the eagerness of those living elsewhere to participate in the excitement of the growing city, paralleled the migratory impulse evident in other ancient and modern cities. Were there other reasons why urban dwellers came to relish both horizontal and vertical constraints on lines of sight? And why do we accept that "boxed-in" feeling today? Given the intense social and economic opportunities of cities that represent many more choices and more opportunities for multitasking than was ever faced by any of our village-living ancestors, the physical compartmentalization of cities provides a subconscious feeling of relief. Overstimulation is physically constrained by the creation of restricted physical neighborhoods, pathways, and places to channel the range of human activities. There is still plenty of autonomy available; after all, one can choose to get to a location by turning right and then left, or left and then right. Yet the selection is narrowed by the human actions that have taken place prior to our setting off for any day's destination. Those constraints paradoxically increase the rate of urban flow, enabling commuters and residents to more precisely pinpoint their areas of movement through the constraints of the built environment, directing their footsteps to places that are "famous" or at least useful.

Show and Tell

Social scientists have not often viewed consumption in a positive light, instead approaching human-artifact interactions with a certain skepticism and disdain. Thorstein Veblen is among the most famous of the moralists who have taken a long, dim view of acquisitions. He published *The Theory of the Leisure Class* in 1899, a book that still has a strong hold on the economic imagination through its use of the term "conspicuous consumption" to deride the use of material objects as class signifiers. Like most scholars, Veblen assumed that consumption was relatively wasteful and regrettable and that the creation of mass-manufactured objects fueled the capitalist race to keep up with the Joneses. Veblen was not the first, or the last, of the great detractors about material objects. Most religious traditions are at odds with the concept of consumption; in the end, they are probably right (after all, you can't take it with you). But that is not the point of urban existence, where the dynamic potential of the here and now is profoundly encoded in the material world.

Archaeologists are constantly unearthing artifacts from cities that we—as well as their long-ago original owners—recognize as having come from a distance. The ancient world's version of globalism was most frequently seen at seaports, where shipwrecks and dock-yard dumps like Monte Testaccio give evidence of the scale and scope of exchange. But there was plenty of trade into landlocked urban areas as well. At the ancient city of Yinxu in China during the Bronze Age of the second millennium, many items were direct imports of stylistic copies of items coming from diverse cultures, including the regions of Henan, Shanxi, Shaanxi, Shandong, and Inner Mongolia. At the inland Maya site of Caracol, Belize, ancient people brought in obsidian from Guatemala, marine shells from the coast, and jadeite and colorful pottery from numerous manufacturing locales. Caracol's obsidian trade, like that at other New World sites such as Pukara, illustrates that long-distance goods often formed the basis of ordinary household assemblages and weren't limited only to the upper classes.

At the central Mexican metropolis of Teotihuacan more than a thousand years ago, the distinctive pottery vessels known as Orange Ware were brought in from southern Puebla, a distance of more than sixty miles (and remember that there were no beasts of burden on the North American continent; each one of those fragile vessels would have been brought in by a person carrying it in a backpack or slung in baskets over a shoulder for a multiday journey). Archaeologists have found so much of this pottery that they have had to think about how it all ended up there. In the days before hotels, how did traveling salespeople spend the night in their destinations? One answer was through the personal contacts that people maintained through social networks from back home; another answer is from the creation of enclaves by migrants who then sponsored newcomers. People came from considerable distances beyond Puebla in numbers high enough to create their own neighborhood within the city, including the "Oaxaca barrio," named for the profusion of materials from there and a parallel to the Chinatowns and Little Indias of our own cities.

One of the distinctive (and delicious) results of ethnic and social diversity comes in the form of ready-made meals. "Takeout" is a mainstay of urban life today, from Manhattan and Paris to Nairobi and Bangkok. And this mode of eating is distributed across the income spectrum; you're just as likely to see a construction worker or a postal employee enjoying a slice of pizza or a plate of pad thai by the side of the road as you are to see a uniformed delivery person taking a packet to a posh residence. But like everything else about our cities, it's not a new concept. Archaeologists have documented the presence of take-out food in ancient cities too, revealed in the discovery of marketplaces heaped up with containers and the ubiquitous discard of individually sized containers. And what was that Mesopotamian bevel-rim bowl for, anyway? With its rough surface that made it easy to handle even when greasy, that cheap and sturdy ceramic container actually had a few advantages over our plastic ones.

In Pompeii, archaeologists have found hundreds of shops, among which takeaway food shops constituted a prominent component. In fact, everywhere in Roman settlements there were so many takeaway establishments and other vendors that the archaeologist Steven Ellis has spoken in wonder about a streetscape "dominated more so by shops." The result was a scene that would have felt very familiar to us as we walk along our own urban streets en route to home, work, or school in which a typical day leads us to pass dozens of restaurants, kiosks, sidewalk vendors, and food trucks. The experience was repeated in ancient cities across the globe. In the lavishly illustrated books of the Aztec Empire, there are images of tamale vendors in the marketplaces, where people ate a quick bite in between their other commercial endeavors, choosing from among a varied selection: meat tamales, plain tamales, barbecued tamales, fish tamales, fruit tamales, turkey egg tamales, rabbit tamales . . . and, for the more delicate palate, tamales made with beeswax, honey, and maize flowers. Angkor's magnificent thirteenth-century Bayon Temple is covered with sculptural depictions that take into account the daily realities of eating and drinking, with bas-relief images of people preparing cauldrons of food and grilling skewers of meat over an open fire. At Bangkok's Grand Palace, the courtyard of the fourteenth-century Emerald Buddha is richly decorated with paintings of everyday life that include images of food vendors casually setting up shop outside the palace wall, where the clientele is a mix of soldiers, travelers, and local youth.

Take-out food is popular for both consumers and producers because it provides more diverse choices for consumers and more economic opportunities for producers. It's a bridge to prosperity for migrants who arrive in urban locales with few resources other than their own two hands; with a small start-up investment in ingredients, they can capitalize on their labor to start earning income. In particular, it's an important urban entrepreneurial niche for women, who can thereby support families. One image from Bangkok's Grand Palace tells the story of women vendors everywhere: sitting on a mat with two large pots of food, a water jar, and an array of bananas, with a tidy stack of bowls to hand, the vendor engages with a female customer and a child who points excitedly at the tasty opportunity. A ubiquitous urban scene, the vignette is reminiscent of the cumulative economic capacity encompassed in the modern tea stalls of India, the *pupusa* stands of San Salvador, and the food kiosks of Ghana, where 90 percent of the street vendors are women.

After vendors are well established and move from mobile carts and

makeshift stands into more permanent quarters, "ethnic" neighborhoods often have food as their focal point of integration with the wider
city, as seen in the world's many Chinatowns, Koreatowns, and Little
Ethiopias. Takeout has other economic benefits as well, because it
is more cost-effective and efficient for people to consume ready-made
meals than it is for each person to gather groceries and cooking equipment for use in their own crowded dwelling. Food vendors' engagement
in economies of scale results in specialties that enable people to enjoy
a wider range of tastes, especially at the cheapest end of the culinary
spectrum. Bagels in New York, *dosas* in Delhi, congee in Shanghai, tamales in Mexico City, croissants in Paris, and *coxinha* in São Paulo are
all cheap foods to buy yet difficult to make in small quantities. None of
them would have become as popular, or as iconic for their cities of origin, if they were prepared exclusively at home.

Where Did All the Money Go?

The cost of living is something that occupies the thoughts of nearly
every city dweller. With urban prices being what they are for everything from a loaf of bread to monthly rent or mortgage payments,
there are few people who feel as though they have enough money for
all of the things that they want and need. Those needs rarely include
saving: in cities, we want more money not because we want to save it
but because we want to spend it! A bonus in a paycheck or an unexpected gift of cash is just what we want in order to take up some enticing urban opportunity that was just out of reach before, whether
it's a pair of theater tickets or a mealtime splurge or a day at the
amusement park.

We've already thought about all of the things that first came about in cities, such as infrastructure that linked people, the development of an attenuated supply of food, and the acceptance of strangers as neighbors. Yet there's something else you would have thought to be part of the initial development of cities but wasn't: money. For thousands of years, people engaged in the myriad, daily complexities of urban economic life without the cash that we would regard as an essential economic lubricant. Nor was cash invented in short order upon the development of urbanism. Because of the intense upswing of economic, social, and ritual activities, we might have expected that there should also have been the invention of an easy form of payment, and one that could render transactions across unequal types of goods (even if you can imagine bargaining a sheep for a bag of grain, what would you do if you only wanted *half* a bag of grain?). Yet long after the development of writing, entrepreneurship, the middle class, and the taste for urban bling, there was still no cash. For more than three thousand years, there were perfectly viable cities all over Mesopotamia in which all of the cattle, sheep, goats, wheat, bread, beer, and slaves moved around through a barter system. Likewise, the inhabitants of Teotihuacan, the Maya cities, the Aztecs, and the entirety of South America had *no* coinage whatsoever prior to European contact.

The vibrancy of urban economies in the absence of money means that we have to think a little more about transaction mechanisms without letting our preconceived notions about the utility of cash get in the way. In the history of economics, we might think that coinage came first and that abstract debt instruments such as bills of lading and credit cards and bank loans came later. But it's actually the reverse, because the idea of debt and repayment was in existence long before the development of coined money. Since time immemorial, concepts of debt and reciprocity were sealed with words and a hand-shake. Only later did writing and other types of record keeping enable people to delegate their memories of a transaction to durable form, and much later than that came the physical representations of value, such as coins and bills.

Barter systems are good for the here and now in which equivalencies are worked out according to the needs of the moment: I'll give you these three potatoes for that length of rope, or this handful of beans for that cow. But such systems also work well for long-term debts and exchanges that involve fluctuating value, such as the use of a piece of land or the access to specialized expertise in times of need. Barter systems are still very much with us, although most of our barter arrangements today are for time rather than objects: I'll pick the kids up from school today if you can do it tomorrow, or I'll write the first part of our department's report if you can do the figures and tables. Barter also can be actualized over the long term through the use of memory, as in "It's my turn to pay for coffee." In fact, most social engagements are about the reciprocation of time and resources, including going to others' homes for meals and exchanging birthday gifts. All of those transactions would be extremely awkward if reduced to money (we have developed the concept of "gift cards" precisely to *avoid* the appearance of using cash as part of friendly transactions).

Barter systems not only encompass individual transactions but also can link entire groups within structures of interdependence, an example of which is provided by the *jajmani* system of the Indian subcontinent. Starting around two thousand years ago, the concept of *jajmani* was a socially encoded set of reciprocal obligations sustained within the caste system. Although there were different social hierarchies among castes, each group, from agricultural laborers to artisans to priests, was expected to provide specialist products to one another without a specific payment on each occasion. Thus, farmers presented their produce at harvest time and throughout the year received other people's services, such as priests' blessings, on an as-needed basis. The resultant mutual obligations kept a wide variety of goods and services flowing within communities without the need for cash transactions.

Once people did develop cash, it caught on quickly both in cities and in the countryside. The first coinage, in the terms that we conceptualize it today in the form of standardized pieces of metal or paper that could be used to distill and transfer value, was invented by the ancient Greeks in the seventh century B.C., long before the emergence of the Roman Empire. Within a hundred years, the Chinese—who had no direct contact with the Greeks and became part of the newly monetized global economy through the Silk Road—also took up coinage in the form of standardized round metal units, as did the Buddhist-majority nations of the Indian subcontinent whose coins came in a variety of shapes and sizes. As the historian David M. Schaps tells us, coinage was "revolutionary." After it was invented, it became a concept and a substance that people couldn't live without—like writing, clocks, and, as we can now add, broadband internet.

Whenever people started to make and use coins, they spread rapidly throughout networks of urbanism, including the ports along the Mediterranean, the cities of the Indian Ocean littoral, and the long sandy camel tracks of central Asia. We might thus think of coinage as being particularly useful for that kind of long-distance trade, but the fact that there were no official mints and many ways to counterfeit coins probably meant that money was viewed more suspiciously than goods but was accepted in trade anyway because its ease of use led to a certain willing sense of disbelief (or an intent to pass anything suspicious off to the next gullible recipient). Coinage probably had a much more profound economic shift within cities and their immediate surrounding hinterlands, where credulity was enhanced by the fact that subtle differences in minting practices could be compared and confirmed among large quantities of coins that exchanged hands and not just in the small mixed groups that characterized trade across vast distances.

Because coinage was a reliable way to transform bulky goods into portable symbols of purchasing power, rural inhabitants' calculations of costs and benefits also changed. Although a shift to cash-based farming and monocropping introduced new risks associated with a lack of diversification, rural people could mitigate other types of risks by transforming seasonal bounty and cash crops into durable coinage that could be stored, hoarded, and accumulated against wants and needs of varying length in the future. Money serves as a long-term store of value in a way that a pregnant cow or a silo of perishable grain cannot, and cold, hard cash can feel more reliable than a verbal promise or written contract. Cities as a source of money also provided a backup plan for those who took risks in the countryside and failed, as well as those who lacked land in the first place and those who had land but elected not to engage in the difficult life of farming.

In addition to expanding the options for rural dwellers, money provided new opportunities to wealthy merchants, religious institutions, and petty traders in cities. Cash also expanded the options for beggary as a job option and economic niche within the urban realm.

Panhandlers had the choice of how and when to render donated money into food, clothing, or other perceived needs. Like day laborers and buskers, or in fact like any other merchant, panhandlers engaged in just-in-time labor inputs in order to survive in the city, where there was a constant source of ready-made food and opportunistic shelter that could be used to keep body and soul together (consider, for example, the way that homelessness in the modern world is primarily an urban phenomenon rather than a rural one, simply because of the many literal niches in which homeless people can survive in a city).

Coins served other purposes, too, in providing a handy symbol that carried the aesthetics of their place of manufacture. In the Mediterranean, the earliest coins were graced with the faces of deities or the symbols of ancient cities, like the famous Athenian "owl" coinage. But it wasn't long before coins became a pocket-sized propaganda machine. Alexander the Great was one of the earliest rulers to use coins to spread his fame and likeness throughout his urban-connected empire from his capital of Pella in Greece to the Mesopotamian cities of Babylon, Susa, and Persepolis—all of which had been occupied for centuries or even millennia before he conquered them—and as far as the metropolis of Ai Khanum in present-day Afghanistan. His example was soon followed by other rulers, including those in the Roman Empire who used frequent changes of portraiture (and the marvelous capacity of the Roman script to abbreviate religious titles and military victories) to circulate the news of their achievements.

Some coins were bold proclamations of victory in faraway lands, like the ones that a young Augustus had inscribed with "ASIA RECEPTA" after his victory over Antony and Cleopatra, as though an entire continent had bent to his will. Others were declarative with the intent of making something true through a repetitive insistence, like the coins of the ever-cautious emperor Claudius that bear the text "S•P•Q•R•P•P•OB•C•S," a careful acronym of consensus that lauds him as Father of the Country and for serving citizens, awarded by the "Senate and Roman People" ("SPQR" as the collective of Roman identity has lasted to this day, stamped on manhole covers and other bits of infrastructure in the Eternal City). Many subsequent emperors studded their coins with the powerful abbreviation "SC," for "senatus consulto," a telling reference to senate affirmations that in practice had little restraint against the true wishes of an emperor. But for those who could not read, there was still plenty of propaganda to be had, like the depictions of the Roman Colosseum that appeared only on small-value coinage—a concept that echoes today in our depiction of feel-good symbols like the Olympics, national parks, and famous people on our pennies and rupees.

Cash systems, once invented, did not displace other types of economic transactions. The Indian *jajmani* system had emerged alongside development of cash economies, illustrating how there could be parallel forms of economic interaction in simultaneous use, and demonstrating that robust economies thrive through the addition and substitution of different payment strategies. While systems of mutual obligation enabled consumers to regularly acquire needed goods and services without having to pay at each instance, producers also used the concept of reciprocity to their advantage, as we can see in the living *jajmani* economies that persist to the present day. Contemporary ceramic artisans studied by the Indian researcher Archana Choksi describe how they make differential investments in their wares depending on the type of payment they receive. One potter named Suman revealed a sliding scale of quality: "For traders or the normal market, we make quite rough pots. For customers with a yearly contract, who give us grain and money in exchange for water pots, we take care and make better pots. But the best products are in our own houses, and our pots have the finest painting too."

Payment strategies continue to evolve today. Cash can be supplanted by a variety of low-tech and high-tech approaches, whether it's a tab at a local market that's written down in a notebook, a plastic card that debits a bank account or adds to a credit card balance, or a wave of a device in the new accountancies that vie for our attention in the form of Apple Pay, Samsung Pay, Walmart Pay, and other mobile wallet apps. When we become completely cashless, it won't be anything new. It will just be a return to those early days of Mesopotamia, where people undertook the greatest and the smallest of transactions through abstract accounting without any coins changing hands at all.

Everyday Bling

Most of the innovative product developments by humans in the past six thousand years have been in cities. In urban locales, there are more people representing more levels of socioeconomic status and differentiation that drive a spirit of entrepreneurship. More consumers mean more opportunities for producers to experiment with novel shapes and styles that might appeal to only a few individuals at first but become more popular, in turn sparking new trajectories of production. Almost everything had a cost, but the urban idea of spending money or other resources in service of fashion wasn't limited to the acquisition of physical goods (although there were certainly plenty of those, including all of those things that were used, discarded, and provided the wonderful accumulations of trash that are the archaeologist's stock-in-trade).

Of all the ways that people could stand out in a city crowd, hair constituted one of the most ephemeral yet telling. Just as we do today, everyone in the ancient world had to do something with their hair, whether revealed or concealed. And there are more ways of recovering information about hairstyles than one might assume: thanks to portraits, statues, and wall paintings in both houses and tombs, we can get a fairly good look at the styles prevalent in different eras. The abundant statuary of the Roman world, for example, shows that elite women took up different styles from one decade to another, from tight pin curls to loose, messy waves and elaborate updos. Hairstyles are intensely personal creations that require continual upkeep and maintenance by the individual and those who help her, and Roman households had hair-care paraphernalia that looks very similar to our modern electrical counterparts of curling irons and scissors. Within cities, women quickly adopted trendsetters' styles, as we know from the small portraits on modest family tombstones and the frescoes from sites such as Pompeii, where wall paintings were preserved by volcanic ash. And mosaics are a giveaway of fashion trends, too, with portraits made of tiny stone squares that look to us now like a low-resolution, pixelated selfie.

The urban rate of production was partially incumbent on making things fast and cheap. Copied goods resulted in diminishing marginal costs through the production of many hundreds of identical exemplars. Although for us today copying raises questions about artisanship and authenticity and the extent to which copying is a legitimate form of creation, ancient people had no such qualms: they were happy to get new goods that looked exactly like what everyone else had. In fact, their ready acceptance of look-alikes and cheap knock-offs indicates that our own feelings about the authenticity of "copies" are somewhat unrealistic. In an article in the campus publication *Business Today*, Audrey Ou has noted that today's consumers and producers are equally complicit in the act of making and accepting counterfeits. Her focus is particularly on the contemporary world of fashion, about which she notes, "As most consumers buy clothes out of desire and not necessity, they appreciate trends more than creative achievement." Although very little actual clothing survives from the ancient world, we do have visual images from sculptures and statues that enable us to see the effect of look-alike fashion. The Roman world's sartorial codes are on full display in sculptures at every scale, from the larger-than-life statues of emperors in togas to the intimate portraits of family groups on tombstones and sarcophagi. Han Chinese tombs show a veritable hierarchy of clothing that demonstrates the social station of each individual portrayed, with the volume of fabric a marker of both substance and savoir faire. In India, stone sculptures similarly illustrate the fashions of the time, in which there's a great deal of ornamentation in addition to diaphanous, flowing garments on both deities and devotees.

Clothing still provides one of the most powerful everyday statements of identity and belonging. Today, every city in the world has a T-shirt industry that enables people to buy a relatively inexpensive piece of clothing emblazoned with the city name: Hong Kong, Miami, Sydney, Cape Town. Visitors can find those souvenir T-shirts in predictable locales: shops in the airport and the train station, and hawked by itinerant vendors at venues such as the zoo and the ballpark. Inter-

estingly, the shirts are worn not only by tourists who take their souvenirs home with them as proof of their adventures but also by locals
who presumably already have a sense of identity with their city. What
is it about a city that leads us to wear a token of its existence even as
it stands all around us? And is the city branding us, or the other way
around?

In ancient times, there weren't T-shirts, of course, but there were
many fabrics and styles of clothing that were known to be associated
with distinctive locales (why is it called the Silk Road, after all?). And
there were beads and turbans and tattoos and beards and hairstyles
and hats that all linked insiders and outsiders through the simple acts
of purchase and display. It was a bespoke familiarity made possible by
mass production, enabling newcomers to act as though they had lived
there all along. And it was not just the things that people wore that
made them "belong." In their homes, they used trinkets and tchotchkes
to show where they had been and how they thought of themselves. In
ancient Rome, there was an incredible variety of kitschy souvenirs
that people could bring home from urban gladiatorial games, like clay
lamps with famous gladiators' images and molded blown-glass cups
that commemorated particular matches. Today, that same spirit is
found in the sports team T-shirt or souvenir event cup that is cheap
enough for almost everyone to afford. Starting in the seventh century
A.D., China became a fountain of porcelain manufacturing, with kilns
in places like Jingdezhen producing millions of exemplars. The potters altered their designs to suit their faraway customers, making different vessels and designs for Middle Eastern, Japanese, European,
and East African markets. Yet the most amazing thing was the way in
which consumers across that vast expanse delighted in something

that was so mundane in its point of origin that Chinese porcelains were primarily used as ballast on ships to counterbalance the lighter and costlier cargoes of tea and silk.

Today we are exhorted to view consumption as a guilty pleasure, and we seek out opportunities to feel less ashamed about the rate of acquisition and discard. The most prevalent remedy is found in the mantra "reuse, reduce, recycle," but each concept has decidedly variable popularity. Let's face it: reuse is icky. If we are on the go with that take-out coffee cup or used yogurt container, where do we keep it until we can bring it somewhere where we can wash it in preparation for reuse? And the recommendation to reduce is no fun at all, especially with the enticements of urban consumption opportunities both large and small that help to make a bad day acceptable and a good day great. So, recycle is the only real option. And it comes with a bonus that plays right into our sensibilities of wanting more stuff, because recycling actually endorses *more*—rather than less—consumption. For recycling to be an effective option, we need special bins to throw the recycling into, special recycling trucks to haul it away, and special facilities to triage, sort, process, and sell the recycled materials. If we think of recycling as being somehow different from the treatment of other kinds of "trash," we are fooling ourselves. And legitimate critiques of recycling have emerged, with researchers noting that most of the recyclables that we so carefully triage are actually relatively inert (like glass and paper) and that the melting down of plastics into new shapes consumes a considerable amount of water.

So is trash a positive? Yes. On the scale of human existence, trash is a great problem to have as a product of human creativity. And the makers and sellers and buyers of that creativity overwhelmingly live in cities. All of the most avant-garde social, artistic, musical, and creative movements either occur in cities or make essential reference to the urban experience, but that process is not static: change is an essential component of the urban experience, and nearly everything in cities is in a process of change, from foodways to clothing styles to architectural embellishments and art. Today there are good programs for waste reduction that make a real dent in the amount of discards and that provide employment to workers who repurpose restaurant scraps into animal feed and industrial cooking oil into biofuel. And anything that helps to reduce the waste of edible food, like recovery programs from markets and restaurants, can address food insecurity for vulnerable urban populations and reduce the structural injustice of food access. But overall, we have to ask ourselves whether a little extra trash isn't a small price to pay for the stretching of creativity, of satisfaction, of intensity of feeling—of "flow" in the form of feeling fully alive in the urban context.

And who does the *most* consuming? As we've already seen, objects can be "consumed" without being bought or possessed, and just seeing them in a market is enough to acquire knowledge about them. Experiences also can be "consumed" through the encapsulation of a week's worth of vacation memories into a single souvenir, or without any tangible by-products at all. By far the greatest impact of consumption, in the traditional sense of acquiring objects and taking them home, is carried out by middle-class households. For the first time in history, cities were places where there were more people who could afford more stuff. They used their discretionary income to acquire both tangible possessions and intangible experiences and used those acquisitions to demonstrate their claims of identity and belonging. With a greater proportion of resources coming from steady, salaried employment as scribes, accountants, and shop managers, the middle classes of ancient cities put their discretionary income on display. While the uppermost elites may have more items per person, the kinds of things that they purchase has a far smaller effect on the economy than middle-class consumption does. It's not surprising that today the majority of marketing and advertising and shopping square footage is designed for middle-class (and middle-class aspirations of) consumption that is not just about getting goods but about making a performance out of selecting those goods and displaying them for others to see.

Portrait from Egypt, c. A.D. 100

THE MOJO OF THE MIDDLE CLASS

I n the ancient Mesopotamian city of Nippur, written documents reveal that the urban temples had an inventory of 350,000 sheep and goats. Keeping track of them would have rivaled any modern corporation's organizational chart! Herders had to be contracted to watch over animals in flocks of manageable sizes, and the herders themselves needed oversight to ensure that the animals stayed healthy and weren't diverted into a rural stew pot. Someone had to organize the information about supply and demand and keep track of annual fluctuations of winter rains and summer droughts that affected the grazing lands far beyond the city walls. Someone also had to calculate when the animals should come into the settlement (you couldn't have a few thousand hungry sheep milling around in the market square all at once or absorb a glut of wool if there were not enough weavers to handle the influx). And someone probably had to be employed to "separate the sheep from the goats" as it were.

The intensive activities at Nippur—and every other Mesopotamian city—could only have happened because of a professional class of managers employed to account for, enumerate, and keep track of all those animals. Trained and educated in accountancy and medicine and animal science, and equipped with the skills of writing and record keeping, middle managers had to answer for the past, present, and future of their decisions. They had to know about weather, seasons, and grazing conditions, and they had to calculate the ancient equivalent of wool futures in which the relative value of leg of lamb today could be reckoned against the need for fiber and leather tomorrow. The complexities of each single component of the economy were enormous, but the sum total of interactive activities was truly impressive. Not only were there sheep and goats to be counted and directed toward markets, but there was also everything else that urban residents needed and that came from the surrounding countryside: vegetables and fruits, grain and fodder, fuel and water, timber and thatch for construction, and raw materials like clay and ore and pigments. The goods that came into cities were accompanied by a steady stream of migrants who also had to be counted and acknowledged, even if those newcomers could not be provided with any civic services and were simply expected to tuck themselves away into the hazardscape of the city's growing slums and shantytowns.

Only through the advent of middle managers—a category of persons that never existed before cities—could the private and public parts of a place like Nippur maintain any sense of order. The managers of Nippur carefully inscribed clay tablets that served as the printouts and ledgers of the urban economy and that also kept track of workers and their relative expectations of productivity. Nippur is also famous as the place from which the world's earliest known city map came, more than three thousand years ago. The map revealed the infrastructure of canals and the emplacement of the main temple that were a credit to the organization of human labor into teams supervised by architects and priests. Along with the accountants and supervisors, those managers received bigger rations than laborers, indicating the relative value of knowledge work compared with physical toil. The emergence of this new group of people who made their living on the basis of their education, knowledge, and training—brain work instead of brawn—resulted in the emergence of the middle class as an entirely new social and economic group for the very first time in human society.

The term "middle class" is certainly one that comes with a great deal of baggage, and many archaeologists hesitate to use it because the idea of a middle class seems to be very modern, or at least something that started with the Industrial Revolution in the eighteenth century and all of those Dickensian factories. But my use of the term "middle class" refers to the broad category of intermediate consumer-producers who are between the top of the heap and the physical laborers. Those individuals, who are primarily information specialists and middle managers, were exactly the types of people who were indispensable in the new social and economic configuration of cities. With cities, as we've already seen, there were not only more people but also a bigger scale of every kind of investment, from residential housing to the size of temples. There were more types of physical integrative mechanisms, from water pipes and sewers to roads and marketplaces, all of which needed someone to oversee the workers and to implement the abstract goals that city leaders had proclaimed. And managers were essential within the new productive spaces of the city as well, in which entrepreneurs were successful because of their coordination of raw material, production technologies, and specialized craftspeople.

The anthropologist Mark Liechty, who studies the realities of the middle class in the modern world, has suggested that the development of a middle class is not the result of a particular type of economic system or an exclusive characteristic of the modern nation-state. After all, there has been the functional equivalent of a middle class in Soviet-era Russia and in places like Cuba and China, where those with education had a distinct lifestyle that could be measured in access to particular types of goods and housing as well as a keen interest in having their children educated. Even when people did not have access to money or other forms of wealth, there were many ways that the intermediate stratum distinguished itself from physical laborers: through mannerisms, speech patterns, hairstyles, the way that clothing was worn, and expressions of preference in music and entertainment. What enabled these developments is not the existence of capitalism but instead what Liechty has identified as the "conditions of possibility" that occur when there are new, shifting modes of production and consumption that include salaried and credentialed professional employment. In those circumstances, he argues, an intermediate stratum forms itself, making use of expertise to become "simultaneously sellers of labor and owners of capital" such as skills, education, and achievements.

Liechty's perspective on the middle class enables us to see how ancient cities and the middle class developed together as essential adjuncts to each other. Before cities, people kept track of things in their own houses and storerooms and could see what was moving into the local temple or saved up for an occasional feast just by looking around within their own local village. They relied on family memory and word of mouth to recall debts and to admonish people against misbehavior. But in urban locales, there were too many activities, too many newcomers, and too many opportunities for simple memory to suffice. People in cities instead developed new strategies of record keeping, among which writing was particularly revolutionary because it did not depend on the memory or credibility of a single individual. Once something was written down on a clay tablet or a strip of bamboo or a piece of papyrus, anyone who could read could have access to the information. Nor did everyone have to be able to read in order for writing to be effective: illiterate people could have the message read to them, and the message would be equally binding.

Whether handwritten or a printed text, writing was an impartial mediator of facts and figures to which multiple individuals could have recourse whether or not they were present at the time of the transaction. Writing was also all-purpose, and once a person could write and read, information of all kinds could be inscribed. Small wonder, then, that the development of writing brought an explosion of text in the form of receipts, lawsuits, medicines, and ritual incantations that were all locked into a fixed and exact form that could be consulted again and again. But writing also required a new way of thinking and planning, because people had to be taught to read and write, a factor that in turn spawned a whole new profession of learned folk in the form of teachers and tutors.

In ancient Egypt, education was part and parcel of professional life, as seen in *The Satire of the Trades,* an Egyptian document of the Eleventh Dynasty. The document details the many different types of jobs that people did four thousand years ago, sequentially describing the dangers and unpleasantness of each. Barbers, reed cutters, potters, bricklayers, carpenters, gardeners, and sandal makers were ugly, worn down by physical toil, and had bad breath. The trader faced

dangers from lions, the coppersmith's work gave him fingers that resembled crocodile skin, and the jeweler's "arms are destroyed by his
exhaustion." Students were warned against every type of work, with
one exception:

> Be a scribe, that your limbs may be smooth and your hands
> languid, that you may go out dressed in white, being exalted
> so that the courtiers salute you. When a trustworthy person
> is sought, you are found. No one knows an insignificant per-
> son, but finds the one who is skilled. He arises step by step
> until he reaches the (position of) an official, in favor corre-
> sponding to his talents.

The *Satire* was so popular that it was copied over and over again,
serving no doubt as an object lesson to children and to their parents.
Writing as a sign of education and as a practical, erudite craft made
an impact on the social configuration of other regions as well. As a
precursor to the history of modern law, the Mesopotamian Code of
Hammurabi shows the tight relationship between the law and political power, and between the law and property. Hammurabi was a
ruler of Babylon, the legendary city along the Euphrates River nearly
four thousand years ago in what is now modern Iraq. Like many
other rulers whose names have come down to us, he had the good
fortune of a long life coupled with an unashamed claim of authority
(the top of the stone manifestation of the code shows Hammurabi
receiving the laws from the sun god, Shamash).

In Mesopotamia, the culture of writing was so tightly integrated
into the formation of career-minded youth that educators used the
Code of Hammurabi for writing practice, resulting in an archaeologi-

cal scatter of textual fragments across a wide swath of the Middle East. The exercise neatly tied together both the concept of writing and the code's content while preparing students to become officeholders and magistrates. Copies of the code were made for a thousand years afterward, signaling that the inscribed laws reflected cultural traditions that had achieved longevity and relevance through the process of middle-class repetition. Internalized by generations of schoolchildren training to be clerks and bureaucrats, the "real thing" still held subsequent rulers in thrall. In the twelfth century B.C., more than five hundred years after it was initially carved, a local ruler of the Iranian Elamites carried the stone two hundred miles eastward to Susa, where it was proudly displayed among other Mesopotamian trophies. The rest of the code's story reads like a textbook case of archaeological intrigue and political capture. Eventually lost to the sands of time, the stone was rediscovered at Susa by archaeologists in the winter of 1901–2. Grabbed by a French expedition and hauled away to Paris, the monolith is now housed in the Mesopotamian galleries of the Louvre. As an icon of capture and knowledge control recycled into the modern postcolonial world, the code has been interwoven into urban life for nearly as long as urbanism itself has existed.

The Code of Hammurabi was popular for the ancients and for the centuries of legal theorists who followed, and provided the appearance of equal access to the law by anyone who could read or could cajole someone else to read it for them. But for whom was the code written? The ruler himself certainly didn't need to have recourse to the law (after all, he had the sun god on his side). And people who were at the lowest end of the social scale would have been unlikely to have the means to pay the lawyers and courts that were bound up in the administration of justice. While the existence of so many copies of the code suggested a democratic approach to justice, the system was organized to favor some socioeconomic groups over others. Rights were graded according to the social standing of the petitioner, with the law recognizing that people had different quantities of means against which to make a judgment. A man seeking to divorce his wife was to give her a mana of silver, unless he was a workman, in which case he would give her one-third that amount—likely representing a much greater proportion of a laborer's wages and thrusting him further down the socioeconomic ladder. Similarly, punishments were graded according to the status of the aggrieved, such that "if a man has knocked out the tooth of a man who is his colleague, they shall knock out his tooth. . . . If he has knocked out the tooth of a working man, he shall pay a third of a mana of silver."

Calculated in terms of purchasing power, the implication is that people with a bit of social and economic status had financial rather than moral obligations to the people whom they transgressed. While repeated acts of violence against peers would quickly have rendered a person toothless, an infinite amount of wealth could mean an unending cycle of abuse to people lower down on the social ladder. Even today, by virtue of the possession of some discretionary income, middle-class people can buy into and uphold the maintenance of inequality using the law to make distinctions between themselves and others, and criminalizing behaviors that they imbued with moral overtones (such as vagrancy, alcohol consumption, begging, and debt). When lower-class people elicit a claim of equality under the law, they still must submit to the intervention of educated, middle-class practitioners of the law to create the opportunity for contestation.

The more a lawyer knows, the greater benefit can be accrued to a client. Nowhere is this more evident than in the realm of property. As the legal scholar Rachel Van Cleave has noted, a concept like property is not about the "doctrine and the rules, but rather the theories, assumptions, histories, and biases upon which the doctrine and the rules have traditionally been based." Expectations of social behavior related to material objects and tangible assets continue today, with property being subdivided into an entire realm of different perspectives that reflect evolving standards and expectations. There's real estate, movable assets, and intangibles such as "intellectual property" in the form of patents and copyrights. Intellectual property rights are neatly tied into the urban realm in many ways: in recognizing the entrepreneurial spirit of invention that occurs in cities, in expanding the role of law beyond a single guild or craft-making group to a general principle of behavior, and in the branding of commodities that constitute urban style. It is for this reason that concepts of "copying" and the varying legalities and perceptions of copies are so difficult to pin down, not only because it is challenging to decide when something is too close to be original, but also because the punishment and recompense can be calculated in so many different ways.

The effects of urban-based laws weren't limited to the metropolis itself, as the examination of other parts of the globe makes clear. In the Roman world, water laws had a spillover effect on the countryside that tightened the mutual ties of the rural and the urban realms. The historian Andrew Wilson highlights the Spanish example of the *lex rivi Hiberiensis,* which was a consortium of three administrative communities that drew off a common water channel coming from the Ebro River. End users had votes as well as obligations in proportion to the water that they drew from the system along a twelve-mile stretch that would have irrigated thousands of acres of farmland. As in the case of the Code of Hammurabi, laws regulating conduct and outlining expectations provided a time-saving shortcut that made it possible for individual interactions to occur without each pair of participants having to come to their own agreements. Writing—in the form of laws—enabled the concept of language to grow beyond the level of gossip and suggestions to a scaffolding of interaction that in turn underwrote other strategies of social and economic profit with expectations about belonging and rights. The law became, as noted by the seventeenth-century jurist Juan de Solórzano Pereira, "like an eye" guarding the city.

Urban Entrepreneurship

The earliest urban dwellers recorded their entrepreneurial intent for us in their own words. Let's take, for example, the Greek writer Demosthenes, who provides a vignette of the diversity of middle-class property and investments in Athens in the fourth century B.C.:

> My father left two factories, each of them a decent-sized business: thirty-two or -three sword makers worth five or six hundred drachmas apiece . . . from whom he got an income of three thousand drachmas per year free and clear; then sofa makers, twenty in number, who were security for a loan of four thousand drachmas, who brought him twelve hundred drachmas free and clear and about a talent of silver lent out at twelve percent, from which the interest every year came out to more than seven hundred drachmas. Beside this, there were ivory and iron, which were used as raw

materials, and sofa-quality wood worth eight thousand drachmas and gold and clothing, my mother's jewelry . . . there was also a maritime loan of seven thousand drachmas to Xuthus, two thousand and four hundred at Pasio's bank, six hundred at Pylades', one thousand six hundred deposited with Demomeles, the son of Demon, and about a talent lent out at two- and three-hundred-drachma loans.

The activities described in this account of Demosthenes reveal a sophisticated understanding of income, risk, and the interconnection of economic activities that nonetheless involved only relatively modest amounts of cash. A drachma was the equivalent of a daily wage for an infantryman, so the sums expended by Demosthenes's father indicated the cautious, diversified portfolio of a small-scale venture capitalist. He lent money for specific purposes, like trade, and kept multiple accounts against the risk of fraud or bank failure. He made loans for maritime purposes as well as terrestrial ones and used both silver and people as collateral for the loans he made to others.

The archaeological record of ancient Greek cities enables us to flesh out this busy picture of middle-class life. Archaeological excavations throughout Athens, and in other cities as well, show the many ways that people exhibited their middle-class status to others. There was a range of housing styles and sizes and a tremendous variety of consumer goods that people bought, used, and discarded to show their sense of style and urban savvy. There were fancy pottery drinking cups and vases decorated with popular scenes of mythology, sporting events, and sex. There were personal-care goods and furniture that made for a cozy home life, as well as ornaments and clothing for going out that sparkled in the bright Mediterranean sun. And people demonstrated their household's standing by investing in tombstones inscribed with pretty words about the piety of the beloved deceased. You can't take it with you, as they say, but an attractive grave marker was the next best thing. There were publicly visible markers for other things as well, like foundation plaques and dedicatory offerings (much as today patrons of a museum or library or hospital can have their names inscribed on the architecture or a commemorative paving stone). For every object and experience, ancient Greek urbanites—like any city dwellers—faced a series of choices among available options at different prices.

The idea of choice is near and dear to economists, as seen in the work of marketing experts like Michael J. Silverstein and Neil Fiske, who have assessed contemporary choice making both within and among categories of objects and experiences. Their book, *Trading Up: Why Consumers Want New Luxury Goods,* examines the way that people engage in a continual reevaluation of consumption choices. They note that marketing is successful when it entices a person to acquire something or when it prompts a person to consider acquiring a particular item *instead of something else.* An intent of status and utility is on display throughout the consumption process, from the moment of education about what potential goods could be acquired through everything from formal advertising to simple word of mouth. In the past as in the present, consumption decisions and emotional states were on display in the process of acquisition, whether haggling in the bazaar over a gem that one went to buy on purpose or suddenly being enticed by the wares spread out on a blanket by the side of the road by an itinerant peddler. There's also an aspirational aspect to consumption: one might buy an object to signal wealth, or scrape together a greater proportion of assets to purchase an item that serves as a social signal of where an individual or household would *like* to be on the socioeconomic ladder.

The aspirational component of consumption fuels both the middle class and those whose socioeconomic status is a little lower. Silverstein and Fiske note that consumers at the lower end of the wealth spectrum (people whom other economists have called BOP, or "bottom of the pyramid") also engage in the occasional selection of goods that are more expensive. The difference from middle-class consumers is that lower-income groups tend to upgrade in only one or two categories of goods, a strategy that the authors call "rocketing." Silverstein and Fiske's ideas about consumer selection are powerful for their universality. Around the world and in every time period, people can and do elect to spend more on a particular category of consumption while accepting a trimmed budget for other things. People even *talked* about trading up. Remember that Roman wine advertisement, which declared that a person could consume wine for one *aes* but that they could also, at the same place, choose the Falernian by spending four times more? As in Silverstein and Fiske's book, the upsell comes with adjectives. That cheap stuff is just wine, but the "premium" implies that it's the consumer and not just the drink itself that is more refined.

In every ancient city, there are both genuine "imported" items and locally made imitations that let people keep up with the Joneses. In the ancient subcontinental cities of the Indus valley four thousand years ago, archaeologists have discovered stunning red carnelian beads that would have taken hours and hours of laborious drilling, shaping, and polishing. There were also similarly shaped beads in red clay, which would have been cheap and expedient, made in just a few minutes. Nor were they the only examples of costly ornamentation juxtaposed with cheap goods; there were also light-colored and expensive faience beads that had their imitations in fired soapstone covered with paint. As the Indus scholar Mark Kenoyer astutely observes, the use of shared style is a powerful demonstration of social cohesion: "The reproduction of identical shapes and styles using different raw materials helps to unify people within a single culture and belief system, although not everyone enjoys the same wealth or status."

If your salary is good, you can afford to buy the "real thing," but even if your salary is not so good you can get something that looks like the real thing. And for those who are in the middle class—a socioeconomic category that was born along with urbanism—cities were also the perfect place to "trade up" in an increasing variety of goods, as well as to contribute to the creation of new styles and production techniques in a dynamic, churning round of everyday consumption. All over the world today, the middle classes are still the key component of globalism and the world economy. Nowhere is this more evident than the mall as a gleaming, air-conditioned shopping center in which there is both the display of goods and the performance of consumption. From Rio and Manila to Shanghai and Dallas, the mall is an arena of purchasing as well as the knowledge of what to buy. When you go to the mall, you might buy one or two things—or nothing at all—but you are consuming information in abundance as you stroll the storefronts learning about the latest fashions.

There wasn't a mall in ancient times, of course, although there were equivalents in the form of the bazaar. Bazaar economies are in some ways very different from malls, because malls have a variety of shops under one convenient roof, while bazaars concentrate multiple shops that all sell the same goods. There might be a jewelry bazaar, a hardware bazaar, a vegetable market, and a shoe bazaar. Although it might seem odd that shops would want to compete side by side instead of having a captive audience through monopoly, the idea of the bazaar was to enable people to peruse a wide variety of goods with the certainty that they would be able to find something that worked for them among all of the different shopkeepers. The bazaar also was a place where social connections were maintained by generations of shopkeepers who inherited generations of customers. Not only did they sell the goods that people wanted to buy, but those merchants were also a handy source of information in a social network.

The bazaar concept still exists. Special-purpose markets still spring up to serve clients at particular venues, whether it's the clusters of photocopy shops and bookstores around universities or the suburban "auto malls" where manufacturers congregate in the hopes that the proximity to competitors will result in a higher overall sales rate than if their showrooms were randomly distributed throughout the city. Farmers' markets are a kind of bazaar, too, in which there's conversation as well as money changing hands and where, in addition to fruits and vegetables, there's a whole range of tag-along goods and services from ready-made food to handmade jewelry. One rarely goes to a farmers' market just to *look* at the items for sale there; the experience of being in an unusual, festive place results in many spontaneous purchases. Much as a fair or a carnival entices us to acquire things that are out of the ordinary (giant turkey leg, oversized stuffed toy, funnel cakes), a bazaar is a social occasion as well as an economic one that enables us to experience the excitement of shopping just as ancient urban dwellers did.

In sum, urbanism offers something for everyone. If you are in the elite upper class, you have more opportunities to show off among your peers with the range of new things that can be purchased and displayed, from architecture to objects to lavish displays of philanthropy. If you are in the bottom range of earners, you can engage in the "purchase" of experiences through the everyday life of flowing through the city streets and making knowledgeable use of its infrastructure. If you are at the very bottom of the socioeconomic ladder, at least you can find some kind of work to get by and some kind of shelter to keep body and soul together. The greatest boost of all occurs if you are in the middle class. For the first time in history, cities provided the opportunities that go along with production, consumption, and discard on a large scale, with a large number of people, and with a nearly infinite amount of variation. Mobility and upward social movement can be signified through something as simple as a take-out beverage or the display of a trendy ornament, even if it's a copy (who's to say whether the Rolex on the wrist next to yours in the subway is real or not?).

Urban consumption was, and is, a constant upward cycle of production *by* middle-class people *for* middle-class people. Before cities, everything that was esoteric, from ritual to education to craft making, was limited to people like chiefs and shamans. And the weight of tradition meant that any innovations were viewed with skeptical conservatism unless proposed by a charismatic leader. With such a small group of people engaged in the support of innovation, new knowledge emerged and spread with an aching slowness. In cities, all of that potential forcefully sprang loose and exploded into an entirely new socioeconomic realm. The middle classes emphasized formal education and cultivated new kinds of mannerisms while seeking new forms of entertainment and participating in new types of secular and religious rituals and while living in upgraded quarters with new consumer goods. They focused on their children and on education to solidify and validate their skills portfolio across generations. Using writing, they relied on newly emergent concepts like insurance and contracts to safeguard their modest investments and to protect the inheritances that they intended for their children.

The Fall of the Magician, Pieter van der Heyden, A.D. 1565

9

ANXIETY, RISK, AND
MIDDLE-CLASS LIFE

I f you have ever been a middle manager, you know that you represent the most essential function of any complex enterprise precisely because you are squeezed between the top and the bottom of the work chain. Higher bosses establish lofty goals and visions, with the expectations that their vague directives will be turned into tangible results—and quick! You're responsible not only for interpreting their goals but also for organizing people to actually get the work done and for responding to their needs and demands in the process. If you supervise salespeople, you've approached each of them with a combination of carrot and stick to meet targets. If you manage office staff, you have to deal with each person's capacities and limitations. Or perhaps you supervise employees who are on the factory floor or the suppliers who are sourcing the raw materials. Along with them there's a whole army of support personnel whose work you oversee as well: the maintenance staff who clean and service the equipment, the people who pack and transport the finished objects, and the accounting staff who track shipments and record invoices.

It doesn't matter what type of people you've supervised or at what level. Whether it's the snack stand at your high school ball game or a Fortune 500 company, the challenges are the same. There's every kind of headache in the management of a team. Hiring people can be a fraught and tense process in which employees' shortcomings may not appear until after they have signed on the dotted line, whereupon their problems become your problems, too. Sometimes people are hired onto your team without your knowledge, and you have to figure out how to integrate them. When the hiring doesn't go well, and sometimes when it does, you might have to fire the employee, which provides another kind of stress. In between hiring and firing, there are all of the other challenges of management, from absenteeism and slacking to subterfuge and pilfering to abrupt changes of company policy, that you have to defend and implement to those working under your supervision.

Yet none of these challenges are new. Compare your experiences of middle management with those of your counterpart four thousand years ago in Mesopotamia, a person named Kibri-Dagan who sent this message to the boss:

> My lord has sent me an order to get to Mari to appear before the junior *ugbabtum*-priestess. I have to direct work here and the field on which I am directing work is in actual danger. . . . If I stay here myself right now I can certainly keep the entire crew together, but once I have dropped the work and have left, the crew will disperse, the work will be aban-

doned, and the country of my lord will be in dire need of irrigation water. . . . I just cannot possibly leave.

Never mind that the memo in that case was a clay tablet, compared with the email or text message that you would get. The sentiment is the same. You and Kibri-Dagan and every other middle manager are caught by a boss who wants you to do two diametrically opposed things at the same time.

When we have extant texts, middle managers speak for themselves. Yet even when we don't have the written word and rely on our observations of structures and city plans, we can sense the stress of the middle manager. The Aztec city of Tenochtitlan, which today lies under Mexico City, is a magnificent example of what happens when middle managers have to contend not only with human bosses but also with the caprices of Mother Nature. Tenochtitlan was in the very center of one of the world's most commanding landscapes, the high-altitude volcanic caldera of central Mexico. The mountains channeled water from all sides into the gentle bowl of the valley floor, resulting in a geologic mud flat interspersed with lakes and marshes. Over generations, people continually built up the city through the engagement with those swampy lands, from the outlying barrios of the raised-field system that provided food to the core of the urban center with its central temple zone. In the heart of that zone was the Templo Mayor, a soaring pyramid structure that also was the scene of ritual dread. From Spanish accounts, we know that human sacrifices took place there, and Aztec picture books show that the plaza had as a prominent feature the *tzompantli:* the Rack of Skulls. Taken from warriors and other sacrificial victims, the heads on the rack were a vivid reminder of the dense, violent power that sometimes inter-weaves its way through the urban fabric.

The Templo Mayor—smoky, imposing, terrifying—was a living en-tity, and each new Aztec emperor was expected to add to its height and wealth. As a result, the structure itself is a series of architectural shells in which each reconstruction completely covered the previous structure. Just as in the case of any other building, sacred or secular, there were engineering realities to overcome. Every time more struc-tural weight was added, there had to be additional shoring and pilings driven into the substrate. Yet almost immediately, the newly enlarged buildings obeyed the law of gravity and began to sink. This problem is certainly known to modern engineers, who account for subsidence in their constructions (the most recent infamous cases are the luxury high-rise Millennium Building in San Francisco, which has tilted and sunk more than sixteen inches, and the Mandalay Bay hotel in Las Vegas, Nevada, which sank an equal amount due to an underlying aquifer). When new construction happens at an empty field site, there is already a lot to contend with in the form of soil quality, bedrock, and earthquake faults; the problems are compounded when it's a ren-ovation of an existing structure in which additions are supposed to address old problems but end up causing new ones.

Like their modern counterparts who inherited a built environ-ment not of their own making, engineers and architects and other project managers at Tenochtitlan were tasked with several things si-multaneously. They had to make the building taller, put the emperor's glory to evidence, mitigate subsidence, and plan for the unforeseen while keeping in mind that each generation's construction was des-tined to be covered over in the next building episode. At the Templo Mayor construction site, middle managers had to be able to explain the constraints and opportunities both to their bosses and to the workers responsible for hauling dirt and quarrying stones. It was impossible to predict how much farther the Templo would subside and difficult to pinpoint the exact cause. Maybe soils. Maybe groundwater. Maybe the other nearby constructions with their own pilings or foundation trenches that had interfered with the unstable ground structure. And it was equally impossible to predict the chances of success through any particular course of mitigation. Those ancient engineers' conversations probably echoed the concerns expressed about the Millennium Building, where there is not only the slow problem of subsidence but also the unknowable timing of earthquakes that could cause radical and catastrophic shifts to the sediments underneath. Knowing how one building could be fixed wouldn't necessarily help another, as the engineer Steven Sanders said about applying the Mandalay Bay hotel's solution to San Francisco: "It may be tough to really go down the road and identify possibilities based on historical knowledge. I think it would be hard and probably dangerous to say, *This is done here, why don't you do the same thing there?*"

Middle managers of the Templo Mayor and its adjoining plazas were at the heart of the building dilemmas of the ancient "business district" of Aztec Tenochtitlan, which, like San Francisco, had a geology that was subject both to prior human construction decisions and to the vagaries of nature. Engineers and architects had to manage the emperor's directives (make it taller!) with the realities of day-to-day tasks and unknowable long-term goals. Promoted to the ranks of managers, they enjoyed a higher status than workers while enduring many more headaches. For the rest of their lives they carried with them the weighty responsibility of accounting for their decisions and living with the consequences; failure could even haunt

22 2

them after death, if some catastrophe struck for which blame was assigned in hindsight.

And failures *did* happen. In the past as in the present, there were many natural and cultural conditions of geology, topography, landforms, weather, climate, and other natural frames of the design process that interfered with human intent. Experts are not infallible, and the mundane realm of infrastructure illustrates how communication and educational processes can fall short in the face of the unforeseen or the unacknowledged. The challenges of engineering are seen not only in high-rise buildings but also in entire systems of infrastructure, as prominently seen in drought-prone regions such as the western United States. Many cities there rely on water imported from long distances, with the biggest example being the city of Los Angeles, which has far outstripped its natural water capacity. The Los Angeles River holds enough water to support about 150,000 people, but the current population of the city is more than twenty times greater than that (and the population of the greater Los Angeles region, which stretches out across five counties, is close to 20 million). The only reason that L.A. can be supported is through the extensive networks of canals and conduits known as the Los Angeles Aqueduct, a grand engineering project started in 1907.

Chief among the authorities engaged to bring water from the mountains to the seaside city of Los Angeles was the charismatic figure William Mulholland, who designed the network of conduits that brought water from hundreds of miles away. Because storage systems are as integral to the provision of water as the canals themselves, Mulholland also built a dam on the outskirts of the northern side of Los Angeles at the point where the captive waters of the western United States entered the city. Squeezed in between two walls of a canyon, the St. Francis Dam was filled to near capacity in short order. Not long afterward, on the fateful night of March 12, 1928, the accumulated water put pressure on the dam's bonding with the friable canyon wall, and the structure gave way. The resulting blowout released twelve billion gallons of water, scouring a path to the sea for fifty miles and obliterating the farms and homes that stood in the way of the floodwaters. Hundreds of people died as a result of the dam rupture in a tragedy that remains, to date, the worst "natural" disaster in California after the 1906 San Francisco earthquake.

Ancient engineers often fared no better, with grandiose projects that outran the capacity of humans and materials to succeed. Archaeological traces of construction show that buildings that started with robust foundations of quarried stones were sometimes finished off with cheap and shoddy brickwork. Sometimes entire projects came to naught, as seen in the part of the world with the best preservation for such things, Egypt. Egypt was the land of pyramids, and not just the ones that we think of most readily at the Giza Plateau on the outskirts of Cairo. There were actually over a hundred pyramids throughout Egypt, and their chronology shows a long period of trial and error. The first pyramids were simple sets of blocks one on top of another, like stacked shoe boxes. That yielded a stepped profile that didn't quite fulfill expectations, so the next set of pyramid builders set about trying to make a smoother triangle shape. They experimented with the angle of the sides of a pyramid and in at least one case changed the angle as the structure got taller (resulting, not surprisingly, in the structure that we know today as the Bent Pyramid).

At the site of Meidum, about forty-five miles south of the Giza Plateau (where the Great Pyramid had not yet been built), engineers tried a different strategy. Rather than building the structure in horizontal layers, they innovated a construction technique that involved encasing the core of the pyramid with successive shells. Work proceeded apace on the structure, and it got taller and taller with an almost conical profile. One fine day, the entire outer shell gave way. The catastrophic failure happened in an instant, perhaps as the workers were straining on a rope, or eating their meal in the shadow of the structure, or as the engineer was congratulating himself, Mulholland-style, on the forthcoming success of his creation. In an instant, all of that hubris came crashing down. The resulting halo of architectural debris is so large that it can be seen in satellite images from outer space, with a visual effect that looks like what happens when a raw egg is dropped from the height of a kitchen counter.

The huge debris field, with blocks of stone larger than a person, serves as mute testimony of a catastrophic engineering failure that caught workers unaware and led to a complete abandonment of the project (I've been inside the fallen pyramid's tunnels and at the time wondered whether the pyramid had finished collapsing or whether there was a likelihood that I would become a permanent part of the Egyptian archaeological record myself). Middle managers were probably the most chagrined about the failure, asking themselves over and over again if they had missed a calculation or overlooked a harbinger of doom that they should have perceived in their inspections and conversations. It's also equally possible that some of the long-ago construction workers at Meidum had already cast a wary eye toward their towering creation, with its shell-upon-shell construction like a megaton set of Russian nesting dolls. Some of them might have tried, unsuccessfully, to communicate with the intermediate manager. Others just drifted away from employment in nervousness, leaving the construction process understaffed but saving their own skins in the process.

The Middle Manager at Home

Being a middle manager is stressful, even if it comes with the rewards of a better salary and the opportunity for the good feelings of team building and a job well done. And that's just the part that involves work. Home life provides plenty of other opportunities for people to be insecure about their achievements, and particularly about the consumption activities that they have undertaken with their salaries. Because there are so many new things that can be obtained in the cities that house middle-class customers, how should a person choose among the myriad new goods and new styles of goods that appear in every shop or bazaar? As the economist Sheena Iyengar reminds us, too many choices result in a kind of consumer paralysis, in which we become overwhelmed by selection. And it's not just that choices take up money or time; they also leave us vulnerable to the dismissive glances of strangers and the chiding admonitions of family: "What did you buy *that* for?"

Income and spending capacity aren't the only constraints on decision making. Ian Steedman's *Consumption Takes Time* provides a brilliant insight into the economics of time management that come along with a surfeit of choices. He notes that time is the one unchangeable factor in human life and that all of the outcomes of decision making are inescapably bound up in the fact that there are only twenty-four hours in a day. Educating oneself about the best way to spend resources is in and of itself a time-consuming occupation among people in the middle class (just think about how much time you've spent looking for that "perfect" gift). In the past, going into debt for bling was different from the hand-to-mouth debt of day laborers, and it still is: payday loans and car-title loans cater to an entirely different socioeconomic spectrum from credit cards and home-equity loans that can be expended for an infinitely large number of purposes . . . including, ironically, the consolidation of other debts.

The challenges of choice are not new to the modern age. Two thousand years ago, the Roman writer Petronius gave a firsthand glimpse of the social awkwardness that comes with choosing the wrong things. In his work *The Satyricon,* he narrates the story of Trimalchio, a newly wealthy man who liberally hands out invitations to a dinner party. Trimalchio tries too hard to impress his guests, starting with the army of household staff who are instructed to treat each arriving guest with a pedicure as a start to the festivities. In the subsequent course of the hours-long meal, Trimalchio provides an enormous quantity of fanciful, peculiar foods like honeycomb on a piece of turf and a roast pig with a hat, all laid out on expensive trays borne by lavishly dressed servants. In addition to the glut of food and drinks, Trimalchio has filled the dining hall with jesters, storytellers, and an orchestra to entertain the guests, with each performance outdoing the ones before. The meal ends with each person receiving a parting gift of a perfumed massage while the host reads his will out loud to demonstrate his wealth and generosity.

Trimalchio's approach to hosting was absurd enough to have kept ancient Roman audiences laughing, but it was probably a nervous laughter. Everyone was in danger of going over the top with their menus and invitations at a time when trade winds enabled people to access the delicacies of places as far away as Britain and India. Just as we experience the awkwardness of attending a wedding or a birthday party where the host has spent so much that it backfires into derision, overspending had to be done just right. And there were many other worries that occupied ancient middle-class lives that seem very familiar today. Were they getting promoted fast enough? Were they getting the work-life balance that they wanted, with enough time to take care of others as well as to take care of themselves? Had they picked the best neighborhood to live in, the best school for their children, the best nursing care for their elderly parents? And what is the risk that their hard-earned gains would be eroded by illness or crime?

Today, the fear of crime has driven middle-class urban dwellers to enclaves that enable them to remove themselves from the perceived hotbeds of lawlessness downtown, whether through distance (by commuting to the suburbs) or through exclusivity (such as gated neighborhoods with guard shacks, or high-rises with security personnel and elaborate entry procedures). Yet, like nearly everything about urbanism, the tendency to seek out enclaves seems to be not a modern phenomenon but one that came along with the very first cities. In Mesopotamia, the contrast between the ritual site of Göbekli Tepe and the city of Tell Brak is stark: while highly symbolic decorations and constructions at Göbekli are indicative of cohesive social connections, Brak presents a darker view. In excavations of one of the suburban mounds, Augusta McMahon and her colleagues have revealed a grim underside of urban life in the form of hundreds of human skeletons, many of which were brutally dismembered and thrown into a trash heap at the edge of the city. Many victims of the violence had evidence of previously healed traumas such as head wounds and broken limbs, indicating that they were probably a minority or slave group repeatedly subjected to abuse. Although we don't have written documents from that early period of settlement, the skeletons of Brak suggest that ethnic tensions and physical crimes have long been a simmering undercurrent of urban life.

Cities certainly provide the scope for more and novel types of crime. New opportunities for malfeasance occur in part because economies are more complicated and there are more people involved in any given enterprise, providing the cover of anonymity amid the crowd. In a village, a pickpocket doesn't last long, because he's soon found out and chased from the community. But in an urban setting, with its many neighborhoods, a pickpocket can keep moving from one place to the next while staying just ahead of the curve of recognition. And while we don't often perceive of crime as a kind of economic specialization, being a successful crook involves work, planning, energy expenditure, risk taking, and strategy, just like any other kind of job. Criminologists have commented that urban crime can be thought of as a kind of "optimal foraging": like wolves on the prowl, criminals head to the parts of town where there's the least deterrence and the greatest reward for petty theft or breaking and entering.

Other types of activities, such as panhandling, prostitution, and homelessness, whether they are actually defined as a crime, are a nuisance for urban middle-class residents. Street life may occasionally strike urban dwellers as a charming part of the social fabric of the city, including the musicians who sing and play instruments in public squares and subway tunnels. Their instrument cases artfully positioned on the ground in front of them to collect tips, these urban performers generally elicit much more support from tourists than from locals, however. To a lot of city people, buskers just get in the way of the commute and interfere with the flow of the daily routine of work and education. The so-called colorful characters also generate another kind of anxiety, related to two thought patterns: Will that somewhat innocent-looking beggar by day turn into a menacing pickpocket at night? And, philosophically, could the misfortune of the street person be due to a simple hairpin-turn loss of privilege that could strike anyone, anytime? It's not surprising that we have installed CCTVs at an astounding rate in urban centers: twenty thousand in Mexico City, twenty-seven thousand in Seoul, thirty-two thousand in Chicago. Because there is no way that someone can actually be watching all of that footage, the CCTV is the modern equivalent of the eye idol: a trust that by having them installed and visible, there will be some protective effect.

People in ancient cities took steps to keep themselves safe that resonate with modern urban dwellers in other ways as well. Just as we have doormen and security guards in our residential buildings and offices, ancient walled cities had guard platforms at their gateways. The Bronze Age city of Harappa, four thousand years ago, had walls around individual neighborhoods to protect the merchant families who had their homes and workshops within those enclaves. Walking through those gateways today, one can easily imagine the presence of a few truncheon-wielding heavies who kept order by day and by night, aided by torches and guard dogs. At the ancient city of Teotihuacan in central Mexico, each apartment complex had a solid, windowless wall around it to enclose the dwellings, the temples, and the two hundred or so people who lived there. There was only one entrance in that wall, with a corridor that allowed people to circulate freely only when they were inside. One can imagine that the watchful tending of the compound entrance was probably done by the old men; perhaps they were in retirement from their prior employment of building civic structures like the pyramids, or perhaps they were elderly farmers who had been brought into the city by their adult children. Grandpa, armed with a stick and a shrill voice, was the ideal person to keep away the unwanted and keep tabs on the residents. Taking turns with the other elders of the compound, for one or two days a month he could, Socrates-like, quiz each and every person who came through. Keeping a sharp eye out for flashy purchases or suspiciously frequent outings, he could add something to the gossip mill when next he sat with his cronies around a shared jug of agave-derived pulque.

There are many other urban risks besides crime, of course, and the extent and impact of different kinds of stress vary by social class. Low-income residents living in the less desirable topographies of the city tend to be subjected to hazards like flooding, parasitic diseases, and vermin, while middle-income residents have the problem of competing for access to desired goods and services (like top public schools) and suffer from diseases of affluence such as heart disease and cancer. Because of their comparatively greater access to resources, middle-income residents can compensate for some misfortune, such as the economic losses sustained when a child flunks out of college or the unexpected costs of elder care. Other problems are equal-opportunity hazards, like traffic that impacts residents of all socioeconomic status, adulterated foods that are dumped on the market by unscrupulous dealers, and air pollution that threatens the lungs of rich and poor alike. Interestingly, however, it is middle-class problems that seem to get the most press and political action. Writing becomes a power for addressing some needs over others, a strategy of complaint that we see in ancient sources as well.

Two thousand years ago, the Roman writer Juvenal complained constantly about his living conditions, counting among the stresses the challenges of moving around the city: "However fast we pedestrians hurry we're blocked by the crowds ahead, while those behind us tread on our heels. Sharp elbows buffet my ribs, poles poke into me, one lout swings a crossbeam down on my skull, another scores with a barrel. My legs are mud-encrusted, big feet kick me, a hobnailed soldier's boot lands squarely on my toes." In ancient Mesopotamia, inhabitants complained in a cuneiform text about having to eat "bought bread," which was apparently not as good as the homemade variety. Yet the fact that people bothered to write these things down provides a particularly good angle on the relationship between writing, anxiety, and middle-class life. The stresses and strains faced by those who were writing about their urban experiences weren't, for the most part, life threatening, although they did add up to worries that revealed a constant feeling of wear and tear.

In addition to the daily factors of uncertainty, the middle classes feared catastrophic losses of the kind that would bring the fortunes of the household to a halt, like the loss of a cargo ship consignment or the death of the principal breadwinner. As a written counterpart to the laws that codified if-then statements into precisely delineated crimes and punishments, there was another urban development that alleviated middle-class anxiety: insurance. Insurance is a collective pooling of resources that addresses the phenomenon of individual risk under conditions when the probability of an adverse incident can be mathematically calculated. Today, insurance is deeply implicated in banking and credit, but the beginnings of the insurance concept can be traced to some of the earliest urban centers for which we have written records. The Code of Hammurabi itself not only was about the law of conduct but also addressed the risks of commerce and phrased its punishments in terms that functioned like a blanket coverage of insurance: "If a man has given his boat to a boatman for hire and the boatman is careless and sinks the boat or loses it altogether, the boatman shall repay the owner of the boat with another boat." Other early insurance collectives included the Roman "burial societies" in which individuals made contributions that would enable their families to tap into resources for a proper burial upon their demise. We know about maritime insurance in the Roman world, too, in which individuals would pool their resources against the risky business of cargo shipping in the Mediterranean and in which merchants and shippers could borrow money against a safe return.

As a collective entity, insurance is predicated on the knowledge of extant conditions (like actuarial statistics about the frequencies of certain kinds of accidents or the anticipated life span of a person or a piece of equipment) and the phenomenon of risk. For any individual who purchases insurance, the outlay represents a sunk cost that is not unlike the cost of maintenance, in which a modest input is designed to stave off the chance of a catastrophic loss. Yet just as there's never a perfect match between maintenance and the long-term viability of a piece of equipment, there's not an absolute concurrence between individuals' investments in insurance and the payouts that are demanded by those who have borne losses (on the other hand, would you really rather have an accident, a burglary, or a premature death?). Those who manage insurance pools for material goods and fixed-place property take into consideration that not all individuals and households will eventually reclaim their investments. As a result, insurance brokerages can become a very lucrative business in which information about risk and restraint conditions is managed in order to acquire a residual pool of funds that can in turn be invested in other pursuits, a piling of risk upon risk that can turn a handsome profit for those willing to take a chance.

Urban moral codes provided suggestions about behavior beyond the expectations outlined in specific laws or identified in the provisions of insurance. The Indian *Arthaśāstra* text, written about two thousand years ago, outlines the details of house construction and codifies what it means to be neighborly: "He should have the place for carts and animals, the fireplace, the place for the water tank, the grinding mill, or the pounding machine constructed one Pada or one Aratni" (a specified length of distance) from the neighbor's property. The interesting thing about the *Arthaśāstra* is that it is an entirely prescriptive document; unlike with Mesopotamia and the Roman world, where there are numerous legal judgments preserved in cuneiform texts, we have no documents of adjudication or enforcement from the era in which the *Arthaśāstra* was written. Civic governments appear not to have evolved to have enough day-to-day authority, instead relying on the moral codes that are clearly aimed at metropolitan life in which houses were expected to be crowded together.

Strong moral and legal codes in urban environments were both relatively consistent compared with the caprices of political authorities, however. People with education could be the targets of rival political violence, as seen in the ancient Maya Bonampak murals where the scribes of the losing party are depicted with their fingers broken, dripping with blood. In that case, history was literally written by the victors because the losers had lost their capacity to do so. Even when there was political calm, however, middle managers and record keepers faced stress over performance. Revenue had to be kept up through taxation and through the delicate business of bringing in commerce for their city by relief from taxes along with other enticements and emoluments. In the Roman world, city managers had to address the perpetual and pressing need to bring grain into the city of Rome, where it would be handed out freely (along with the entertainment, hence the phrase "bread and circuses"). The result was a combination of carrot-and-stick approaches that involved other professionals, from tax collectors in the provinces who had to siphon off enough local production to Rome, to the ship owners on whose vessels the grain cargo was brought, to the insurance agents who guaranteed against losses incurred in shipwrecks.

A similar cost-benefit analysis is seen in the medieval city of Vijayanagara in India, a place extensively studied by historians and archaeologists. Responding to the entrepreneurial demands of producer groups that sound very similar to our own times, Vijayanagara's managers granted tax breaks to weavers if they agreed to relocate to the city. One tax remission to a newly settled group of weavers stipulated that they would owe no loom taxes for three years; recognizing that the new settlers were savvy about expiring tax breaks, city managers abolished their other taxes permanently. Upward mobility became part of the calculation; having made their mark through the provision of high-visibility goods, the weavers sought out civic and religious privileges as well. They countered the enticements with extra demands: for the troubles of crowding, pollution, and the higher cost of living, they also wanted to partake in the city's ephemeral riches of social recognition through the right of religious participation and other privileges. The move enabled them to become part of a middle class in which production, consumption, anxiety, and wealth were interwoven into the urban fabric.

Like so much else in cities, anxiety itself provided opportunities and was the lubricant of middle-class entrepreneurship and social dynamism. If we were to blame the Industrial Revolution for our own temptations to outsource everything from household cleaning and child rearing to what's on the table for dinner tonight, we'd be wrong. For every urban anxiety, there's always been a solution for hire. Worried about money and taxes? Ancient Mesopotamian city dwellers would say, "Hire an accountant." Worried about your food supply? Hire a caterer or a bespoke organic vegetable service. Worried about your child passing classes or getting higher education? Hire a tutor or a college-applications coach. Worried about being worried? That's what counselors and clergy are for. Middle-class professionals beget more middle-class professionals, each trained in her or his own specialty and trading that expertise for the results of others' knowledge. It's a web of interconnection that first became, in the ancient urban world, a human internet. And like many other conditions that at first glance appear to plague city life, the excess of anxiety is not a flaw of urbanism but a design feature.

Urban worries, far from being detrimental, actually contribute to the creation of cities' distinctive sense of flow. As Mihaly Csikszentmihalyi admits, "Enjoyment appears at the boundary between boredom and anxiety, when the challenges are just balanced with the person's capacity to act." In cities, the middle-class experience is one that involves constant opportunities for changes in employment through the enhancement of skills and new forms of training (a factor that might explain why professionals such as lawyers, doctors, and accountants have continuing-education requirements and recertification), in which the increase in challenges is met by deliberate attention to an increase in the "capacity to act." In Csikszentmihalyi's discussion of flow, we can sense a middle-class approach to life and anxiety that is exquisitely tailored to the realities of urbanism. Before cities there was fear of the outside world and fear of the cosmic unknown that could be propitiated through pilgrimage to a sacred site. But urban misgivings are not so much about the fear of the unknown or the uncontrollable, as is the case of a farmer who can do nothing to change the weather or forestall the onslaught of pests, or the hunter who relies on sympathetic magic to call forth an animal to be hunted. Instead, urban anxieties are internally and socially generated as a result of worrying about the consequences of known and deliberate human actions among an increasing number of choices, ranging from objects and housing to employment, education, and mates.

Even something as simple as choosing basic food items can trigger a bout of mild anxiety. The people in Mesopotamia who complained about eating bought bread revealed themselves to have a diversity of consumption opportunities unavailable to rural dwellers. They could get the ingredients to make bread at home, or they could get bread ready-made. To a Mesopotamian householder, this probably brought a twinge of uncertainty about what people should eat every day, as well as what they would be seen serving to guests (echoing a modern concern about whether it's healthier to eat out or cook at home, more host-worthy to make a meal or buy takeout, more genuine to buy a fancy cake or to bake a less elaborate specimen at home). The decision to get bought bread encompassed a whole range of follow-on questions about the time, money, and labor for cleanup, too. In short, even a simple purchase of daily staples was a point of stress for ancient Mesopotamian urbanites, resulting in a phenomenon that we can sympathize with today.

Did ancient people also face troubles related to middle-class urban lifestyles that resulted in other types of anxieties about getting and keeping their positions of managerial authority? Archaeologists have never seriously considered the impact of sedentary lifestyles on the middle class of the past, although we probably should. Did those cross-legged Egyptian scribes develop painful arthritis over the course of a lifetime stooping over papyrus documents? What happened when a Mesopotamian specialist in cuneiform suffered from alcohol-induced tremors and could no longer keep a steady hand on the thin reed that punctured the wet clay of a tablet? Myopia, so easily corrected with eyeglasses in our modern world, would have been a devastating blow to parents who had expected that their child would be educated to take up the family profession of accountancy or law. Nearsightedness among adults would have brought a wave of household fear as well, and worries for a crippling end to a manager's career as each day brought a terrifying diminution of the ability to see accounts, super-vise workers, or judge the quality of raw materials.

All over the ancient world, the structural envelope of middle-class life went far beyond moral codes, law, or insurance. Physical infra-structure itself stood in as a template for movement and action and the legitimacy of access. Streets and canals could be used to channel food, water, and footsteps in ways that specifically advantaged some groups over others. As the wry saying goes, "Water flows uphill to money," and in ancient cities that and much more were directed in ways that first and foremost benefited those who had the most in-come. When the ancient city of Rome grew, its water needs also grew and were fed by springs, wells, and the construction of aqueducts. Rome's aqueducts were ostensibly a mechanism for providing water for city dwellers' daily needs, but that need was differentially defined by those who desired fountains and gardens and other decorative elements that were more about keeping up appearances than basic issues of health and hygiene. Every time an aqueduct was extended, people downstream had the benefits of better yields made possible by the water. But people upstream had reason to fuss if they perceived that the extension took away some of the abundance that they had previously enjoyed. We can imagine that aqueducts, like our own linear infrastructure of new highways, ring roads, and train lines, were constructed not in an empty landscape but in one that was already inhabited with people who had to contend with the specter of their resources being tapped by the metropolis.

Pathways are another way of privileging some social groups over others. A telling modern example is offered by Charlotte Lemanski in her study of the two adjacent communities of Silvertree and Westlake in Cape Town, South Africa. Green and graceful, Silvertree is a gated enclave of middle-class residents who live in houses widely spaced apart, where being a "good neighbor" means not interfering with other people too much. Westlake, by contrast, is a low-income community that's much less aesthetically pleasing but more socially integrated. Its houses are closely packed, and the community has much less of the infrastructure of roads and schools enjoyed by the middle-class residents of Silvertree. Westlake's limitations are marked by what's found inside the community as well as the neighborhood's link to the rest of the city. Its roads and pathways force residents to travel extra-long distances, with direct links physically barricaded. There's a chain-link fence between the neighborhood and the nearest grocery store, which the residents finally cut through in order to be able to get groceries. Although South Africa's long and damaging history of apartheid is officially over, the logistical challenges of in-

ANXIETY, RISK, AND MIDDLE-CLASS LIFE

frastructure show that the social practices of separation are still being negotiated every day.

In ancient Rome and modern Cape Town and everywhere else, the separation that characterizes middle-class neighborhoods from less well-off areas provides a mental scaffolding as well as a physical one. Middle-classness is about the anxiety not so much of getting ahead—because achieving the uppermost echelons of society is often highly unrealistic—as of not falling behind. Through laws, middle-class anxiety becomes articulated by precise measurements of behavior (the length of a property setback, the age of consent) and a specific prescription for redress (the amount of a fine or settlement, the length of time for servitude or incarceration). These actions are predicated on the existence of an entire realm of middle managers, from scribes who write down the laws to clerks who record the infractions and punishments to wardens who enforce the legal apparatus by making sure that fines are paid and sentences completed.

Peutinger Table; thirteenth-century copy of a fourth-century original

A WORLD OF CITIES

C oming in from an airport after a long flight, I sometimes have to ask myself, "Where am I?" There's a ring road of divided highway, a sprawling suburb of flats and commuter stations, and the ubiquitous presence of glass-fronted office buildings. Maybe it's Bangalore? Or Dubai? Maybe Washington, D.C.? No, hmm . . . Bangkok. The glass-fronted buildings are particularly hard to place. Instantly recognizable as corporate offices, they look the same whether the people inside deal with commodities, raw materials, the products of sooty factories, or the intellectual labor of computer programmers. Although there are certainly nods to national styles and local materials and regional construction expertise, the buildings and lawns and parking lots all substitute for one another. Like a hotel chain whose rooms look the same from Lagos and London to Lincoln, Nebraska, the globalized networked world of commerce looks the same everywhere.

People traveling from one Roman city to another within the

empire would have had the same sense of eye-rubbing déjà vu when coming into a new port. Looking out from the deck of the ship, a person living at the time of Julius Caesar would have seen a harbor and metropolis that looked so similar to the last one that it would have prompted a question to the deckhands to make sure that the ship hadn't just been turning in circles all night. On the shore, there were the same piles of amphora fragments next to the same warehouses of grain and olive oil. Everyone was speaking the same language, and the skyline was crowded with the usual assortment of buildings that included a public bath, an amphitheater, and a forum. Out in the distance, beyond the city wall, was the graceful curve of the aqueduct that brought water from the countryside.

The same double take rang true in every place where networks of shared culture made cities possible. On the Indian subcontinent, bumping along the road by oxcart or sailing down one of the mighty tributaries of the Ganges, the newly arrived visitor could see that the tall arches and lively marketplaces of one city were very much like another. The traveler might ask, am I in Hastinapura? Kaushambi? Vaishali? Pataliputra . . . ? Ancient travelers between cities in China couldn't blame themselves for being momentarily confused whether they were in Luoyang or Chang'an. Travelers in the pyramid-studded Maya realm of Mexico and Central America might have to stop and think carefully, too. Within a day's walk it was . . . perhaps Tikal, perhaps Yaxha, perhaps Uaxactun? And traders approaching the Swahili coast of East Africa, sailing down the coast from Mogadishu to Mozambique, would have checked their charts and their memories carefully, to make sure that they hadn't inadvertently skipped one of the intervening stops or slept their way past a port.

The global network of cities connects each individual metropolis to a broadband network of connected places. Within any given culture, a local distribution of cities was like your company's intranet connection. But your company or institution is linked to others, including those far outside your own culture, ethnicity, or language group, through the phenomenon of the internet that binds us all together in a web of connectivity. With more than half of the world's populations now living in cities, there's an increased concentration not only of people but also of wealth, knowledge, and expertise in urban centers, too. It's not surprising that scientists are increasingly calling for us to acknowledge the significant impact of humans through the development of a special geologic era to be called the Anthropocene: the time when humans' impact has outweighed nature itself.

An Unnatural World?

One of the criticisms of urban life, particularly modern urban life with its plastics and internal-combustion engines and electric lines, is that we have become utterly removed from nature. Ecologists worry that the next generation of children will have no direct experience of an unpaved world and that the rest of us will become progressively disassociated from the realm of other living things. Yet there's plenty of nature within cities, and environmental scientists are now productively exploring the ways in which cities harbor new niches of habitat. Robert McDonald, in his book *Conservation for Cities,* has shown us that in addition to being places of concrete and steel, cities have a "green infrastructure" that integrates the natural world. Stephanie Pincetl and her colleagues have observed that thanks to human acts of planting and water management, the city of Los Angeles actually has many more trees than it would otherwise. And studies of urban animals worldwide show how some animals have adapted to our urban world in ways that make their populations soar.

You might remember the "pizza rat" of New York City whose escapades have been viewed millions of times on YouTube, but what about the booming populations of larger mammals? In Britain, census data on red foxes show that not only are these urban predators thriving, but they are also expanding their ranges to occupy larger and larger areas within cities and more and more cities within the national urban network. They are smart animals, and no doubt they have learned the same tricks of urban living as coyotes in the United States, which in comparison to their country cousins shift their nighttime hours to be most active when vehicular traffic is at its lowest. Carnivores in other places thrive, too: Hyenas in Ethiopian cities and leopards in Indian ones come out at night to hunt down domestic animals and to scavenge from readily available piles of household waste.

Birds are particularly adept at making the three-dimensional world of urban construction their own. The wildlife scientist John Marzluff, in his book *Welcome to Subirdia,* has revealed the way in which urban fringe settlements are an inviting niche for songbirds. Some bird species are particularly good at adapting to life with humans, such as the Brewer's blackbird that flocks to open-air markets and parking lots where vehicle and pedestrian traffic is the environmental equivalent of buffalo that stir up tasty insects in the dust. In addition to blackbirds, there are many urban birds that we take for granted that are doing well, too, like pigeons and sparrows, which join their mammalian cousins the rats and squirrels as ubiquitous urban denizens. Peregrine falcon populations have increased in cities like New York, Boston, Toronto, and Cape Town, South Africa, where they use tall buildings as a good-enough canyon for residence. It turns out that while humans brought cities into existence because our whole cognitive evolution had primed us for the compelling cognitive analogue of the internet, animals came along, too, finding new opportunities for their own preexisting behavioral patterns.

The consistent presence of nature in the urban sphere is good for us. Landscaping is a component of streetscapes, and trees are a ubiquitous part of urban life whether they grow along sidewalks or in the parks that are interspersed with metropolitan cores and suburban sprawls. Trees constitute a living, incremental monumentality that competes with architecture as the only other urban ground-based entity that invites us to look up. Trees are complex in their jurisdiction, with some trees under the direct control of cities and some trees along sidewalks and rights-of-way that are partially the responsibility of individual landowners. Despite the complexities of ownership, control, and maintenance, trees are universally "good to think." Inspired by the inherent link between trees and good governance, urban leaders around the world have started tree-planting programs, including the Million Trees initiatives of New York and Los Angeles, as well as the Green Delhi program and the Huangpu East Bank Urban Forest of Shanghai. And if we want a true measure of the extent to which the presence of nature is understood as a component of urban environments, we need look no further than simulator games like SimCity and Cities: Skylines. No matter how futuristic their constructions, there are always trees in the landscapes of imagined cities.

The inescapability of nature in urban areas confirms that our place in the world as a biological species is hardly budged by the fact that for the past six thousand years we have surrounded ourselves with buildings, paved pathways, city walls, and water and food supplies that come from far away. And even the smallest encounters with wild animals give us an opportunity to philosophize. Not long ago when I was in the sun-washed Mediterranean city of Nice, I was walking down the street and saw an enormous, iridescent bug on the sidewalk that made me pause. I wasn't the only one to stop: two elderly ladies also had noticed it and marveled at it in the midst of all the concrete. Compelled to do something to move it away from the certain doom of pedestrians, carts, and errant motor scooters, one lady emphatically declared, *"Ils vivent comme nous!"* Yes, we all nodded, even these small creatures seek and deserve the consideration of life. We looked around and saw a nice garden across the street where trees and hibiscus would provide a better lodging for the bug. Without further ado, one of the ladies scooped it up, crossed the street, and tucked the tiny beast away in the foliage.

The movements of even the smallest of urban animals—the snails, the crickets, the ants, the rats, the pigeons—confirm that the rhythms of night and day, and the randomness of demise, govern the patterns of every terrestrial creature. However sophisticated we might be in our interactions with the world around us, we humans remain part of the cyclical cadence of light and dark. Like our ancestors a million years ago, we are still a diurnal species tied to the daily disappearance of the sun. Whether in a high-rise apartment or a suburban cul-de-sac, we have retained our species' tendency to be most active outside our residences during daylight hours, a pattern that persisted through a million years of hunting and gathering and through subsequent eras of simple farming life, right up to the present. Although in the past 150 years the advent of electricity has enabled people to lengthen the day, it has not fundamentally changed our concept of what a "day" means.

Nearly everything in our urban culture is still calibrated to a dawn-to-dusk social, economic, and religious life. Office work is still an 8:00–5:00 endeavor, as is the vast majority of formal education from nursery school onward. Family structures reinforce our diurnal programming because children and older people generally are not out and about at night, so those who are their caretakers also expect to be indoors with them from nightfall to dawn. Our entertainment follows the oscillation of the sun, too. Although there are now many more ways to watch television programs, for example, we nevertheless have a sense that the "prime time" for relaxation and entertainment is equivalent to the early evening hours. We are ready prey for those who expect us to be home, as known by telemarketers who target their customers between dinner and bedtime.

Our diurnal patterns set conditions on infrastructure, too. Commuting to the kinds of white-collar work that cities make possible will continue to be between 6:00–9:00 a.m. and 4:00–7:00 p.m., which means that there will always be a need to tailor transportation networks to concepts of a "rush hour" instead of spreading out infrastructure timings as if there were a 24/7 world of steady demand. Seasonality will always play a role in our urban worlds as well, with the realities of wind, rain, snow, and excessive heat being part and parcel of both individual days and civic calendars. Seasonality is not just about the weather; it also encodes religious and secular holidays that punctuate the cycles of work and school. Just as in modern times, ancient cities stretched and groaned to accommodate pilgrims who temporarily doubled or tripled the size of the population in just a short time, putting a strain on every kind of infrastructure. In Jerusalem two thousand years ago, for example, rural herders hurried to get their flocks into market in time for the major seasonal holidays in order to maximize their market share. Archaeologists have discovered just how far-flung this economic network was when they recently discovered a dump of animal bones outside the walls of the Old City. By using a technique called stable-isotope analysis to identify the traces of the kinds of plants that the animals had eaten, researchers discovered that some animals were raised locally but that others came from desert fringes and rocky landscapes as far away as Judaea and Galilee.

Today our urban seasonal population movements are still focused on the punctuated moments of a ritual calendar whether it is the Lunar New Year in China, the Christmas and New Year holidays of Europe and the Americas, or the annual hajj pilgrimage that brings people from every global nation through a worldwide network of airports to the cities of Mecca and Medina. In addition to those holidays, there are plenty of secular holidays—like sporting events or wedding seasons—that govern the patterns of traffic and influence the prices of desired commodities like flowers and plane fares. Less celebratory, but equally predictable, are the annual punctuations of government budget cycles and fiscal closings. As a result, time is structured for us at the daily level through clocks, at the monthly level through paychecks, and at the annual level by seasons and administrative chronologies. The collective biological and meteorological constraints are part of our social and economic lives and are never going to be superseded.

A diurnal social and biological life isn't the only thing we have inherited from our ancestors. We're also a species that relishes being omnivores, with a desire to eat and enjoy a wide range of foods. Even when people choose to restrict their diets for social or religious reasons, or when they are constrained by medical conditions from eating certain foods, there are still many opportunities for novel cuisine: Chinese kosher, vegan barbecue, nondairy ice cream, gluten-free bread. The interesting thing is that we haven't actually domesticated a new plant for thousands of years, and continue to rely on the maize, wheat, rice, and barley that supported the residents of the very first cities. What *does* make our foodways new and different is the incorporation of spices and the blending of ingredients from different parts of the world that continually result in new and innovative cuisines.

We've inherited a creativity in cookery from our urban ancestors, with our global trade networks mirroring the way in which ancient cities such as Rome drew on a vast hinterland of provisioning by shipping wheat, wine, and olives around the Mediterranean or in which the cities of Mesopotamia drew in a web of cattle, sheep, goats, wheat, and beer along the radial roads that we can still see on satellite images. Ancient rivers in India and China were the lifelines of rural grain boats that drifted down the current with their cargoes to the closest downstream megalopolis. In the Andes of South America, sardines were brought up from the sea, and llamas walked their cargoes down from the alpine valleys to the cities of the coastal plains. And in the ancient Valley of Mexico, archaeological excavations have revealed frescoes and codices with the images of porters that show them huffing and puffing up to the high-altitude city of Tenochtitlan with backpacks full of maize to supply creative *tamaleros*.

Those global networks of food trade will only grow in the future. Hidden behind every morning croissant, lunch sandwich, and evening plate of noodles is the stark fact that the cultivation of food requires much more space and water than could possibly be captured within an urban footprint, even when a city's edges are interspersed with pockets of arable land. Although there's a lot of optimism and work toward "urban gardening" today, the foods that are grown by metropolitan food producers are mostly perishables such as fresh fruits, vegetables, and herbs, rather than bulky foods like meat or carbohydrates like potatoes and staple grains, which will have to continue to come from more extensive rural hinterlands. Beyond staple foods, multiple networks give us the variety that we crave and that we can find even in ordinary grocery stores: wine from Italy, Australia, and Argentina; cheeses from France and Wisconsin; coffee from Ethiopia, Colombia, and Java.

Urban Networks

In many parts of the world, in both the present and the past, the question isn't just "Why cities?" but "Why *so many* cities?" This question springs up in Mesopotamia, where cities were dotted up and down the Tigris and the Euphrates in such density that one could have strung along the slowest of boat journeys by landing in a different city every night. In the Maya region of Mexico and Central America, cities were packed so closely together that a person could see the temples of one mighty metropolis from the tall pyramids of another. In the Roman world, particularly along the eastern Mediterranean, the border of the sea had a necklace of dozens of cities that stretched from Leptiminus in Tunisia to Constantinople in present-day Turkey, all of them occupied for hundreds of years. Interchangeable in their economic and social functions, they were all within a day's sail of each other and shared language and customs that would have made any newcomer feel right at home. And while the Mediterranean provided easy access around a single shoreline, the principle of connectivity also worked in more challenging environments such as the North Sea, which linked up medieval Scandinavian cities on the landmasses of Sweden, Norway, and Denmark. All of these configurations were the ancient analogues of today's massive conurbations that crosscut state boundaries and local jurisdictions: the Washington–Philadelphia–New York–Boston corridor that runs through more than a half-dozen different U.S. states; the Rhine–Ruhr metropolitan region of northwestern Germany; and the explosion of interconnected urban sites in East Asia, such as Guangzhou to Hong Kong and Beijing to Tianjin.

Interconnectedness, and our ancestors' ability to fit in easily within cities across cultures, made cities the ultimate point of reference for our species even if it did take us a million years to finally bring cities to fruition. Cities are tangible and real as physical entities that house us, employ us, and protect us. The networked daily experience of cities, the sense of flow that is autonomous within mass movement, and the sense of creating one's own reality result in a greater number of experiences per person per day in urban environments. The networked phenomena of everyday life and the heightened tolerance of strangers are also why cities tend to be more liberal than the nations in which they are housed. People *trust* cities more than they trust states precisely because cities are point-specific locales where there are multiple opportunities to interact with strangers in ways that dissipate the strangeness under the aegis of a shared urban ethos. And cities are places not only of greater entrepreneurial license for the creation of new and different physical objects and fashions but also of greater tolerance of others, whether those are minority groups or ethnic refugees or LGBTQ communities.

In the ancient political world, the real prizes were not the new cities that could be filled on a royal whim, like the Egyptian city of Amarna, which was brought into existence by decree, only to fade away after its founder Pharaoh Akhenaten's death. Most rulers sought instead to be worthy of the cities of long establishment whose cultural pedigrees could be appropriated. Sometimes this was in the form of conquering famous cities within expanding empires, as Alexander the Great did with Babylon and Susa. Sometimes it was through appending new cities right next to famous places, resulting in sequential sprawling urban landscapes like the seven cities of Delhi—so vast as a legacy of ancient urbanism that some of that original group, like Tughluqabad, are still in the wilderness outside the modern metropolis. In other cases, rulers took a symbolic approach and poached the icons of conquered cities to plant anew in their own urban realms. In a move that echoed the removal of the Code of Hammurabi, the fourteenth-century sultan Feroz Shah Tughluq (who started one of the cities of Delhi at a place called Ferozabad) imported a nearly two-thousand-year-old stone pillar from one of the cities of the historical emperor Ashoka.

The Roman emperor Augustus brought back the prize of an obelisk from Egypt to Rome, a "tangible symbol of a conquered foreign land." Our own repurposing of ancient Egyptian obelisks continues that trend, with the iconic spires now distributed far from their place of origin in cities like New York and Paris. Institutions sought the pedigree of history, too. The Catholic Church could have had established its headquarters anywhere in the Mediterranean and might have been more logically housed in ancient Palestine or in one of the eastern metropolitan capitals like Constantinople or Antioch, where we know that there was substantial ancient Christian activity. Yet the Vatican is far to the west of the birthplace of Christ, making use of every atom of atmosphere that was inherited from the heart of the ancient Roman Empire.

The network realities of urban life mean that, from the beginning, cities sustained one another across distances. Networks of provisioning enabled people to overcome the variability of seasons, analogous to the way in which your online supplier of goods might channel your order from its own warehouse or a subsidiary that you've never heard of (what does it matter to you, as long as you get that shirt, handbag, or out-of-print book?). Resilience to household problems of health and welfare also came in the collectivities of infrastructure that enabled people to mitigate problems of potable water and sewage and to access a greater range of medical expertise to address the ailments that did occur in their midst. Although cities with their dense populations were attractive targets of warfare, they were resilient to conflict, too. Some cities had walls that provided a defined perimeter, and even those without walls still had "safety in numbers" where leaders could call upon both middle manager subordinates and entrepreneurs to mitigate the challenges of siege. Cities saw powerful leaders come and go whose effects on the metropolis (however positive or negative) were often temporary compared with the ongoing synergy of place sustained by thousands of ordinary inhabitants.

Cities were, for the first time in the human experience, places that fundamentally reorganized people's relationships to the environment and to each other by making networks of communication permanent in the landscape. Like any new technology, cities came with costs and risks that might be familiar to us as we consider the effects of being the first generation that has ever lived with the internet. We are now accustomed to being accidentally exposed to distressing content or running the risk of fraud and identity theft through our use of the web. For the first inhabitants of cities, the risks and dangers would have been just as easy to discern. Cities are places where diseases can spread faster and where pockets of crime can result in being stabbed or beaten up or shot if you're in the wrong neighborhood. Yet we aren't thinking of going off-line permanently (or at least most of us aren't), just as ancient metropolitan residents couldn't conceive of stopping urbanism; the only solution was to make things better. Today we're forestalling the risk of harmful internet exposure through filtering software and cyber-crime bureaus and awareness campaigns. And like the first urban inhabitants, we're forestalling the negative effects of cities by thinking about what makes them good, in order to make them better.

Juan de Solórzano Pereira engraving showing "walls as the eyes of the city," A.D. 1653

THE NEXT 6,000 YEARS

Today our global urban population is reaching what seems to be staggering and scary proportions: more than half of the world's population now lives in cities. We may be surprised by that number, or feel as though we are entering into some entirely new frame of reference for civilization. We worry about the configuration of concentrated populations, and we worry about how high that percentage could go without causing a complete system collapse. But we needn't worry. Archaeological evidence suggests that past eras might have had a higher proportion of population in cities than we do! During some of its long eras of urbanism, ancient Mesopotamia—the areas now mostly encompassed in Iraq, Syria, and southeastern Turkey—had more than 75 percent of its population in cities. And if we are worried about crowding and high rent and homelessness, archaeological remains provide a perspective on that, too: in Rome's port city of Ostia, it's estimated that 95 percent of the population was housed in shops, small flats, subdivided apartment suites, and out on the street.

Making our own cities better, given that they are inevitable, is likely to involve investments in three things highlighted in this book. One is the acknowledgment that infrastructure has the inherent capacity for framing social interactions and for contributing to social justice. Ancient cities show us that the conscious melding of different social and ethnic groups has a long history. At the three-thousand-year-old site of Yinxu in China, Zhichun Jing and colleagues have used texts and archaeological remains to show how the city was "intentionally and actively created to serve the needs and interests of socially and culturally differentiated groups . . . previously separate peoples who may have come from local communities and/or distant territories and spoken different dialects." Teotihuacan's suburbs included places like the Oaxaca enclave and the "Merchants' Barrio," settled by people from distant areas elsewhere in Mexico.

Today we know that ethnic differences will never be completely erased; they too often serve as a positive force for community cohesion and individual identity, particularly through the kinds of material consumption of clothing, hairstyles, music, and leisure activities that enable individuals to thrive and succeed. So the idea of complete assimilation is both impractical and illogical; in addition, the retention of distinct cultural traditions has a positive spillover into urban identity for all residents. An abundance of different kinds of ethnic cuisines serves to affirm a city's cosmopolitan nature and the entrepreneurial promise of household advancement and collective coexistence; an abundance of people from different regions, speaking different languages and bringing their own cultural backgrounds, enhances not only cultural institutions like schools and museums but also the effectiveness of globalized economic outreach and business growth.

Archaeological evidence also affirms that although cities have many different economic, political, and social roles, their cultural core still includes religious architecture. The ziggurats of Mesopotamia or the pyramids of Teotihuacan and Aztec Tenochtitlan are echoed in the cathedrals, mosques, and temples of cities that have sprung up since and that continue to anchor our downtowns even in very secular nations. The impulse is exactly the same as what we find at the earliest cities of Mesopotamia like Ur, where Woolley's excavations dramatically showed that the centrality of the temple was a key factor in its continued longevity. When the congregation grew too large (or too wealthy) to be accommodated in the sanctuary of the goddess Ningal, they didn't move out to the suburbs, where land might have been cheaper and more easily available: instead, they rebuilt the temple, over and over again, in the exact same spot. Today, the thriving future of urban religion is seen everywhere from the megachurches of downtown Seoul to the new cathedrals planned in Africa's growing cities, like Accra's new National Cathedral, whose design includes a new "ceremonial route" linking it to government buildings and Independence Square.

On the more mundane level, by including social awareness in the creation of the built environment, we can reap the soft benefits of secular infrastructure long into the future. To the knowledge of engineers and architects can be added the knowledge base of anthropologists, sociologists, and historians, who remind us of the way that the built environment shapes urban flow. Longitudinal planning should take into account the demographic and social changes that we will face in the future, including the fact that many more people are reaching old age. Coupled with improved medical care and longer life spans, infrastructure that proactively addresses the needs of the elderly can start with simple actions such as removing physical steps and lighting up streets for better visibility and security. Infrastructure can be designed with multifunctional use in mind for a fraction of additional cost, and in the United States we have already seen that laws such as the Americans with Disabilities Act (originally intended to make sidewalks and buildings more accessible to people in wheelchairs) have provided benefits to everyone who uses wheels, from stroller-pushing parents to time-pressed delivery people. And why not turn schools—which are physically distributed throughout cities—into community centers and places for exercise once the school day is done?

A second useful observation from ancient cities is that there are always socioeconomic hierarchies. Every city that we've ever dug has disparities of housing, from rulers' palaces to merchants' compounds to the slums of makeshift residences occupied by newly arrived migrants and vast numbers of low-income workers who survived on daily wages. The "conditions of possibility" identified in the growth of urban life do not mean that class no longer matters or that all people can realistically expect to move up in the social hierarchy in the course of their or their children's lifetimes. At the same time, the need for manual labor for manufacturing, caregiving, cleaning, maintenance, and other essential activities means that a world of only white-collar professionals would be extremely dysfunctional. Instead, what is needed are wages that enable a dignified life achieved through both brain work *and* brawn work.

The tale of the ancient city of Tushan provides a compelling opportunity to evolve our thinking about ancient cities to look at the ways in which people of all socioeconomic statuses are essential. Located in Turkey near the modern village of Ziyaret Tepe, Tushan was part of the powerful Assyrian Empire that held sway over Mesopotamia in the first millennium B.C. By this time, there had already been cities in Mesopotamia for about four thousand years; for the Assyrians, *The Epic of Gilgamesh* was already archaic, much as Chaucer is to us today (we know that *The Canterbury Tales* are an important example of medieval literature, but how many of us can recall a single story from the collection?). Archaeologists have been excavating at Ziyaret Tepe for more than a decade to understand its place in the network of urban centers of the Assyrian Empire. Along with the inevitable tons of pottery that inform us about the urban economy, archaeologists have recovered fragile ancient cuneiform tablets that tell the story of everyday lives as well as the events that we typically associate with history. One remarkable tablet conveys the confusion and angst of an official named Mannu-ki-libbali who had been tasked with assembling a unit of chariots at the moment that the Assyrian Empire was crumbling and as the city's population was fleeing. The complexities of this request overwhelmed him as he contemplated the loss of so many of the necessary personnel:

> Concerning the horses, Assyrian and Aramean scribes, cohort commanders, officials, coppersmiths, blacksmiths, those who clean the tools and equipment, carpenters, bow-makers, arrow-makers, weavers, tailors and repairers, to whom should I turn? . . . Not one of them is there. How can I command?

Note that the writer of this tablet enumerates not just those with technical skills, such as bow makers and coppersmiths, but those whose work is equally essential if less glamorous—the cleaners and repairers. These personnel were all coordinated by the "cohort commanders," but they, too, had left. Lacking middle managers and their multilingual scribes, everyone was left to fend for themselves, and the tablet itself ends with the plaintive cry "Death will come out of it. . . . I am done!" Although the message is ostensibly about the momentary failure of the city, it actually reveals something far more interesting in its view of urban life that transcends a fateful moment of warfare. The scribe's lament points to the central premise of urban life: that a city survives, and an administration functions, only when a range of expertise is present that can be networked into a team.

The third observation that we can glean from the ancient world is the need to acknowledge and celebrate the spirit of consumption that has been part and parcel of every urban center ever known. The amount of goods per person increases in cities because of the capacity for specialization and the acceleration of manufacturing to cater to urban populations' increased diversity of social and biological needs. By seeing, buying, borrowing, and displaying objects, people express both their actualities and their aspirations. The pursuit of long-distance ordinary goods, some of which were cheaply available due to economies of scale and others of which were produced specifically for foreign markets, is a concept that comes straight from the archaeological past. Over three thousand years ago, the fledgling cities of the Mycenaean Bronze Age, dotted along the shorelines of Greece, pulled in trade goods from all over Europe and North Africa: ivory, tin, copper, ostrich eggshells, amber, and murex shells. But there were some also fairly mundane things, like clay wall brackets used as lamps. Puzzling over the appeal of these rather unattractive objects, the archaeologist Eric Cline has suggested that it was their very exoticism that made them of interest. He calls the phenomenon "distance value," a factor of attraction that explains why the wall brackets turned up in both elite and non-elite contexts.

By the Roman period a thousand years later, the shipping capacity around the Mediterranean had become capable of staggering quantities, including not only wine and olives for connoisseurs and wheat in a great enough quantity to feed the population of Rome but also sacks of pepper coming from the Indian subcontinent. Among the most desired objects of that era was the shiny red pottery known as terra sigillata, which was produced in central France at the rate of tens of thousands of vessels per kiln firing. Just like today when we get our cheap goods from abroad, the objects that came out of ancient factories encoded distance value as well as aspirational claims, souvenir status, touchstones of memory, and talismans of emotion and gift-giving in urban households. So what if there is a little extra trash? If Descartes was alive today, he might well say, "I discard, therefore I am."

Plus Ça Change

The long-term continuity of many archaeological cities, along with their demonstrated changes over time, illustrates that cities are compelling and successful because they are never "finished." Whether you look at infrastructure or parks or buildings or neighborhoods in transition, living cities are always a work in progress. Inheriting the concept of physical renewal that had driven the reconstructions of Göbekli Tepe and the expansions of Stonehenge, cities are living canvases that combine both architectural inheritance and plenty of scope for change. At Teotihuacan, the height and mass of the site's three massive pyramids were continually upgraded. Yet those reconstructions weren't just a matter of brute force, as we can see with the successive changes of the Feathered Serpent Pyramid. Grand and imposing, the pyramid was a late addition to the Avenue of the Dead, decorated with a starkly different aesthetic that included a series of garish animal masks. A generation or so later, the detractors had their way, and the surreal feathered serpents were entombed behind a new facade that brought the look of the building in line with that of the older Sun and Moon pyramids. After a hundred years or so, the building's frightening masks, long since removed, would have been almost completely forgotten, a snapshot moment rather than an enduring urban reality. Our experiences today echo those moments, in which a rapid turnover of construction leaves newcomers with the feeling that they have just missed something that once caused a flutter of social commentary.

Just as Teotihuacan's intense, glaring feathered serpent sculptures were covered in favor of a more benign facade, urban sensibilities were coded and recoded into public architecture elsewhere. In the ancient Aztec capital, the king was obliged to add to the layers of the Templo Mayor, as the ideological and political center of town, a regular enlargement that included adding height to the temple as well as new pavements that resulted in a complete face-lift at every royal succession. At Tikal, the excavation of the marketplace shows that the inhabitants put in a floor patch where a pronounced dip had developed, the ancient equivalent of fixing a pothole but for the benefit of foot traffic because there were no wheeled vehicles in the New World. Those simple acts of maintenance included upgrades in masonry styles: before A.D. 600, the architecture of the marketplace consisted of small, flat-laid stone blocks; by the end of that century, the prevailing style shifted to the use of on-edge blocks that were nearly twice the size. Those bigger blocks were used in the market galleries as well as in other civic structures like temples and ball courts, lending a strikingly different appearance to the built environment. Christopher Jones links this stylistic upgrade to the reign of a ruler named Jasaw in the early eighth century A.D. who had the good fortune of having not only a sense of style but also enough longevity to carry out extensive renovations. Jasaw's building programs also included the paving of causeways that led into the plaza and its marketplace, all wrapped up in a grand program of urban renewal carried out under the watchful eye and generous patronage of the city overlord.

Lavish, distinctive architectural styles have appeared over and over again in cities, often identified with some great ruler, like the Roman emperor Augustus, the Angkorian ruler Jayavarman VII, or Queen Victoria. The development of a stylistically distinctive "era" associated with a ruler wasn't due to the fact that the ruler was herself or himself an architect or engineer or had much to do with the construction process. Instead, the presence of a long-reigning monarch in times of relative prosperity provided the conditions under which creative entrepreneurs introduced new styles. Patrons were charmed by the opportunity to put their stamp on the urban realm, and down-the-line consumers, particularly the middle class, took up the new styles, too. Then as now, they constantly scrutinized their residences to see how they might be improved (and sometimes with the exact same materials, as one can discern today from the parallels in bathroom fixtures and flooring types that can be found in both airport restrooms and private homes, an echo of the link between civic architecture and ordinary households that archaeologists have noted even in ancient Mesopotamia, where the same impressive stonework styles of public buildings could also be found in lavatories!). The concept of remodeling our own kitchens and bathrooms stems from an impetus for change that reverberates from the urban realm inward; in almost every case, the structure and its rooms are perfectly functional, yet we can't help but subject them to our architectural restlessness.

Renovation and renewal are continually expressed in the materials and designs of urban surroundings. Although archaeologists see modern examples no matter where they live, sometimes our eyes focus most clearly on the patterns of change when we're away from home. In India, where I do my research, the construction types of contemporary houses range from solid stone to the most ephemeral constructions of bamboo and thatch. Each building comes with its own set of benefits to occupants, like being easy and cheap to build or being solid enough to stay cool in the hot summers. Each of those types of construction comes with trade-offs of cost and risk as well, including variable susceptibility to earthquakes, landslides, water damage, and other disasters. I remember that one day at Sisupalgarh while we were excavating with our team of local farmers, there was suddenly a loud shout from one of the workers. He and the other men jumped out of the dig trenches and began running furiously to the horizon, where billowing smoke signaled a house on fire. It was only the roof that could burn, because the walls of the structure were made of solid mud-packed earth. The workers' urgency was focused on a single task: to rip down the burning parts of the rice stalks that constituted the thatch roof in order to keep the fire from spreading to the stored grains, clothing, school certificates, and other valuable flammables that were the markers of a family's aspirational achievements. Throughout the archaeological record as well, there is ample evidence of fires and roof collapses and floodwaters, resulting in the need to clear away what archaeologist Gregory Possehl called the "unhappy grist of daily life . . . erased by the process of cleaning up the mess and rebuilding."

Episodes of reconstruction, thus, are not prompted just by the need to upgrade style or aggrandize a ruler, as we've seen for the pyramids of Tenochtitlan or the face-lifts of Tikal's marketplace. Builders might need to mitigate new hazards or seize the opportunities to take advantage of new materials and technologies. For the ancient Romans, this included the invention of concrete, which suddenly made it possible to build multistory buildings; for us today, it includes the development of solar technology that can enable individual residences not only to contribute to a city's power grid but also to be independent of it as a factor of self-reliance and resilience.

But What About Collapse?

There's a considerable fashion for the concept of ancient "collapses" of civilization. After all, if we have to dig up the evidence for early urbanism, it must be because premodern cities suffered demise. And if some of the mightiest ancient cities went away, perhaps we should be concerned for the eventual fate of our own. However, I'd like to suggest that the "collapse" part of ancient urban life is greatly overplayed. After all, many of the world's most successful ancient cities are still underfoot: Athens, Rome, London, Kyoto, Delhi, Baghdad, Cairo, Mexico City, Lyons, Carthage, Marseille, Quito, Xi'an, Jakarta, Istanbul, Samarkand, Cuzco . . . the list goes on. Wearing their ancient remains as a pedigree of urban legitimacy, they are right where our ancestors left them.

Other ancient cultures that had cities might have lost some of them in sequence, but the idea of urbanism was carried along from one place to another. Pompeii and Herculaneum were wiped out by a volcanic eruption, but the survivors had many other cities to choose from as they relocated to other parts of the Roman Mediterranean. Many Maya urban centers disaggregated into smaller rural settlements after the ninth century A.D., but the urban idea lived on in other places, like the Yucatán settlements of Mérida and Chichén Itzá, which kept on building pyramids and had large and diverse populations until the Spanish appeared on the horizon hundreds of years later. On the Indian subcontinent, cities along the Ganges plain were subjected to tectonic shifts, sometimes in the form of earthquakes and sometimes in the form of slow uplift that gradually left nearby rivers high and dry. When that happened, people made use of trade networks and pilgrimage routes as paths to find new places to live.

The urban idea was so compelling that once cities began—whether in China, Europe, Africa, or South America—the concept never went away. And the individual cities whose populations drifted away were retained in collective memory through poetry and drama even if their physical surroundings had suffered hard times due to warfare or environmental assault. The Aztecs paid homage to the much older city of Teotihuacan as an especially sacred site within their network of tributary cities. And just as the Aztecs had named Teotihuacan (Place Where the Gods Emerged) to suit their own purposes, the Spanish in turn rechristened the Aztec's own capital of Tenochtitlan as Mexico City. Rome's motto in the Punic Wars against Carthage was that the city needed to be completely destroyed; in reality, the Romans just took over without so much as a name change. Cuzco in Peru retained its name, too, a banner that covered the city's tremendous political shifts from ancient Inka times through the tumultuous Spanish period and into the modern nation of Peru.

Systems of cities in the ancient world meant that while individual urban centers might suffer great convulsions, they rarely disappeared altogether, or when they did, other nearby cities were the beneficiaries of a population influx. Some of them continued to have natural advantages (like being located along a river as London and Paris were) or displayed the palimpsest of cultural significance that was transacted through new institutions, just as the Catholic Church held on to Rome as the seat of its religious authority and eventually propelled its reemergence as a seat of political power. All over the Mediterranean, there was an unbroken phenomenon of urbanism that started three thousand years ago and continues today. Across the Sahara, there are more than a thousand years of continuity from the first appearance of cities to their thriving modern descendants. And in Mesopotamia, where the first urbanism began, there are the longest-lived cities of all, many of them continuously occupied since Day One.

Archaeological vestiges show that urban centers are remarkably sustainable despite their apparent vulnerabilities. Cities are able to withstand occasional shortfalls and periodic warfare because of transportation networks that bring goods in from all over (think about your food supply today: it's only when you squint at those tiny little stickers that you learn whether your garden-variety apple comes from New Zealand, Belgium, or your own home state). Cities started in some places that were sometimes very unpromising natural locales—the Fragile Crescent of Mesopotamia being just one example. Yet because of the multiple routes that fanned out into the surrounding countryside, there were many ways by which any particular city could be supplied with food, people, and raw materials.

In ancient Jerusalem, the demand of pilgrims for sacrificial animals fueled an entire hinterland economy that stretched out into the desert fringes. At the site of Sisupalgarh, we learned that even the most basic foods like rice were grown across a wide swath of the landscape, brought into the city along the same transport routes that ferried durable goods like pottery and iron objects. When catastrophe struck—a prolonged drought, a flood that wiped out one set of fields, or a war in a distant region—city dwellers hardly felt the pinch because some other supply zone could always fill the breach.

Urbanism, once it starts, is extremely hard for people to abandon even when individual cities lose their viability or desirability. Again, the internet analogy comes in handy. We might lose our connection for a short while in the course of travels, or collectively due to a natural disaster, yet that doesn't mean that the concept goes away. Quite the opposite: we work to restore connectivity as soon as possible. In ancient times, while there are plenty of examples of individual cities that lost their populations and became abandoned, there are almost no cases of overall regional urban collapse. People never forgot about urbanism or ceased to see cities as a great enticement. For those few places where urbanism seems to have been profoundly eclipsed, we might look at them to see whether they really were "urban systems" or best described as something else. Two of the most commonly identified areas of urban collapse are the Bronze Age Indus civilization of what is today Pakistan and western India, and the Angkor region of northern Cambodia. Both of these are poster-children cases of ancient urban demise. And while the sites are certainly as large as we would expect cities to be, there are some things about them that seem decidedly odd.

The Indus case has only four cities spread out in an area that is twenty times larger than the entire Egyptian civilization. With population centers spaced too far apart to be a functioning urban network, the Indus culture might instead have been the result of a series of millennial movements predicated on a social system that was not truly urban but instead more like a long-lived commune that happened to be densely packed with people. When life became unviable in cities like Harappa and Mohenjo Daro (currently thought to have been abandoned because of tectonic uplift), those urbanites might have fled to central Asia, the Iranian plateau, or as far away as Mesopotamia, where they assimilated with groups already living there. Like other urban migrants who calculate that it's better to blend in, those Indus migrants were likely to have given up distinct markers of their culture, such as stamp seals (perhaps because they became accustomed to cuneiform writing, which was more precise in the use of an alphabet instead of symbols) and perforated jars (because the foods that were prepared in them in the Indus were prepared some other way in their new urban locales, or perhaps the raw ingredients were not available).

Further research on Angkor relies on technical as well as theoretical adjustments of our expectations. Settled in the hot and humid northern regions of Cambodia, the massive temples and waterways of the extensive settlement of Angkor seem at first glance to be an exquisitely evocative case of urban fragility, abandonment, and oblivion. Though it certainly presents a picturesque point of global comparison, two things about Angkor can set the record straight. First of all, the site was occupied for five hundred years—hardly an indication of urban hubris or a flash in the metropolitan pan. And second, Angkor only looks like a lonely outpost of urbanism on the basis of what we can see using traditional archaeological methods in which we are beguiled by the towering heights of temples like Angkor Wat rising above the otherwise impenetrable vegetation. Recent research using LIDAR has illustrated that within Cambodia there were many large and densely populated settlements that were contemporaneous with Angkor, if somewhat less visible to the traditional archaeological eye. And if we look beyond Cambodia itself, there was also plenty of urbanism that continued in Thailand to the east, in Myanmar (Burma) to the west, and in Indonesia to the south right through the medieval period and into the modern era.

So, the idea of urban collapse is a good story line for a movie but is hardly a blueprint for the eventual fate of our own urban areas. If ancient cities didn't really collapse and simply morphed into other forms or sent their populations scurrying to the shelter of another metropolis, we shouldn't be surprised that modern cities are going strong despite the poor conditions in which many of their residents live. Many parts of our current cities are already quite dystopian, especially from the perspective of people living in slums, but the steady influx of people to these areas of abject poverty demonstrates that even when city life is very unattractive, there's still plenty that draws people in. Their calculations to stay in cities despite urban disadvantages are logical moves, given that cities attract a disproportionate amount of resources when things do go bad. In 2017, there were three major hurricanes in the United States: in Texas, in Florida, and on the island of Puerto Rico. Although the damage to Puerto Rico was in many ways far greater for its lasting potential effect, it received much less federal recognition than the other areas. Political pundits suggested that the comparatively limited attention was due to factors of disaster fatigue or racism; although those elements might have played a role, the fact is that the population of Puerto Rico was much more dispersed, and the main city of San Juan was considerably smaller than the affected metropolitan areas of Houston, Tampa, and Miami.

Large cities draw in nationalized resources because, having been integrated into the national fabric, they are "too big to fail." In fact, there seems to be only one way to kill off a modern metropolis, and that's through a nuclear catastrophe: Chernobyl in Ukraine is the only city in the past thousand years that has come to a complete stop.

A Full Circle to the Past

A few years ago while doing archaeological fieldwork in Bangladesh, I spent some time in a little administrative town on the banks of the great river that bisects the country. One night there was a fashion show organized by the local youth. Under a brightly lit canopy in the town's little park, young women and men paraded up and down the catwalk displaying their latest clothing to the rhythm of pulsing electronic music. It seemed completely out of character for a small, conservative rural place, and the clothes that were modeled were never seen in the local marketplace, let alone actually worn on the streets of the town. Yet it was not just the clothes themselves that were on display: it was an attitude and a declaration of urban savoir faire that made the youths fully *of* the city, although they were hundreds of miles away.

The pull of cities is so powerful today that everyone on the planet is affected in ways that provide a model for the past as well. Those who don't live in cities grow food for urban residents and supply raw materials for urban factories. And those who don't live in cities look toward them for light-hearted reasons when they seek what is in fashion, and for intense and heartfelt reasons when they seek a new course of life. Rural areas provide a psychological opposite of urban ones, a kind of temporary refuge for urban dwellers who take adventurous or restful holidays in remote, scenic areas (at least before they hurry back to cities with a sigh of relief). Cities are transformative because they are architecturally and economically distinct in the landscape, and because they provide the opportunity for individuals to grow, change, or augment their identities. Cities allow the scope for aspirational consumption of all kinds and the exercise of multiple identities through kinship, friendship, work, leisure, and play. Cities continue to grow regardless of the types of nations in which they are found. Mumbai and New Delhi, both in democratic India, are projected to be the world's biggest cities by 2050 with nearly forty million inhabitants each. But cities in "failed states" also are set to grow: Kinshasa, located in the perpetually dysfunctional Democratic Republic of the Congo, had half a million people in 1960, a population of ten million now, and is projected to have thirty-five million people by 2050.

The fact that nations don't tend to matter for city growth is an important insight into ancient cities, too. Although we often think of ancient states and empires as holistic and well organized, that's really just because of the successful propaganda of ancient rulers who also wanted their own subjects to believe that. Authoritarians were very good at depicting themselves as being firmly in control of their subjects, whether in the form of monuments and sculptures that showed them in larger-than-life poses vanquishing their enemies or in the form of poems and histories that celebrated their great achievements. In truth, however, even the most successful of ancient leaders had only a limited effect on daily life compared with the cumulative outcomes of routine actions by ordinary inhabitants. So, too, does the modern world give us cities that have been much longer lived than the national configurations in which they are embedded. Consider, for example, the metropolis of Warsaw, which in the past two and a half centuries has been sequentially in the territory of the Polish-Lithuanian Commonwealth, Napoleon's Duchy of Warsaw, Prussia, the Kingdom of Poland, Imperial Russia, Germany, the Soviet Union, and the present-day Republic of Poland.

The tenacity of Warsaw—and of other cities possessed by sequences of nations, like Malacca, Colombo, Beirut, and Asmara—speaks volumes about the durability that is the kernel of every metropolis from the first moment that people brought cities into being. In this book, I've written a lot about Tell Brak, located on the dusty plains of Syria and a long-lived anchor of Mesopotamia urbanism. But Tell Brak is not just the story of the first city; it is the story of every city that has ever existed. Today, from London and New York to Johannesburg and Mumbai, cities exist because of the everyday decisions of millions of people who consciously make the trade-off from rural life to urban life, creating cities through a consensus of thought and action. As a result, we've inherited cities not only from the first urban dwellers in the dusty metropolis of Tell Brak but also from every urban center since then. The continual process of growth, renewal, and reinvigoration of our modern cities also results in an archaeology of the present. Whether we are newcomers to a metropolis or longtime residents, we can read the story of urban evolutions and revolutions in the material traces of the world around us. I hope that you'll feel inspired to use your archaeological vision to puzzle over the palimpsest of the city that is all around you, from the disjuncture of grand architecture to that abrupt little cut in the sidewalk where something else used to be.

Just like ancient sites, modern urban centers have patterns of open public spaces and monumental architecture, private compounds and public markets, temples and ritual spaces, and recording systems and managerial innovations. Those developments started six thousand years ago in places as far apart in time and space as Mesopotamia, China, Egypt, Mexico, South America, and the Indian subcontinent. For the first time in human history, and over and over again, the people who created the cities of these disparate civilizations developed a physical infrastructure that linked residents together for the provision of water, the transportation of goods and people, and the conformation of the landscape to drain sewage and take away trash. For the first time in human history, there was a production and consumption trajectory of goods that provided the largesse to enable a sophisticated social signaling of both belonging and aspiration for all sectors of society, from the poorest to the wealthiest urban dwellers. And for the first time in human history, people engaged in educational and entrepreneurial specialization to create a middle-class stratum that used written language to manage the construction, upkeep, and expansion of the city's economic and political configurations.

Urban spaces channeled flow into crowded, dense spaces by drawing upon the long-ago practices of ritual that made crowded spaces an occasional event. What cities did for the first time was make those crowded spaces a regular, daily occurrence and a permanent human-created landscape. From a primordial cognitive capacity for integration, migration, interaction, and material display, our ancestors created the ultimate template for human physical space and the ultimate network for human existence.

Cities are here to stay, for good.

ACKNOWLEDGMENTS

This book has been more fun to write than just about anything I've ever done. Like any writing project, the ripple effect runs deep, and there are many people to thank. To all of the people who have ever been with me on an urban dig project, a hearty thank-you for the companionship and camaraderie at the sites that read like a compendium of the exotic: Wroxeter, Leptiminus, Ostia Antica, Ziyaret, Mahasthangarh, Coptos, and Sisupalgarh. To all of my students past and present, thank you for your freshness of inquiry that inspires better answers to your questions.

Touching base with the long-ago, I would like to thank the late Philip Barker, from whom I learned how to wield a pickax, and Stafford Betty and the late Michael Flachmann, from whom I learned how to wield a pen. Much warmth of appreciation goes to Melinda Zeder of the Smithsonian Institution; to companions from the University of Arizona for their good cheer and mentorship, especially Michael Schiffer, Jeff Reid, and Arthur Jelinek; to Dick Drennan, my first academic boss; and to the completely dedicated individuals with whom I've crossed paths at the National Geographic Society: John Francis, Christopher Thornton, Catherine Workman, and Andrea Lewis. For the continued intellectual companionship that stems from those days, too, a special thanks to Jonathan Losos and Jan Nijman. For the much-appreciated encouragement for this book, thanks go to my UCLA colleague Jared Diamond.

Sincere appreciation goes to the U.S. National Science Foundation, the National Geographic Society, the Wenner-Gren Foundation, and UCLA and the University of Pittsburgh for support of the archaeological fieldwork at Sisupalgarh and surrounding regions, and to my colleague Rabindra Kumar Mohanty for wisdom and shared vision during our fifteen years of co-directing projects in India. To the many students and colleagues who have worked with us there, a profound gratitude for all of the hard work and genuine dedication that you brought to the field while braving sudden downpours, windstorms, mosquitoes, power outages, and invasions by langurs.

Many thanks go to Wendy Wolf at Viking for the cheerful exactitude that has made this a much better book than it would have been otherwise; thanks also to Terezia Cicel at Viking for her spot-on comments, and to Max Brockman, my agent, for making it all possible.

To Tacita and Mathew and Rufus, thanks for sharing Los Angeles; to James and Aidan, thanks for sharing . . . everything.

NOTES

EPIGRAPH

vii **"The amalgamation of numerous villages"**: Matthew Dillon and Lynda Garland, *Ancient Greece: Social and Historical Documents from Archaic Times to the Death of Alexander the Great*, 3rd ed. (London: Routledge, 2010), 3.

CHAPTER 1: WHY CITIES?

5 **It's predicted that by 2030**: For Africa, see "African Urbanization," *Population Connection*, www.populationconnection.org; for other regions, see "Percentage of Global Population Living in Cities, by Continent," *Datablog* (blog), *Guardian*, Aug. 18, 2009, www.theguardian.com.

10 **the minimum number of people**: For Cuba and Senegal, see Robert B. Potter, *Urbanisation and Planning in the 3rd World: Spatial Perceptions and Public Participation* (New York: St. Martin's Press, 1985); for Ohio, see Chapter 703.01 Classification, Title VII Municipal Corporations, Ohio Revised Code, codes.ohio.gov.

11 **"a center of population concentration"**: Richard G. Fox, *Urban Anthropology: Cities in Their Cultural Settings* (Englewood Cliffs, N.J.: Prentice-Hall, 1977), 24; V. Gordon Childe, "The Urban Revolution," *Town Planning Review* 21, no. 1 (1950): 8, 12.

CHAPTER 2: CITY LIFE, PAST AND PRESENT

23 **"We saw the aqueduct"**: Bernal Díaz del Castillo, *History of the Conquest of New Spain*, cited in Jacques Soustelle, *Daily Life of the Aztecs on the Eve of the*

Spanish Conquest, trans. Patrick O'Brian (1955; Stanford, Calif.: Stanford University Press, 1961), 10.

24 **"the city of Cuzco":** Michael J. Schreffler, "Inca Architecture from the Andes to the Adriatic: Pedro Sancho's Description of Cuzco," *Renaissance Quarterly* 67, no. 4 (2014): 1191.

25 **ball courts as a distinctive form:** Eric Taladoire, "The Architectural Background of the Pre-Hispanic Ballgame: An Evolutionary Perspective," in *The Sport of Life and Death: The Mesoamerican Ballgame*, ed. E. Michael Whittington (New York: Thames and Hudson, 2001), 97–115.

30 **earthquakes that frequently toppled:** Lee Mordechai and Jordan Pickett, "Earthquakes as the Quintessential SCE: Methodology and Societal Resilience," *Human Ecology* 46, no. 3 (2018), 335–48.

30 **The earliest city plan:** Elizabeth C. Stone, "The Spacial Organization of Mesopotamian Cities," *Aula Orientalis* 9 (1991): 235–42.

31 **"The Gate of the Unclean Women":** F. Vass Maic, "The Map of Nippur," *Cartography* 9, no. 3 (1976): 174.

31 **Known as the Severan Marble Plan:** David Koller et al., "Fragments of the City: Stanford's Digital Forma Urbis Romae Project," in *Imaging Ancient Rome: Documentation, Visualization, Imagination: Proceedings of the Third Williams Symposium on Classical Architecture, Held at the American Academy in Rome, the British School at Rome, and the Deutsches Archäologisches Institut, Rome, on May 20–23, 2004*, ed. Lothar Haselberger and John Humphrey, *Journal of Roman Archaeology*, Supplement Series, no. 61 (2006): 237–52.

32 **Pietro Forrier, who in 1741:** "The Severan Marble Plan of Rome," *Stanford Digital Forma Urbis Romae Project*, formaurbis.stanford.edu.

32 **run-of-the-mill shops and gathering places:** Steven J. R. Ellis, *The Roman Retail Revolution: The Socio-economic World of the Taberna* (New York: Oxford University Press, 2018).

34 **He calls this concept flow:** Mihaly Csikszentmihalyi, *Flow: The Psychology of Optimal Experience* (New York: HarperCollins, 1990).

34 **"By far the overwhelming proportion":** Ibid., 49.

37 **At the archaeological city of Kerkenes:** Scott Branting, "The 2004 GIS Studies on Transportation," in *The Kerkenes Project: A Preliminary Report on the 2004 Season*, by Geoffrey Summers, Françoise Summers, and Scott Branting (Ankara: Middle East Technical University, 2004), 25–36.

38 **the archaeological site of Sisupalgarh:** Rabindra Kumar Mohanty and Monica L. Smith, *Excavations at Sisupalgarh* (New Delhi: Indian Archaeological Society, 2008).

38 **the phenomenon of "architectural dependence":** Jeremy Till, *Architecture Depends* (Cambridge, Mass.: MIT Press, 2009) 1–2, 45–46, and Chapter 7.

39 **In Chang'an, a great ancient capital:** Nancy Shatzman Steinhardt, *Chinese Imperial City Planning* (Honolulu: University of Hawai'i Press, 1990).

39 **"the street became a substantive building":** Frank Edward Brown, *Roman Architecture* (New York: G. Braziller, 1961), 30, cited in Heather N. Lechtman and Linn W. Hobbs, "Roman Concrete and the Roman Architectural Revolution," in *High-Technology Ceramics: Past, Present, and Future,* ed. W. D. Kingery (Westerville, Ohio: American Ceramic Society, 1986), 81–128.

39 **larger than entire villages:** For the idea of neighborhoods as a village-sized entity within an urban context, see Elizabeth C. Stone, "The Development of Cities in Ancient Mesopotamia," in *Civilizations of the Ancient Near East,* ed. Jack M. Sasson (New York: Charles Scribner's Sons, 1995), 235–48.

CHAPTER 3: HOW TO DIG AN ANCIENT CITY

46 **One good example of an entrepreneurial change:** Mark D. Stansbury-O'Donnell, *A History of Greek Art* (Chichester: John Wiley & Sons, 2015), 206.

49 **"Let us not forget":** John Marshall, *Taxila: An Illustrated Account of Archaeological Excavations Carried Out at Taxila Under the Orders of the Government of India Between the Years 1913 and 1934, vol. 1, Structural Remains* (Cambridge, U.K.: Cambridge University Press, 1951), xv.

51 **we've been searching for the pieces:** Koller et al., "Fragments of the City."

51 **an ancient hole in the ground:** Henry T. Wright, Richard W. Redding, and Susan M. Pollock, "Monitoring Interannual Variability: An Example from the Period of Early State Development in Southwestern Iran," in *Bad Year Economics: Cultural Responses to Risk and Uncertainty,* eds. Paul Halstead and John O'Shea (Cambridge, U.K.: Cambridge University Press, 1989), 106–13.

52 **Phosphates reveal the traces of ancient toilets:** Heather B. Trigg et al., "Archaeological Parasites as Indicators of Environmental Change in Urbanizing Landscapes: Implications for Health and Social Status," *American Antiquity* 82, no. 3 (2017): 517–35.

54 **"I saw the great mound":** M. E. L. Mallowan, "Excavations at Brak and Chagar Bazar," *Iraq* 9 (1947): 1.

56 **more than twenty years of painstaking work:** Jonathan Mark Kenoyer and Richard H. Meadow, "The Ravi Phase: A New Cultural Manifestation at Harappa," in *South Asian Archaeology 1997,* eds. Maurizio Taddei and Giuseppe de Marco (Rome: Istituto Italiano per l'Africa e l'Oriente, 2000), 55–76.

57 **"commenced on March 26, 1899":** Robert Koldewey, *The Excavations at Babylon,* trans. Agnes S. Johns (London: Macmillan, 1914), 26–28.

57 **"my view of the purpose of the various buildings":** Ibid., ix.

61 **In Mesopotamia, they routinely recycled:** C. Leonard Woolley, *Ur of the*

Chaldees: A Record of Seven Years of Excavation (Great Britain: Ernest Benn, 1929), 149–54.

63 **A more high-tech approach:** Arlen F. Chase et al., "Airborne LIDAR, Archaeology, and the Ancient Maya Landscape at Caracol, Belize," *Journal of Archaeological Science* 38 (2011): 387–98.

63 **The French-Cambodian team:** Research at Angkor has been a multi-country effort for decades, focused not only on major temples such as Angkor Wat and the Bayon but also on the extensive suburban and rural landscapes of the ancient city; see, for example, Mitch Hendrickson, "A Transport Geographic Perspective on Travel and Communication in Angkorian Southeast Asia (Ninth to Fifteenth Centuries AD)," *World Archaeology* 43, no. 3 (2011): 444–57.

64 **He used declassified 1960s:** Jason Ur, "CORONA Satellite Photography and Ancient Road Networks: A Northern Mesopotamian Case Study," *Antiquity* 77, no. 295 (2003): 102–15.

CHAPTER 4: BEFORE CITIES, THERE WAS . . .

69 **Like a prehistoric Woodstock:** No less than the musicians, the mud and rain at Woodstock in 1969 were legendary. See Hendrik Hertzberg, "What Woodstock Was Really Like," *New Republic*, Aug. 28, 1989, newrepublic.com. In an equally intense recollection from a modern pilgrimage in India, the anthropologist E. Valentine Daniel tells the tale of pilgrims bathing communally in an impossibly dirty pool of water as a moment of sublime transition. See *Fluid Signs: Being a Person the Tamil Way* (Berkeley: University of California Press, 1984), 261–63.

69 **most remarkable is Göbekli Tepe:** Charles C. Mann, "The Birth of Religion," *National Geographic*, June 2011, 39.

69 **nearby province of Diyarbakir:** For a delightfully readable book about the archaeological project, see Timothy Matney et al., *Ziyaret Tepe: Exploring the Anatolian Frontier of the Assyrian Empire* (Edinburgh: Cornucopia, 2017).

69 **"first structure human beings put together":** Mann, "Birth of Religion," 39.

70 **an entire zoology of local wild animals:** Oliver Dietrich et al., "The Role of Cult and Feasting in the Emergence of Neolithic Communities: New Evidence from Göbekli Tepe, South-Eastern Turkey," *Antiquity* 86 (2012): 674–95.

71 **at least four iterations:** "Göbekli Tepe: World's Oldest (12,000 Years Old) and Biggest Temple," *Ancient History Encyclopedia*, www.ancient.eu.

71 **Stonehenge was surrounded:** Timothy Darvill et al., "Stonehenge Remodelled," *Antiquity* 86 (2012): 1021–40.

76 **the best candidate:** While archaeologists agree that the earliest cities were in Mesopotamia, it was long thought that the southern cities of Uruk and Ur were earlier until recent research at Brak provided more data about urban

origins. For a comprehensive discussion, see Jason Ur, "The Birth of Cities in Ancient West Asia," in *Ancient West Asian Civilization: Geoenvironment and Society in the Pre-Islamic Middle East,* eds. Akira Tsuneki, Shigeo Yamada, and Ken-ichiro Hisada (Singapore: Springer, 2017), 133–47.

76 **they created the brand-new dichotomy:** For the concept of "rurality" that came into existence along with urbanism, see Norman Yoffee, "Political Economy in Early Mesopotamian States," *Annual Review of Anthropology* 24 (1995): 281–311, p. 284; and George L. Cowgill, "Origins and Development of Urbanism: Archaeological perspectives," *Annual Review of Anthropology* 33 (2004): 525–49, p. 527.

77 **Among the most startling:** Mallowan, "Excavations at Brak and Chagar Bazar," 32.

78 **Mark Kenoyer has observed:** Jonathan Mark Kenoyer, "Eye Beads from the Indus Tradition: Technology, Style, and Chronology," *Journal of Asian Civilizations* 36, no. 2 (2013): 1–22.

80 **Ur needed no process of rediscovery:** Jason Ur, "Southern Mesopotamia," in *A Companion to the Archaeology of the Ancient Near East,* ed. D. T. Potts (Chichester: Wiley-Blackwell, 2012), 533–55.

81 **"the inner court and the sanctuary":** Woolley, *Ur of the Chaldees,* 151.

82 **Uruk—another famous Mesopotamian site:** Eva Strommenger, "The Chronological Division of the Archaic Levels of Uruk-Eanna VI to III/II: Past and Present," *American Journal of Archaeology* 84, no. 4 (1980): 479–87.

82 **the world's first indoor toilet:** Augusta McMahon, "Waste Management in Early Urban Southern Mesopotamia," in *Sanitation, Latrines, and Intestinal Parasites in Past Populations,* ed. Piers D. Mitchell (Farnham: Ashgate, UK, 2015), 22.

83 **Uruk's ancient construction crews:** Ur, "Birth of Cities in Ancient West Asia."

83 **By the fourth millennium B.C.:** Guillermo Algaze, *The Uruk World System: The Dynamics of Expansion of Early Mesopotamian Civilization,* 2nd ed. (Chicago: University of Chicago Press, 2005); Gil J. Stein et al., "Uruk Colonies and Anatolian Communities: An Interim Report on the 1992–93 Excavations at Hacinebi, Turkey," *American Journal of Archaeology* 100, no. 2 (1996): 205–60.

84 **flowering of the earliest urbanism:** Melinda A. Zeder, "Provisioning Early Cities in Mesopotamia: The Role of Pastoralism in the Development of Specialized Urban Economies," in *The Social Construction of Ancient Cities,* ed. Monica L. Smith (Washington, D.C.: Smithsonian Institution Press, 2003), 156–83. Many years ago, the urban theorist Jane Jacobs proposed that cities provided the main impetus for domestication in the first place, a "cities-first" perspective that has occasionally been revived, most recently by Peter J. Taylor in *Extraordinary Cities: Millennia of Moral Syndromes, World-Systems, and City/State Relations* (Cheltenham, U.K.: Edward Elgar, 2013). It should be

emphasized, however, that archaeological evidence in both the New World and the Old World clearly supports the fact that people domesticated plants and animals thousands of years before the emergence of the first cities.

84 **the "Fertile Crescent":** Thomas Scheffler, "'Fertile Crescent,' 'Orient,' 'Middle East': The Changing Mental Maps of Southwest Asia," *European Review of History* 10, no. 2 (2003): 253–72. Scheffler notes, however, that Breasted's nomenclature not only was about archaeology but also reflected racial prejudices and Orientalist claims of the Middle Eastern region by Europe and America in the early twentieth century.

85 **the "Fragile Crescent":** T. J. Wilkinson et al., "Contextualizing Early Urbanization: Settlement Cores, Early States, and Agro-Pastoral Strategies in the Fertile Crescent During the Fourth and Third Millennia BC," *Journal of World Prehistory* 27, no. 1 (2014): 44.

86 **If any particular link was broken:** Monica L. Smith, "The Origins of the Sustainability Concept: Risk Perception and Resource Management in Early Urban Centers," *Research in Economic Anthropology* 35 (2015): 215–38.

CHAPTER 5: URBAN BUILDING BLOCKS

91 **The division of corporeal labor:** Monica L. Smith, *A Prehistory of Ordinary People* (Tucson: University of Arizona Press, 2010).

92 **Dunbar has evaluated the ways:** Robin Dunbar, *Grooming, Gossip, and the Evolution of Language* (London: Faber and Faber, 1996).

95 **One of the most challenging:** Chris Stringer's *Lone Survivors: How We Came to Be the Only Humans on Earth* (New York: St. Martin's Press, 2012) contains a thorough discussion of studies of both mitochondrial DNA and the Y chromosome that illustrates the back-and-forth movement of our human ancestors across Eurasia.

96 **In a remarkable study:** Marcy Rockman, "Landscape Learning in Relation to Evolutionary Theory," in *Macroevolution in Human Prehistory: Evolutionary Theory and Processual Archaeology*, eds. Anna Marie Prentiss, Ian Kuijt, and James C. Chatters (New York: Springer, 2009), 51–71.

98 **Mark Granovetter coined a term:** Mark S. Granovetter, "The Strength of Weak Ties," *American Journal of Sociology* 78, no. 6 (1973): 1360–80.

100 **Our species' first real social:** Marek Kohn and Steven Mithen, "Handaxes: Products of Sexual Selection?," *Antiquity* 73 (1999): 518–26.

100 **we have inherited our ancestors' willingness:** For more about the materiality of everyday life and the inescapable impact of objects in even our most intimate moments, see Michael Brian Schiffer, *The Material Life of Human Beings*, with Andrea R. Miller (London: Routledge, 1999), 46–49.

101 **About 100,000 years ago:** Francesco d'Errico and Lucinda Backwell, "Earli-

est Evidence of Personal Ornaments Associated with Burial: The Conus Shells from Border Cave," *Journal of Human Evolution* 93 (2016): 92.

102 **In her study of the natural environments:** Mary C. Stiner, "Finding a Common Bandwidth: Causes of Convergence and Diversity in Paleolithic Beads," *Biological Theory* 9 (2014): 58.

103 **Clothing, because it is relatively easy:** Because ancient clothing has not survived, archaeologists are creative about proxy evidence. Needles suggest the crafting of sewn items that would have included baskets and netting as well as clothing; stone scrapers can be identified as having been used to work leather; and the genomic study of the human body louse suggests that heat-holding clothing that would have provided the louse's ideal temperature would have come along by about seventy-five thousand years ago. For the latter, see Ralf Kittler, Manfred Kayser, and Mark Stoneking, "Molecular Evolution of *Pediculus humanus* and the Origin of Clothing," *Current Biology* 13 (2003): 1414–17.

103 *inconspicuous* **consumption came into existence:** Monica L. Smith, "Inconspicuous Consumption: Non-Display Goods and Identity Formation," *Journal of Archaeological Method and Theory* 14 (2007): 412–38.

104 **Among the most famous:** Marcel Mauss, *The Gift,* trans. W. D. Halls (New York: W. W. Norton, 1990).

106 **Physical buildings increasingly became the place:** Credit to David M. Carballo for the phrase "cooperation and collective action," in his book *Cooperation and Collective Action* (Boulder: University Press of Colorado, 2013).

106 **"The idea to come here":** Gail Webber et al., "Life in the Big City: The Multiple Vulnerabilities of Migrant Cambodian Garment Factory Workers to HIV," *Women's Studies International Forum* 33 (2010): 164.

106 *"buscar la vida":* T. D. Wilson, *"Vamos para Buscar la Vida: A Comparison of Patterns of Outmigration from a Rancho in Jalisco and Internal Migration into a Mexicali Squatter Settlement"* (Ph.D. diss., University of California, Los Angeles, 1992).

106 **"when you are of working age":** Nguyen Tuan Anh et al., "Becoming and Being Urban in Hanoi: Rural-Urban Migration and Relations in Viet Nam," *Journal of Peasant Studies* 39, no. 5 (2012): 1103–31.

107 **"I did not know where Xilunguine was":** Jeanne Marie Penvenne, "Seeking the Factory for Women: Mozambican Urbanization in the Late Colonial Era," *Journal of Urban History* 23, no. 3 (1997): 365.

108 **Today, Shanghai is a paragon:** Hanchao Lu, "Creating Urban Outcasts: Shantytowns in Shanghai, 1920–1950," *Journal of Urban History* 21, no. 5 (1995): 563–96.

108 **"When a boat became too decrepit":** Ibid., 570.

109 **Squatters might hope:** Ibid., 574.

109 **"a slum in the very center"**: Tyler Anbinder, *Five Points: The 19th-Century New York City Neighborhood That Invented Tap Dance, Stole Elections, and Became the World's Most Notorious Slum* (New York: Free Press, 2001), 20.

109 **"had no infrastructure"**: David P. Jordan, "Haussmann and Haussmannisation: The Legacy for Paris," *French Historical Studies* 27, no. 1 (2004): 100.

109 **And London had plenty**: Stephen Halliday, *The Great Stink of London: Sir Joseph Bazalgette and the Cleansing of the Victorian Capital* (Stroud, UK: The History Press, 1999), 178.

111 **The Peruvian desert city of Chan Chan**: Alexandra M. Klymyshyn and Alexandra M. Ulana, "Elite Compounds in Chan Chan," in *Chan Chan: Andean Desert City*, ed. Michael E. Mosely and Kent C. Day (Albuquerque: University of New Mexico Press, 1982), 119–43.

112 **The inhabitants of Teotihuacan**: René Millon, "Teotihuacan: Completion of Map of Giant Ancient City in the Valley of Mexico," *Science* (1970), 170: 1077–82. For a comprehensive treatment of the site, see George L. Cowgill, *Ancient Teotihuacan: Early Urbanism in Central Mexico* (New York: Cambridge University Press, 2015).

113 **Piecing together data**: Andrew Wallace-Hadrill, "Domus and Insulae in Rome: Families and Housefuls," in *Early Christian Families in Context*, eds. David L. Balch and Carolyn Osiek (Grand Rapids, Mich.: William B. Eerdmans, 2003), 3–18.

114 **It was in Mesopotamia**: Ur, "Southern Mesopotamia," 535.

115 **Margaret Grieco, in a wonderful study**: Margaret Grieco, "Transported Lives: Urban Social Networks and Labour Circulation," in *The Urban Context: Ethnicity, Social Networks, and Situational Analysis*, ed. Alisdair Rogers and Steven Vertovec (Oxford: Berg, 1995), 189–212. For India, see Monica L. Smith and Rabindra Kumar Mohanty, "Monsoons, Rice Production, and Urban Growth: The Microscale Management of Water Abundance," *Holocene* (2018), 28(8): 1325–1333.

115 **Producers also sought efficiencies**: The classic text of Western economics is Adam Smith's *The Wealth of Nations*, interestingly published in the same year as the United States' declaration of independence from Britain in 1776. For an archaeological perspective on manufacturing efficiencies, see Monica L. Smith, "The Concept of Copies: An Archaeological View of the Terracotta Ornaments from Sisupalgarh, India," *West 86th: A Journal of Decorative Arts, Design History, and Material Culture* 22, no. 1 (2015): 23–43.

CHAPTER 6: INFRASTRUCTURE HOLDS THINGS UP

122 **Co Loa in Vietnam**: Nam C. Kim, Lai Van Toi, and Trinh Hoang Hiep, "Co Loa: An Investigation of Vietnam's Ancient Capital," *Antiquity* 84 (2010): 1011–27.

122 **Co Loa has an encircling rampart**: N. C. Kim, "Lasting Monuments and

Durable Institutions: Labor, Urbanism, and Statehood in Northern Vietnam and Beyond," *Journal of Archaeological Research* 21, no. 3 (2013): 217–67; Kim, Toi, and Hiep, "Co Loa."

124 **The first settlement in Rome:** Malcolm Todd, *The Walls of Rome* (London: Paul Elek, 1978), 13–14.

125 **Under Aurelian, the walls were completed:** Ibid., Chapter 2.

125 **the walls themselves are visible:** Graham Connah, "Contained Communities in Tropical Africa," in *City Walls: The Urban Enceinte in Global Perspective*, ed. James D. Tracy (Cambridge, U.K.: Cambridge University Press, 2000), 19–45; Jesse Casana and Jason T. Herrmann, "Settlement History and Urban Planning at Zincirli Höyük, Southern Turkey," *Journal of Mediterranean Archaeology* 23, no. 1 (2010): 55–80.

128 **Ishtar Gate of Babylon:** Koldewey, *Excavations at Babylon*, 26–49. For the reconstruction, see Mirjam Brusius, "The Field in the Museum: Puzzling Out Babylon in Berlin." *Osiris* (Journal of the History of Science Society, University of Chicago) 32(1) (2017), 264–85. Brusius (p. 279) points out that the 30,000 bricks were actually only one quarter of the amount that the excavator initially proposed to bring back.

129 **an urban armature:** For the concept of armature, see Andrew T. Creekmore III, "The Social Production of Space in Third-Millennium Cities of Upper Mesopotamia," in *Making Ancient Cities: Space and Place in Early Urban Societies*, eds. Andrew T. Creekmore III and Kevin D. Fisher (New York: Cambridge University Press, 2014), 32–73.

130 **"surrounded by eight rivers":** P. Du and H. Chen, "Water Supply of the Cities in Ancient China," *Water Science and Technology: Water Supply* 7, no. 1 (2007): 173–81.

131 **a preoccupation that led:** Michael Jansen, *Stadt der Brunnen und Kanäle: Mohenjo-Daro, Wasserluxus vor 4500 Jahren. City of Wells and Drains: Mohenjo-Daro, Water Splendour 4500 Years Ago* (Bergisch Gladbach: Frontinus, 1993).

132 **The city of Rome had 865 baths:** Lechtman and Hobbs, "Roman Concrete and the Roman Architectural Revolution," 84.

133 **Roman tenement housing:** Bruce Woodward Frier, "The Rental Market in Early Imperial Rome," *Journal of Roman Studies* 67 (1977): 27–37.

133 **Ostia had at least fourteen:** Lechtman and Hobbs, "Roman Concrete and the Roman Architectural Revolution."

134 **the Roman author Juvenal grumbled:** Juvenal, *The Sixteen Satires*, trans. Peter Green (Harmondsworth, Middlesex, U.K.: Penguin, 1974), 3.223–25, pp. 87–98.

135 **the famous twelve-seater toilet:** Eleanor Dickey, *Stories of Daily Life from the Roman World* (Cambridge, U.K.: Cambridge University Press, 2017), fig. 41.

135 **a toilet demon called Shulak:** McMahon, "Waste Management in Early Urban Southern Mesopotamia," 21.

135 **"untreated discharge of fouled sewage":** Akira Matsui, Masaaki Kanehara, and Masako Kanehara, "Palaeoparasitology in Japan—Discovery of Toilet Features," *Memórias do Instituto Oswaldo Cruz, Rio de Janeiro* 98, no. S1 (2003): 134.

135 **"many of the residences":** Ibid.

136 **Uruk in Mesopotamia had its first toilet:** McMahon, "Waste Management in Early Urban Southern Mesopotamia," 22.

136 **Fujiwara's waterways contained:** Matsui, Kanehara, and Kanehara, "Palaeoparasitology in Japan—Discovery of Toilet Features," 135.

137 **"The government office shall direct":** Ibid.

137 **the sentiment "*tout à l'égout!*":** Matthew Gandy, "The Paris Sewers and the Rationalization of Urban Space," *Transactions of the British Institute of Geographers* 24 (1999): 23–44.

138 **"the flow of water in Paris":** Ibid., 23–24.

139 **All of that changed in 1815:** Halliday, *Great Stink of London*, 106–7.

139 **conversations about the Los Angeles River:** Blake Gumprecht, "Who Killed the Los Angeles River?," in *Land of Sunshine: An Environmental History of Metropolitan Los Angeles,* eds. William Deverell and Greg Hise (Pittsburgh: University of Pittsburgh Press, 2005), 115–34n14.

142 **And it certainly didn't diminish:** Gungwu Wang, "The Nanhai Trade: A Study of the Early History of Chinese Trade in the South China Sea," *Journal of the Malayan Branch of the Royal Asiatic Society* 31, no. 2 (1958): 3–135; John F. Robertson, "The Social and Economic Organization of Ancient Mesopotamian Temples," in Sasson, *Civilizations of the Ancient Near East,* 446.

142 **The Spanish chroniclers who arrived:** Bruce H. Dahlin et al., "In Search of an Ancient Maya Market," *Latin American Antiquity* 18, no. 4 (2007): 363–84.

143 **Maya people constructed a type:** For discussions of different ancient road networks, see papers in James E. Snead, Clark L. Erickson, and J. Andrew Darling, eds., *Landscapes of Movement: Trails, Paths, and Roads in Anthropological Perspective* (Philadelphia: University of Pennsylvania Museum of Archaeology and Anthropology, 2009).

145 **The initial settlement of Houston:** See the map of Houston that accompanies chapter 1.

148 **a cascade of other changes:** For the concept of an invention cascade, see Michael Brian Schiffer, *Power Struggles: Scientific Authority and the Creation of Practical Electricity Before Edison* (Cambridge, Mass.: MIT Press, 2008), 91.

149 **"arena for all of a community's activities":** Kurt F. Anschuetz, Richard H. Wilshusen, and Cherie L. Scheick, "An Archaeology of Landscapes," *Journal of Archaeological Research* 9, no. 2 (2001): 161.

NOTES

CHAPTER 7: THE HARMONY OF CONSUMPTION

152 **Known affectionately as the BRB:** Daniel Potts, "Bevel-Rim Bowls and Bakeries: Evidence and Explanations from Iran and the Indo-Iranian Borderlands," *Journal of Cuneiform Studies* 61 (2009): 1–23.

154 **Temples then redistributed:** Robertson, "Social and Economic Organization of Ancient Mesopotamian Temples."

154 **At the site of Chogha Mish:** Potts, "Bevel-Rim Bowls and Bakeries," 13.

154 **the archaeologist Vivian Broman:** Christopher Jones, "The Marketplace at Tikal," in *The Ancient Maya Marketplace: The Archaeology of Transient Space,* ed. Eleanor M. King (Tucson: University of Arizona Press, 2015), 83.

156 **our own "baby carrot" phenomenon:** Gary Lucier and Biing-Hwan Lin, *Factors Affecting Carrot Consumption in the United States* (Washington, D.C.: USDA, Economic Research Service, 2007); also thanks to Glenn C. Smith, personal communication.

158 **figurines were made to be broken:** Christina T. Halperin, "Circulation as Placemaking: Late Classic Maya Polities and Portable Objects," *American Anthropologist* 116, no. 1 (2014): 119.

158 **Jewish weddings include:** Ana Prashizky, "Breaking the Glass: New Tendencies in the Ritual Practice of Modern Jewish Orthodox and Alternative Weddings," in *Between Tradition and Modernity: The Plurality of Jewish Customs and Rituals,* ed. Larissa Remennick (Ramat-Gan: Sociological Institute for Community Studies, Bar-Ilan University, 2008), 89–110.

158 **Chinese funerals and Ghost Festivals:** C. Fred Blake, *Burning Money: The Material Spirit of the Chinese Lifeworld* (Honolulu: University of Hawai'i Press, 2012).

161 **this form of consumption:** Suzanne Scheld, "Youth Cosmopolitanism: Clothing, the City, and Globalization in Dakar, Senegal," *City and Society* 19, no. 2 (2008): 232–53.

162 **"You can get a drink here":** Brian K. Harvey, *Daily Life in Ancient Rome: A Sourcebook* (Indianapolis: Hackett, 2016), 284.

162 **The lowest-priced drink:** Ibid.

162 **Among the most famous:** Pausanias, *Guide to Greece,* trans. Peter Levi (New York: Penguin, 1979).

163 **Tourist circuits, entirely aimed:** Kevin Bond, "The 'Famous Places' of Japanese Buddhism: Representations of Urban Temple Life in Early Modern Guidebooks," *Studies in Religion* 43, no. 2 (2014): 232.

164 **over six hundred new religious sites:** Ibid., 230.

164 **Religious spaces were socially approved:** Laura Nenzi, *Excursions in Identity: Travel and the Intersection of Place, Gender, and Status in Edo Japan* (Honolulu: University of Hawai'i Press, 2008).

166 **At the ancient city of Yinxu:** Zhichun Jing et al., "Recent Discoveries and Some Thoughts on Early Urbanization at Anyang," in *A Companion to Chinese Archaeology,* ed. Anne P. Underhill (Chichester: Blackwell, 2013), 343–66.

166 **Maya site of Caracol:** Arlen F. Chase et al., "Markets Among the Ancient Maya: The Case of Caracol, Belize," in King, *Ancient Maya Marketplace,* 231; Diane Z. Chase and Arlen F. Chase, "Caracol, Belize, and Changing Perceptions of Ancient Maya Society," *Journal of Archaeological Research* 25, no. 3 (2017): 215.

166 **New World sites such as Pukara:** Elizabeth Klarich, Abigail Levine, and Carol Schultze, "Abundant Exotics and Cavalier Crafting: Obsidian Use and Emerging Complexity in the Northern Lake Titicaca Basin," in *Abundance: The Archaeology of Plenitude,* ed. Monica L. Smith (Boulder: University Press of Colorado, 2017), 139–64.

166 **Mexican metropolis of Teotihuacan:** Cowgill, *Ancient Teotihuacan,* 128.

167 **"dominated by shops":** Ellis, *Roman Retail Revolution,* 4.

167 **In the lavishly illustrated books:** Fray Bernardino de Sahagún, *General History of the Things of New Spain Book 10,* trans. Charles E. Dibble and Arthur J. O. Anderson (Santa Fe, N.M.: School of American Research, 1961), p. 69 and plate 127.

168 **Bayon Temple is covered:** "Satay Kebab Cooking, Ancient Sculpture, Angkor, Cambodia," FeaturePics, www.featurepics.com.

168 **food kiosks of Ghana:** FAO, "A Women's Business: Street Food Vending in Accra," www.youtube.com.

171 **the *jajmani* system:** William L. Rowe, "Changing Rural Class Structure and the Jajmani System," *Human Organization* 22, no. 1 (1963): 41–44.

172 **The first coinage:** David M. Schaps, "War and Peace, Imitation and Innovation, Backwardness and Development: The Beginnings of Coinage in Ancient Greece and Lydia," in *Explaining Monetary and Financial Innovation: A Historical Analysis,* eds. Peter Bernholz and Roland Vaubel (Cham, Switzerland: Springer, 2014), 32.

172 **Within a hundred years:** Peter Bernholz, "The Development of Small Early Money in Western Antiquity and Early China," in *Money in Asia (1200–1900): Small Currencies in Social and Political Contexts,* eds. Jane Kate Leonard and Ulrich Theobald (Leiden: Brill, 2015), 80.

172 **coinage was "revolutionary":** Schaps, "War and Peace, Imitation and Innovation, Backwardness and Development."

174 **inscribed with "ASIA RECEPTA":** Clive Foss, *Roman Historical Coins* (London: Seaby, 1990), 43.

175 **the coins of the ever-cautious emperor:** Olivier Hekster, "Coins and Messages: Audience Targeting on Coins of Different Denominations," in *Representation and Perception of Roman Imperial Power,* eds. Lukas de Blois et al. (Amsterdam: Gieben, 2003), 20–35.

175 **depictions of the Roman Colosseum:** Ibid., 30.

175 **sliding scale of quality:** Archana Choksi, "Pottery Manufacturing Techniques: The Role of Technical Constraints and Personal Choices," *Man and Environment* 23, no. 2 (1998): 107–18.

177 **The abundant statuary of the Roman world:** Elizabeth Bartman, "Hair and the Artifice of Roman Female Adornment," *American Journal of Archaeology* 105, no. 1 (2001): 1–25.

178 **consumers and producers are equally:** Audrey Ou, "Copying and Pasting in Fast Fashion: Just the Sellers' Fault?," *Business Today* (Fall 2016): 20–21.

179 **incredible variety of kitschy souvenirs:** Yuko Minowa and Terrence H. Witkowski, "Spectator Consumption Practices at the Roman Games," *Journal of Historical Research in Marketing* 4, no. 4 (2012): 510–31.

179 **kilns in places like Jingdezhen:** Stacey Pierson, "Production, Distribution, and Aesthetics: Abundance and Chinese Porcelain from Jingdezhen, AD 1350–1800," in Smith, *Abundance*, 229–50.

180 **Chinese porcelains were primarily used as ballast:** Susan Gal, "Qualia as Value and Knowledge: Histories of European Porcelain," *Signs and Society* 5, no. S1 (2017): S134.

180 **If we think of recycling:** Livia Albeck-Ripka, "Your Recycling Gets Recycled, Right?," *New York Times,* May 30, 2018, B1.

180 **legitimate critiques of recycling:** Lester B. Lave et al., "Municipal Solid Waste Recycling Issues," *Journal of Environmental Engineering* 125, no. 10 (1999): 944–49; Jefferson Hopewell, Robert Dvorak, and Edward Kosior, "Plastics Recycling: Challenges and Opportunities," *Philosophical Transactions of the Royal Society B* 364 (2009): 2115–26.

CHAPTER 8: THE MOJO OF THE MIDDLE CLASS

185 **350,000 sheep and goats:** Robertson, "Social and Economic Organization of Ancient Mesopotamian Temples," 446.

186 **hazardscape of the city's growing slums:** Daanish Mustafa, "The Production of an Urban Hazardscape in Pakistan: Modernity, Vulnerability, and the Range of Choice," *Annals of the Association of American Geographers* 95, no. 3 (2005): 566–86.

186 **kept track of workers:** Robert K. Englund, "Hard Work—Where Will It Get You? Labor Management in Ur III Mesopotamia," *Journal of Near Eastern Studies* 50, no. 4 (1991): 255–80.

188 **anthropologist Mark Liechty:** Mark Liechty, "Middle-Class Déjà Vu: Conditions of Possibility, from Victorian England to Contemporary Kathmandu," in *The Global Middle Classes: Theorizing Through Ethnography*, eds. Rachel Heiman, Carla Freeman, and Mark Liechty (Santa Fe, N.M.: School for Advanced Research Press, 2012), 271–99.

188 **"simultaneously sellers of labor":** Ibid., 279.

189 **Barbers, reed cutters, potters:** *The Satire of the Trades,* www.ucl.ac.uk.

190 **"Be a scribe":** Ronald J. Williams, "Scribal Training in Ancient Egypt," *Journal of the American Oriental Society* 92, no. 2 (1972): 218.

190 **the top of the stone manifestation:** J. Dyneley Prince, "The Code of Hammurabi," *American Journal of Theology* 8, no. 3 (1904): 601–9.

191 **In the twelfth century B.C.:** "Law Code of Hammurabi, King of Babylon," Louvre, www.louvre.fr.

192 **A man seeking to divorce his wife:** H.-Dieter Viel, *The New Complete Code of Hammurabi* (Lanham, Md.: University Press of America, 2012), 537.

192 **"if a man has knocked out":** Ibid., 635.

193 **"doctrine and the rules":** Rachel A. Van Cleave, "Property Lessons in August Wilson's *The Piano Lesson* and the Wake of Hurricane Katrina," *California Western Law Review* 43, no. 1 (2006): 101.

193 **In the Roman world:** Andrew Wilson, "Water, Power, and Culture in the Roman and Byzantine Worlds: An Introduction," *Water History* 4 (2012): 1–9.

194 **"like an eye":** Juan de Solórzano Pereira (1575–1655), cited in Richard Kagan, "A World Without Walls: City and Town in Colonial Spanish America," in Tracy, *City Walls,* 132.

194 **"My father left two factories":** David M. Schaps, *The Invention of Coinage and the Monetization of Ancient Greece* (Ann Arbor: University of Michigan Press, 2004), 18–19.

195 **A drachma was the equivalent:** Thucydides notes in his *History of the Peloponnesian War,* trans. Richard Livingstone (Oxford: Oxford University Press, 1943), 149, that each infantryman got two drachmas, "one for himself and another for his servant," though we can only speculate the extent to which the infantrymen truly split their earnings fifty-fifty with those who assisted them.

196 **the work of marketing experts:** Michael J. Silverstein and Neil Fiske, *Trading Up: Why Consumers Want New Luxury Goods—and How Companies Create Them,* with John Butman, rev. ed. (New York: Portfolio, 2005).

197 **other economists have called BOP:** C. K. Prahalad, *The Fortune at the Bottom of the Pyramid* (Upper Saddle River, N.J.: Wharton School Publishing, 2005).

197 **the authors call "rocketing":** Silverstein and Fiske, *Trading Up,* 6.

197 **In the ancient subcontinental cities:** Jonathan Mark Kenoyer, *Ancient Cities of the Indus Valley Civilization* (Karachi: Oxford University Press, 1998), 143.

198 **"The reproduction of identical shapes":** Ibid.

CHAPTER 9: ANXIETY, RISK, AND MIDDLE-CLASS LIFE

204 **"My lord has sent me":** A. Leo Oppenheim, *Letters from Mesopotamia* (Chicago: University of Chicago Press, 1967), 104.

206 **The Templo Mayor:** Eduardo Matos Moctezuma, "Archaeology and Symbolism in Aztec Mexico: The Templo Mayor of Tenochtitlan," *Journal of the American Academy of Religion* 53, no. 4 (1985): 797–813.

206 **the most recent infamous cases:** James Tarmy and Kartikay Mehrotra, "Who Will Pay for San Francisco's $750 Million Tilting Tower?," Bloomberg, Feb. 1, 2017, www.bloomberg.com.

207 **"It may be tough":** Ibid.

208 **The Los Angeles River holds:** Gumprecht, "Who Killed the Los Angeles River?," 121. For the current population, see "Los Angeles, California, Population 2018," *World Population Review,* June 12, 2018, worldpopulationreview.com.

208 **the Los Angeles Aqueduct:** William L. Kahrl, "The Politics of California Water: Owens Valley and the Los Angeles Aqueduct, 1900–1927," *California Historical Quarterly* 55, no. 1 (1976): 2–25.

209 **the fateful night of March 12, 1928:** James E. Snead and Ann Stansell, "'The Lurking Power': Archaeology, Water Wars, and the St. Francis Dam Disaster of 1928 (paper presented at the Eighty-second Annual Meeting of the Society for American Archaeology, Vancouver, 2017).

209 **At the site of Meidum:** Mark Lehner, *The Complete Pyramids: Solving the Ancient Mysteries* (London: Thames and Hudson, 1997).

211 **too many choices result:** Sheena Iyengar, *The Art of Choosing* (New York: Twelve, 2010).

211 **only twenty-four hours in a day:** Ian Steedman, *Consumption Takes Time* (London: Routledge, 2001).

212 **In his work *The Satyricon*:** Petronius: The Satyricon and Seneca: The Apocolocyntosis, rev. ed., trans. J. P. Sullivan (Harmondsworth, Middlesex, U.K.: Penguin, 1986).

213 **In excavations of one of the suburban mounds:** Augusta McMahon, Arkadiusz Sołtysiak, and Jill Weber, "Late Chalcolithic Mass Graves at Tell Brak, Syria, and Violent Conflict During the Growth of Early City-States," *Journal of Field Archaeology* 36, no. 3 (2011): 201–20.

214 **like wolves on the prowl:** Shane D. Johnson and Kate J. Bowers, "The Stability of Space-Time Clusters of Burglary," *British Journal of Criminology* 44 (2004): 55–65. I would like to thank my departmental colleague Jeff Brantingham for our many interesting conversations about crime and urbanism over the years.

215 **we have installed CCTVs:** For Mexico City, see Carlos J. Vilalta et al., "A Descriptive Model of the Relationship Between Police CCTV Systems and Crime: Evidence from Mexico City," *Police Practice and Research* (2018), doi:10.1080/15614263.2018.1473770; for Seoul, see Joon Tag Cho and Jisun Park, "Exploring the Effects of CCTV upon Fear of Crime: A Multi-level Approach in Seoul," *International Journal of Law, Crime, and Justice* 49 (2017): 35–45; for Chicago,

see Robert Draper, "They Are Watching You—and Everything Else on the Planet," *National Geographic*, Feb. 2018, www.nationalgeographic.com.

215 **At the ancient city of Teotihuacan:** Estimates of compound populations range from 60-100 on the basis of the amount of human burials found in the compounds (Suburo Sugiyama, *Human Sacrifice, Militarism, and Rulership: Materialization of State Ideology at the Feathered Serpent Pyramid, Teotihuacan.* Cambridge, U.K.: Cambridge University Press, 2005: 2) and overall population density estimated from surface remains at the site, which still remains mostly unexcavated. Cowgill suggests that the ancient city had up to 200,000 people overall, housed within an estimated 2,300 compounds (*Ancient Teotihuacan*, p. 141). Walking around in the excavated compounds and keeping in mind my own experience with tightly-packed Indian villages, my sense is that they could have been much more crowded, perhaps up to 300 people or so per compound.

216 **middle-class problems that seem:** David Satterthwaite and Sheridan Bartlett, "Editorial: The Full Spectrum of Risk in Urban Centres: Changing Perceptions, Changing Priorities," *Environment and Urbanization* 29, no. 1 (2017): 3-14.

217 **"However fast we pedestrians hurry":** Juvenal, *Sixteen Satires*, 3,223-25, pp. 95-96.

217 **In ancient Mesopotamia, inhabitants complained:** Kathryn Keith, "The Spatial Patterns of Everyday Life in Old Babylonian Neighborhoods," in Smith, *Social Construction of Ancient Cities*, 69.

218 **"If a man has given his boat":** Viel, *New Complete Code of Hammurabi*, 662.

218 **maritime insurance in the Roman world:** Peter Temin, "The Economy of the Early Roman Empire," *Journal of Economic Perspectives* 20, no. 1 (2006): 133-51.

219 **"He should have the place":** Patrick Olivelle, *King, Governance, and Law in Ancient India: Kauṭilya's Arthaśāstra* (New Delhi: Oxford University Press, 2013), 195.

220 **the medieval city of Vijayanagara:** Carla M. Sinopoli and Kathleen D. Morrison, *The Vijayanagara Metropolitan Survey*, vol. 1 (Ann Arbor, Mich.: Museum of Anthropology, 2007); Carla M. Sinopoli, *Pots and Palaces: The Earthenware Ceramics of the Noblemen's Quarter of Vijayanagara* (New Delhi: Manohar, 1993); Kathleen D. Morrison, *Fields of Victory: Vijayanagara and the Course of Intensification* (New Delhi: Munshiram Manoharlal, 2000).

220 **Vijayanagara's managers granted tax breaks:** Carla M. Sinopoli, *The Political Economy of Craft Production* (Cambridge, U.K.: Cambridge University Press, 2003), 269-70.

221 **"Enjoyment appears at the boundary":** Csikszentmihalyi, *Flow*, 52.

224 **Every time an aqueduct was extended:** Wilson, "Water, Power, and Culture in the Roman and Byzantine Worlds," 2.

224 **Pathways are another way:** Charlotte Lemanski, "Spaces of Exclusivity or Connection? Linkages Between a Gated Community and Its Poorer Neigh-

bour in a Cape Town Master Plan Development," *Urban Studies* 43, no. 2 (2006): 397–420.

CHAPTER 10: A WORLD OF CITIES

229 **geologic era to be called the Anthropocene:** For variable definitions of the Anthropocene, see P. J. Crutzen, "The 'Anthropocene,'" in *Early System Science in the Anthropocene,* eds., Eckart Ehlers and Thomas Krafft (Berlin: Springer, 2006), 13; and Will Steffen, Paul J. Crutzen, and John R. McNeill, "The Anthropocene: Are Humans Now Overwhelming the Great Forces of Nature?," *Ambio* 36, no. 8 (2007): 614.

229 **Ecologists worry that the next generation:** Richard Louv, *Last Child in the Woods: Saving Our Children from Nature-Deficit Disorder,* rev. ed. (Chapel Hill, N.C.: Algonquin Books, 2008).

229 **cities have a "green infrastructure":** Robert I. McDonald, *Conservation for Cities* (Washington, D.C.: Island Press, 2015), 4 and Chapter 4.

229 **Los Angeles the city of:** Stephanie Pincetl et al., "Urban Tree Planting Programs, Function or Fashion? Los Angeles and Urban Tree Planting Campaigns," *GeoJournal* 78, no. 3 (2013): 475–93.

230 **census data on red foxes:** Lourraine A. Tigas, Dirk H. Van Vuren, and Raymond M. Sauvajot, "Behavioral Responses of Bobcats and Coyotes to Habitat Fragmentation and Corridors in an Urban Environment," *Biological Conservation* 108 (2002): 299–306.

230 **Hyenas in Ethiopian cities:** Gidey Yirga Abay et al., "Peri-Urban Spotted Hyena (*Crocuta crocuta*) in Northern Ethiopia: Diet, Economic Impact, and Abundance," *European Journal of Wildlife Research* 57 (2011): 759–65; Alexander R. Braczkowski et al., "Leopards Provide Public Health Benefits in Mumbai, India," *Frontiers in Ecology and the Environment* 16, no. 3 (2018): 176–82, doi:10.1002.

230 **The wildlife scientist:** John M. Marzluff, *Welcome to Subirdia: Sharing Our Neighborhoods with Wrens, Robins, Woodpeckers, and Other Wildlife* (New Haven, Conn.: Yale University Press, 2014).

230 **bird species are particularly good at adapting:** John M. Marzluff, "Small Birds Use Their Brains to Live Among Us," *Psychology Today,* Feb. 25, 2013, www.psychologytoday.com.

230 **Peregrine falcon populations:** Marcel A. Gahbauer et al., "Productivity, Mortality, and Management of Urban Peregrine Falcons in Northeastern North America," *Journal of Wildlife Management* 79, no. 1 (2015): 10–19.

231 **SimCity and Cities: Skylines:** "Amazingly Detailed Metropolises Recreated in Cities: Skylines—in Pictures," *Guardian,* July 15, 2015, www.theguardian.com.

234 **a technique called stable-isotope analysis:** Gideon Hartman et al., "The

Pilgrimage Economy of Early Roman Jerusalem (1st Century BCE–70 CE) Reconstructed from the δ15N and δ13C Values of Goat and Sheep Remains," *Journal of Archaeological Science* 40 (2013): 4369–76.

238 **as Alexander the Great did:** Waldemar Heckel, "The Conquests of Alexander the Great," in *A Companion to the Classical Greek World,* ed. Konrad H. Kinzl (Malden, Mass.: Blackwell, 2006), 560–88.

238 **"tangible symbol of a conquered":** Molly Swetnam-Burland, "Aegyptus Redacta: The Egyptian Obelisk in the Augustan Campus Martius," *Art Bulletin* 92, no. 3 (2010): 135.

CHAPTER 11: THE NEXT 6,000 YEARS

243 **more than 75 percent:** See Ur, "Southern Mesopotamia," 544.

243 **95 percent of the population:** Frier, "Rental Market in Early Imperial Rome."

244 **"intentionally and actively created":** Jing et al., "Recent Discoveries and Some Thoughts on Early Urbanization at Anyang," 362.

244 **Oaxaca enclave and the "Merchants' Barrio":** Linda Manzanilla, "Introduction: Mesoamerican Domestic Structures, Compounds, and Neighborhoods," in *Domestic Life in Prehispanic Capitals: A Study of Specialization, Hierarchy, and Ethnicity,* edited by Linda R. Manzanilla and Claude Chapdelaine (Ann Arbor, MI: Memoirs of the Museum of Anthropology, University of Michigan, number 46: 2009), 32-35.

245 **the thriving future of urban religion:** For churches in Seoul, see In-Hwan Hwang and Jin-Yong Jeon, "Spatiality of Two Urban Religious Spaces in Seoul: A Case Study of Myeong-dong Cathedral and Bongeun Buddhist Temple Precincts," *Journal of Asian Architecture and Building Engineering* 14, no. 3 (2015): 625-32; for Accra, see Natasha Levy, "David Adjaye Unveils Plans for National Cathedral of Ghana in Accra," *Dezeen,* March 7, 2018, www.dezeen.com.

247 **"Concerning the horses":** John MacGinnis and Timothy Matney, "Ziyaret Tepe: Digging the Frontier of the Assyrian Empire," *Current World Archaeology* 37 (2009): 40.

248 **"Death will come out of it":** Ibid.

248 **Over three thousand years ago:** One of the most remarkable cases of underwater archaeology is the Uluburun shipwreck, a vessel from the fourteenth century BC found off the coast of Turkey. See Cemal Pulak, "The Uluburun Shipwreck: An Overview," *International Journal of Nautical Archaeology* 27, no. 3 (1998): 188–224.

249 **He calls the phenomenon "distance value":** Eric H. Cline, "Coals to Newcastle, Wallbrackets to Tiryns: Irrationality, Gift Exchange, and Distance Value," *in Meletemata: Studies in Aegean Archaeology Presented to Malcolm H. Wiener,* ed. Philip B. Betancourt et al. (Liège, Belgium: Université de Liège, 1999), 119–23.

249 **Among the most desired objects:** Michael Fulford, "Gallo-Roman Sigillata: Fresh Approaches, Fresh Challenges, Fresh Questions," in *Seeing Red: New Economic and Social Perspectives on Terra Sigillata,* ed. Michael Fulford and Emma Durham (London: Institute of Classical Studies, University of London, 2013), 1–17.

250 **Feathered Serpent Pyramid:** Cowgill, *Ancient Teotihuacan.*

250 **At Tikal, the excavation:** Jones, "Marketplace at Tikal."

252 **the same impressive stonework:** McMahon, "Waste Management in Early Urban Southern Mesopotamia," 19–39. McMahon discusses the appearance of stone orthostats in bathrooms; for the discussion of orthostats in public buildings, see Ömür Harmanşah, "Upright Stones and Building Stories: Architectural Technologies and the Poetics of Urban Space," in *Cities and the Shaping of Memory in the Ancient Near East* (Cambridge, U.K.: Cambridge University Press, 2013).

253 **"unhappy grist of daily life":** Gregory L. Possehl, *The Indus Civilization: A Contemporary Perspective* (Walnut Creek, Calif.: Altamira, 2002), 49.

254 **On the Indian subcontinent:** Bruno Marcolongo, "Geoarchaeological Observations in Doab Plain," in *Kāmpilya: Quest for a Mahābhārata City,* eds. Gian Giuseppe Filippe and Bruno Marcolongo (New Delhi: D.K. Printworld, 1999), 15–29. For discussion of an earthquake at Taxila, see John Marshall, *A Guide to Taxila* (Karachi: Sani Communications, 1960), 62–70.

254 **The Aztecs paid homage:** Christopher P. Garraty, "Aztec Teotihuacan: Political Processes at a Postclassic and Early Colonial City-State in the Basin of Mexico," *Latin American Antiquity* 17, no. 4 (2006): 363–87.

256 **At the site of Sisupalgarh:** Smith and Mohanty, "Monsoons, Rice Production, and Urban Growth."

256 **The Indus case has only four cities:** Robin Coningham and Ruth Young, *The Archaeology of South Asia: From the Indus to Asoka, c. 6500 BCE–200 CE* (Cambridge, U.K.: Cambridge University Press, 2015), 178. The notion of Indus populations being not quite "urban" echoes the much earlier work of Walter Fairservis, who saw Indus culture as being predominantly rural and wrote that the resultant dispersed Indus settlements were "not a true centralizing factor as it was in Mesopotamia." Walter A. Fairservis Jr., "The Harappan Civilization: New Evidence and More Theory," *American Museum Novitates,* no. 2055 (1961).

257 **When life became unviable:** Wayne R. Belcher and William R. Belcher, "Geologic Constraints on the Harappa Archaeological Site, Punjab Province, Pakistan," *Geoarchaeology* 15, no. 7 (2000): 679–713. For the idea of migration and abandonment of the Indus sites, see Kenoyer, *Ancient Cities of the Indus Valley Civilization,* 174.

258 **many large and densely populated:** Damian Evans, "Airborne Laser Scanning as a Method for Exploring Long-Term Socio-economic Dynamics in Cambodia," *Journal of Archaeological Science* 74 (2016): 164–75.

260 **Cities continue to grow:** For the information on Mumbai, New Delhi, and Kinshasa, see Ann M. Simmons, "Urban Population Growth and Demand for Food Could Spark Global Unrest, Study Shows," *Los Angeles Times,* April 29, 2016, www.latimes.com, from Thomas A. Reardon, *Growing Food for Growing Cities: Transforming Food Systems in an Urbanizing World,* Chicago Council on Global Affairs, April 2016.

260 **the metropolis of Warsaw:** Jerzy Lukowski and Hubert Zawadzki, *A Concise History of Poland,* 2nd ed. (Cambridge: Cambridge University Press, 2006); Paul Robert Magoscsi, *Historical Atlas of Central Europe,* revised and expanded edition (Seattle: University of Washington Press, 2002).

INDEX

INDEX